THE TERROR OF INDIANA

Bent Jones & The Moody-Tolliver Feud

Bob Moody

The Terror of Indiana: Bent Jones & The Moody-Tolliver Feud, Second Edition
Copyright © 2021 by Robert A. Moody.

First Edition: 2018
Second Edition: 2021

ISBN (paperback): 978-1-7327231-2-2
ISBN (hardcover): 978-1-7327231-3-9
ISBN (ebooks): 978-1-7327231-4-6

Front cover: East side of the square in Orleans, Indiana, circa 1908. Thomas Moody was murdered two blocks west of this location on March 2, 1875.

All rights reserved. No part of this book may be reproduced in any form whatsoever without prior written permission from the publisher except in the case of brief quotations embodied in reviews.

Cover Design and Formatting by Streetlight Graphics

Published by Light Bread Press
Louisville, Kentucky

www.bobmoody.com

To Daniel Oliver Spencer, Jr., the gifted reporter known as "D.O.S.", and to all the anonymous newspapermen whose words still live on these pages.

Table of Contents

Preface 7
A Note About Names and Dates 11
Part One 13
    Chapter One: The Unpleasantness 15
    Chapter Two: Despicable Incendiarism 25
    Chapter Three: Now Shoot Him! 35
    Chapter Four: Cowardly Assassination 47
    Chapter Five: Seven Feet of Rope 59
    Chapter Six: A Rude Awakening 68
    Chapter Seven: The Other Side 74
    Chapter Eight: Certain to Swing 84
    Chapter Nine: Oh, I Am Murdered! 96
    Chapter Ten: He Hollered Willfully 110
    Chapter Eleven: The Blood of Abel 118
    Chapter Twelve: Devilish Delight 132
    Chapter Thirteen: Scalp Dance 139
    Chapter Fourteen: The End Is Not Yet 150
    Chapter Fifteen: Tolliver Takes Tall Timber 163
Part Two 175
    Eli Lowry: Unwilling Tool 180
    Lee Jones: A Little Careless 190
    Thomas Tolliver: The Most Dangerous Man 198
    Parks Tolliver: Tricky Tolliver 208
    Bent Jones: The Terror of Indiana 221

Afterword 253
Acknowledgments 257
About the Author 260
Moody-Tolliver Feud Timeline 261
Bibliography 264
Online Resources 274

Preface

My great-great-great grandparents are buried in a Southern Indiana cornfield. Not in a legally recognized cemetery situated on any map, but on private property in the middle of a working farm. Generations of landowners have carefully plowed around the Moody family headstones and respected the graves. The story of how I became aware of them is almost miraculous. It would prompt a forty-year search for the history of my Indiana ancestors and eventually reveal new and dramatic details about the almost forgotten Moody-Tolliver Feud.

In the late Seventies my father received a family Bible from a half cousin in Arkansas. My grandfather Moody had been born in Indiana, but became an orphan at the age of eighteen, so we didn't know much about the family history. The torn and battered Bible had been printed in 1829 and contained handwritten dates of birth, marriage, and death for unfamiliar ancestors. One note mentioned "Orange County" and "Little Orleans". Guessing that this was Orleans, Indiana, just across the Ohio River from my home in Kentucky, Dad asked me to investigate.

Since 1976 I had been working at WAKY radio in Louisville. In early 1981 I traveled to the courthouses in Paoli (Orange County) and Bedford (Lawrence County), where I found several references to the Moody family, including documents related to wills and civil trials. Later I was introduced to a distant relative in Orleans who told me about the murder of my great-great-great uncle Thomas Moody and showed me the house where it had happened.

One day I mentioned my visits to Indiana on the radio and thanked people I had met for their help. The next day I boarded a flight to England to celebrate my thirtieth birthday. When I returned two weeks later there was a message at WAKY from a young farmer in Orleans named Jim Salkeld. He had been driving south to deliver part of his corn crop to New Albany when he heard me mention my search for the Moody family on his truck's AM-only radio. When I returned the call Jim's wife, Sheila, said, "I don't know if they are part of your family, but we have Moodys buried on our farm." Reading off her notepad, she gave me names and dates that turned out to be those of both of my great-great-great grandparents and one of their daughters-in-law.

That inspired my first serious efforts at genealogical research. At that time, long before home computers, it meant hours of scrolling through microfilm in libraries and consulting local history books. Along the way I found brief references to the Moody-Tolliver Feud with specific dates that allowed me to search page by page in old newspapers on file at libraries in Louisville and New Albany. Tantalizing details appeared in those accounts, but the full story and eventual outcome were beyond my grasp, especially after I left Louisville in 1985.

Over the years I was able to learn more about my family tree using Internet resources, but I did not realize that the Moody-Tolliver Feud had been covered in newspapers across the United States and abroad, including the front page of the *New York Times*. Only when it became possible to access indexed newspaper files online did the significance of that feud and the subsequent trials become apparent.

The story of the violent "unpleasantness" between the Moody and Tolliver families had been reported from coast to coast and beyond. It appears to be the first family blood feud to receive immediate national newspaper coverage. Earlier family conflicts had taken place in relatively remote areas prior to coast-to-coast telegraph service in 1861 and completion of the U.S. transcontinental railroad in 1869. Many of those are widely regarded as continuations of hostilities from the Civil

War, while the notorious Hatfield-McCoy Feud did not receive much attention outside the Appalachian region until 1878. The Moody-Tolliver Feud took place in an area with extensive railroad and telegraph service that allowed correspondents to file daily reports for newspapers in New Albany, Bloomington, Louisville, and Indianapolis which were then distributed across the United States. Newspapers in smaller towns – especially the weekly and bi-weekly papers – would re-write reports from the major dailies, usually (but not always) with attribution. Sometimes only the headline was changed.

While newspaper accounts of the time were often sensationalized and occasionally misleading, many were also witty and remarkably engaging. Newspapers were the primary source of public information and entertainment. Daily papers today struggle to survive in even the biggest media markets, but during the nineteenth century the smallest towns might support one or more. The bibliography for this book includes one hundred and sixty-eight different newspapers, representing twenty-five states, two Canadian provinces, and eleven cities in Great Britain, each of which is cited for having provided unique content. Many of them carried multiple stories about the feud over the years.

Even though it was before the advent of truly national press syndication in America, many stories about the Moody-Tolliver Feud appeared in substantially the same wording in scores of additional publications. Newspaper correspondents were seldom identified by anything other than a pseudonym or initials. Consequently, their true identities are rarely remembered today. There were also local writers who used nicknames such as "Snacks" or "Jerry Slapjack" whose comments and opinions were a precursor to modern newspaper columnists. Some of their writing was uneven or overblown – but much of it, as you will see, was brilliant.

There was considerable national interest in the case among the legal profession as they closely observed the sequence of long, expensive, and elaborately eloquent trials. It was an ideal story for the Gilded Age.

Bob Moody

I have maintained the original spelling and punctuation used by each newspaper to capture the original flavor of their reports. Direct quotations appear between quotation marks. Corrections have been made only for obvious typographic errors that did not change the meaning or context. Any additions for clarification appear in brackets; [sic] indicates a quoted word or phrase exactly as it appeared in the original source.

A Note About Names and Dates

Spelling, especially of family names, could be notoriously inconsistent at the time of these events. Sometimes it was a matter of what a clerk or census taker thought they heard, rather than the person's preference, but families and individuals also used flexible spelling when writing in their own hand.

This was especially true with Toliver or Tolliver. Early records tend to use one "L", while many – but certainly not all – family members later chose to use the "double-L" form. A survey of known burials in Orange and Lawrence counties in 2017 included 152 members of that family interred between 1821 and 2017. In Lawrence County the name on the tombstone was almost equally split: 38 Tolivers and 37 Tollivers. Interestingly, every one of the 77 family members buried in Orange County cemeteries preferred Toliver. I have tried to use the name as commonly spelled on legal documents or tombstones except when quoting directly from court records or newspaper accounts. It should be noted, however, that most printed sources standardized the spelling as Tolliver. For consistency, that spelling is used in general references to their feud with the Moody family.

To a lesser degree this is also true for the Moody family. Alexander, the original settler in Indiana, is referred to as Mooday in his will and other early records and at least one of his children continued to use that spelling. It could perhaps be an indication of how this Scots-Irish family pronounced the name, although when he died in 1853 his tombstone read "Alexander Moody". Of the 23 family members found buried in Orange and Lawrence counties between 1853 and 2013, only five used the Mooday spelling. In this case, with apologies to living family members who still include the "A", I have standardized the spelling to "Moody" because very few, if any, relevant documents or newspaper accounts used the alternate spelling after 1870.

Spelling was also inconsistent among many other families in the area, including Lowry/Lowery, Murry/Murray, Tegarten/Tegarden, Hoffstetter/Huffstetter, and Voris/Vorhis/Voorhees/Vories, among others.

The absence of birth certificates often makes it difficult to reliably determine the actual age of many persons mentioned in this account. Some may not have been certain of their own birth date. It was both frustrating and slightly amusing to track the ages given in federal census records and other documents over several decades. Results may vary, but it is safe to say that it was rare to find anyone getting *older* than previous records would suggest. I have made every effort to provide the best possible estimate of their actual ages.

Part One

Chapter One:
The Unpleasantness

WILLIAM TOLIVER HAD NO REASON to think that August 17, 1870, would be the last day of his life. When the 59-year-old farmer and father of thirteen children settled onto his wagon seat and began a routine five-mile trip from Orleans, Indiana, to his farm in Lawrence County he probably expected to have supper that night with Polly, his second wife of less than eighteen months. But that was not his destiny, as reported by the *New Albany Daily Ledger* the following day:

```
"SAD ACCIDENT AT ORLEANS.
   An Old Citizen Falls from a Wagon and
     is Kicked to Death by His Mules.

From a private telegraphic dispatch from
Orleans, Orange county, dated this morning,
we learn that a very melancholy accident
happened in that town late yesterday afternoon,
resulting in the death of an old gentleman
named William Toliver, a very highly esteemed
and wealthy farmer, living a mile and a half
north of Orleans.
   It appears that Mr. Toliver had come into
the town on some business, driving a mule
team, which he usually used in doing his
hauling from the town to his farm. By some
```

means the mules took fright and ran away. Mr. T. was using his utmost endeavors to check the frightened animals, standing in the forward part of the wagon body, when one of the wheels struck an object on the road side, which threw him over the forward end of the body upon the double tree of the wagon, where he clung to the boards and double tree until the mules in their frantic flight kicked him in a most terrible manner, when he loosed his hold upon the wagon and dropped on the road side. Some parties who saw Mr. Toliver when he fell to the ground ran to his assistance, but his injuries were so great that he did not live more than from three to five minutes after he was reached by them....

This terrible accident has cast a gloom over the entire neighborhood where Mr. T. resided, and is so well known. His remains will be interred today."

News of his accidental death would soon appear in newspapers across the U.S. and overseas because William Toliver had died intestate – without a legal will. That simple fact would result in multiple lawsuits, a vicious beating, a midnight firebombing and sniper attack on his wife's home and ultimately a cold-blooded murder. It would trigger a series of trials that would be described at the time as "one of the most celebrated cases in the history of Western jurisprudence".

The Moodys and Tolivers were neighbors living on adjoining farms in Lawrence County, immediately north of the Orange County line. William Toliver was born in Huntsville, Alabama, in 1811. His parents were among the early settlers of Indiana, arriving in 1818. In 1835 he married 19-year-old Delana Burton. Six months later he purchased forty acres of land and added an additional forty acres in 1837. William and Delana would have thirteen children, nine of whom – five boys and four girls – would live to adulthood. A sad calamity struck two years before his death, when Delana died at the age of 53. By that time Toliver was a wealthy and respected farmer. But now he was also a 57-year-old widower in charge of a household that included two daughters, ages 18 and 22, and a 12-year-old boy who would grow up to be a notoriously rambunctious young man.

Alexander Moody had been another early pioneer. He was born in 1780 and left western Pennsylvania sometime before 1803 for Lincoln County in Kentucky. In 1820 he and his wife, Mezza, moved their family across the Ohio River to Indiana, although they appear to have kept their land in Kentucky for another decade. Alexander died in 1853, followed by his wife the following year. In 1870 four of their sons – William, John, Joseph, and Thomas – along with their 51-year-old sister, Mary Ann (called "Polly"), lived adjacent to the Toliver family on land that had been left to them by their parents. William, John, Joe, and Tom were all lifelong bachelors, while Polly was what would have been commonly, if not politely, known as an "old maid".

It is not known when William Toliver first thought of marrying Polly Moody, but it did not take him long to act. Less than six months after Delana's death she was his new bride. Within another eighteen months she would be his widow.

Published reports later claimed that both the Moody and Toliver families had disapproved of the marriage even before the wagon accident that killed William. Polly Moody Toliver found herself without a husband but with three hostile stepchildren living at home and several grown Toliver children who resented the marriage and wanted to make sure they were not cheated out of their inheritance. Equally suspicious and angry were the sons-in-law who had married into the Toliver family. Years later the *New York Sun* described Polly's situation:

> "She was old and her character fixed, so that she and her husband are said not to have agreed well together, while the condition of the Tolliver children at home was almost equal in point of misery to being in Pandemonium."

The Tolivers alleged that William had withdrawn $2,000 in

cash for an intended out-of-state land purchase shortly before his death and had secured it in a safe at his home. Family members would later testify that Polly had gone into that room alone on the night following William's death. Shortly thereafter, they claimed, the cash was discovered to be missing. Polly knew she was not welcome and later told a judge that due to the "unpleasantness" she decided to move back to the Moody farmhouse she shared with "the boys".

Then it was discovered that William had died without a will. By Indiana law, his widow was entitled to a minimum of one-third of the estate, including sixty acres of land. This did not please any of the extended Toliver clan, to say the least. A household inventory was ordered in preparation for an estate sale. Meanwhile, a series of claims and counterclaims were made regarding who would be designated to administer the estate. John Riley, clerk of the Lawrence County common pleas court, had appointed Simpson Toliver, William's eldest son, as administrator. On October 4, Polly (under her legal name of Mary Toliver) filed a complaint asking that Simpson's appointment be revoked on the grounds that she had not abandoned her right to serve in that role, that the clerk had been so advised, and that the action had been illegal to begin with since it had been made *on* the fifteenth day after William's death and the law required the administrator to be appointed *after* the fifteenth day.

The following day Simpson Toliver filed an affidavit in response

```
"...the said Mary, widow of the decedent, is
incapable of performing the duties of such
administrator for the reason that she is
totally unable to read or write and knows
nothing of the rules of Common Arithmetic and
is unable to keep accounts and is mentally
incompetent to transact the business devolving
upon an administrator."
```

He may have had a point. She had signed her complaint with

"X – her mark", although in the federal census taken two months earlier she claimed to be able to read, although unable to write. Simpson Toliver was still listed as the administrator of his father's estate when the final statement from the auction was filed with the court on October 26. He would eventually be replaced by Eli Burton. The Burton family was related by marriage to the Tolivers, but Eli was a respected former Justice of the Peace with previous experience in administering wills. It would be a thankless job.

The auction of William Toliver's personal goods, livestock, farm implements, and harvested crops took place as scheduled at the Toliver farm on September 30, 1870. Court documents indicate "a hundred or more people present" and list 129 lots of goods sold, ranging from $405 for two mules to ten cents for "two sickles". The sales totaled $3415.80. Over half of the lots (72) were sold to Toliver family members, including sons-in-law. John Moody was the only member of Polly's family to make a purchase: $2.20 for a "Grind Stone & fixtures". From their point of view, the Tolivers believed that they were being forced to buy back items that should belong to them from a woman whom they alleged had already stolen two thousand dollars in cash.

Finally, Simpson Toliver loudly proclaimed, "The black-hearted sons-of-bitches have stolen more than they ever brought here." That vulgar accusation prompted a one-sided brawl. Tom Moody was brutally attacked by four Toliver sons and A.B. "Bent" Jones, who was married to their sister, Clarissa. Each of his alleged attackers was more than twenty years younger than Moody.

In March of 1871 Thomas Moody filed two lawsuits at the Lawrence County courthouse in Bedford. The first accused Joseph Toliver, Parks Toliver, Wiley Toliver, Thomas Toliver, and Bent Jones with trespass and assault and battery. Moody charged that:

> "... (the defendants) assaulted the plaintiff and with fists, stones, clubs, and brass knucks beat, bruised, pushed, dragged and pulled about, kicked, wounded and maimed the plaintiff whereby the plaintiff became and was sick,

sore, lame and disordered and so continued for a long space of time."

Later testimony would declare that Tom was confined to his bed for weeks. He asked for $5,000 in damages. Each of the accused filed separate responses to the charges. Bent Jones claimed that Moody had assaulted him first and that he was only acting in self-defense. The defendants were eventually found guilty, but Moody was awarded only $75, with his legal expenses estimated to be around $500.

Thomas Moody's second lawsuit charged Simpson Toliver with slander for his "black-hearted sons-of-bitches" remark on the grounds that he had been falsely accused of larceny. He won that case, too. According to the *Fort Wayne Weekly Sentinel*, the penalty was determined by consensus: "...the jury assessed the damages by each member writing a sum upon separate slips of paper, adding the sums together, and dividing by twelve, thus striking an average, which proved to be $1,400."

The Tolivers retaliated by attempting to have a grand jury indict Thomas and Polly for allegedly stealing the missing $2,000. But "as the law does not contemplate that a wife can commit larceny by taking funds belonging to her husband no bill was found." Instead, Polly filed suit against her late husband's estate to recover money she had brought with her to the marriage and which William had intended to invest on her behalf. The court awarded her $2,100. In 1873 Eli Burton, as executor of William Toliver's estate, appealed the terms of Polly's settlement to the Indiana Supreme Court. That appeal was denied.

Files at the Lawrence County courthouse in Bedford are jammed with papers related to these and other civil cases filed by the Moodys and Tolivers during this time, including original subpoenas, additions, corrections, withdrawals, and responses to charges filed. Even this early in the dispute it was apparent that the immediate beneficiaries were not the parties involved, but rather the legal teams they hired to move the process along. From the outset it was apparent that stubbornness by both families allowed their attorneys to prolong the cases over relatively minor issues.

By today's standards it is perhaps easy to sympathize with the Toliver family's unhappiness at having a major portion of their inheritance fall into the hands of William's relatively recent and unwelcome wife. His children and their spouses saw themselves as victims of the law. They were angry, humiliated, and determined to settle accounts. From the Moody perspective, there was abundant incentive to seek every benefit to which Polly was legally entitled. Polly Moody and the four brothers with whom she shared a home were all unmarried and without children. Their ages ranged from 53 to 65 and there were no "safety nets" to provide for their future. At the time, however, there was no way to anticipate the price both families would pay for their bitter animosity.

The stage was now set for the violent episodes and resulting trials that would generate coverage in newspapers throughout the United States and, eventually, in Canada and Great Britain.

These were the key characters in what became known as the Moody-Tolliver Feud:

Thomas (Tom) Moody was one of the four bachelor brothers who lived with their sister, Polly, on a large farm in Lawrence County. Tom was the sixth of nine children. Brothers James and Walter lived on their own farms in Orange County, while David had moved west to Illinois by 1868, before the feud began. Another sister, Elizabeth "Betsy" Moody Wright had died in 1862. Tom was the family's dominant personality and would be the most prominent member of his family in the forthcoming drama. He was an active member of the Democrat party. An 1875 newspaper account described him as "a man of some sixty years of age, unmarried, large size, weighing about 200 pounds, fair complexion and said to be one of the finest looking gentlemen in that section." Another reporter recalled that "…while a very determined man, [Tom] was jolly and roystering in disposition, who loved a game of cards, and occasionally dissipated."

Alonzo Benton Jones, usually referred to as A.B. or Bent, was a brother-in-law of the Tolivers, having married their sister, Clarissa. He became the main protagonist from the Toliver side. He owned a sawmill and woodworking factory in Mitchell. Like Tom Moody, Bent was active in the Democrat party, having been elected a township trustee in a heavily Republican precinct. Later he would seek the Democratic nomination for sheriff of Lawrence County. He was described as "a man of influence and means, but of strong prejudices and great determination." He was 32 years old in 1870. New research has revealed remarkable details about his later years and the surprising location of Bent's final resting place.

Lee Jones was a younger brother to Bent Jones (by 14 years) and would become a fellow brother-in-law when he married Louisa Toliver in October of 1871. Of all the future defendants, the circumstances of his death would be the most shocking.

Parks Toliver (legal name: Milton Parks Toliver) was a 22-year-old pharmacist living in Orleans with his brother Joseph's family in 1870. Even though state records indicate that he never graduated from a medical school, Parks would later open a practice in Mitchell and was referred to thereafter as "Doctor Toliver". Printed reports emphasized that he did not look or act like a criminal, but he would be indicted and imprisoned on murder charges. His dramatic escape from justice and subsequent life story are among the most fascinating and unforeseen discoveries in this case.

Thomas (Tom) Toliver was the "baby" of his family. Born in 1856, he was only fourteen years old when his father, William, died. His widespread reputation as a "sporting man" would result in a relatively short, troubled life. Tom would make headlines again when he died in sordid circumstances.

Simpson Toliver, known as Sim or Simp, was William Toliver's eldest son. He was 34 years old in 1870 and owned a livery stable in Mitchell. His remarks and actions accelerated the feud, although violence might have been inevitable. His role in the feud diminished over the coming years. By 1880 Simpson and his family had moved to Illinois to join his brother, Wiley. He died there in 1915.

Eli Lowry (or Lowery) was only about 19 years old when he became involved in the feud through his job at Bent Jones's sawmill. He was a single man and was not related to the Toliver or Jones families. It is likely that they intended for Lowry to be the scapegoat. His confession is the most detailed and colorful account of the events of 1875. Lowry would receive unwelcome attention from the press again after he began working in law enforcement following his release from prison.

James Murray (or Murry) was also a Toliver brother-in-law, having married William and Delana's oldest child, Mahala. The Murray farm adjoined the Toliver property to the west. He eventually admitted to having lied under oath and was indicted for his role in the feud but was not convicted.

Two other Toliver sons were named as assailants of Thomas Moody at the estate sale. William Gordon (known as Wiley) Toliver had moved to Illinois in 1858 but returned home briefly following his father's death. Joseph Toliver was a 29-year-old farmer in 1870, living in Orleans with his wife, Ann, and their one-year-old daughter. Joe was a defendant in Tom Moody's 1871 slander suit and would later be charged with arson, but he was never convicted of criminal charges. He moved to Illinois before 1880, then lived in Kansas before settling with his family in Missouri, where he was a longtime member of the Kansas City Stock Exchange.

The Moody farm included 160 acres in the southeast quadrant of section 18 in Marion Township, along with other parcels of land nearby in Lawrence County and extending south into Orange County. They shared a property line to the west with the Tolivers. About one-third of the Toliver land was divided by the Louisville,

Bob Moody

New Albany, and Chicago (later commonly known as the Monon) railroad tracks. These sixty acres, from the tracks east to the Moody section, would soon become the property of William Toliver's widow, Polly. But the Toliver brothers and their brothers-in-law, Bent and Lee Jones, were making plans to get it back – starting with an order for several gallons of highly flammable benzine.

Chapter Two:
Despicable Incendiarism

Shortly after midnight on Sunday morning, June 25, 1871, the Moody farmhouse that was home for Thomas, William, Joseph, and John Moody, along with their sister, Polly Toliver, was firebombed by unknown persons who then fired guns into the house and shot at those who attempted to escape. Thomas and another man were badly injured and not expected to live, while Polly suffered serious burns.

That was front page news in the next day's edition of the *New Albany Ledger*, with a headline proclaiming it as:

```
"Kuklux Outrage in
   Lawrence County.
Dastardly Attempt to Assassinate
       a Whole Family.
    Petroleum and Torpedoes
     Thrown into the House.
    The Family Attempting to
     Escape are Fired Upon.
One of the Victims Mortally Wounded.
    Another Dangerously Wounded
   And a Woman Terribly Burned.
No Clew as Yet to the Perpetrators."
```

The attack began when flaming jugs filled with benzine were

tossed into rooms occupied by the family along with "several very large combustible torpedoes loaded with buckshot, nails, screws, and other missiles of like character." Soon the beds and furniture were burning as multiple shooters fired into the house. Thomas was running toward the door when he was shot in the hip, with "the ball passing upward and entirely through the body, coming out at the upper portion of the breast." The newspaper reported that "There is no possible chance, it is believed, for the recovery of Mr. Moody, as the wound is a most fearful one, and from which he is suffering terribly." Polly was said to have been "terribly burned", while a "hired man" named Robert "Bob" Lee had a bullet pass through his thigh, "causing a very severe and painful wound, but not necessarily fatal." Some versions of the story mentioned "a stranger by the name of Starks" inside the house at the time of the attack, although he was not mentioned in court testimony.

William, Joseph, and John Moody struggled to put out the fire until neighbors arrived to help, at which time an effort to pursue the attackers was made, but it was too late. The newspaper observed that "many of the best citizens are not unwilling that summary punishment should be dealt to the perpetrators."

At the bottom of the front-page story was this update:

"LATER

> Orleans, Ind., June 26,—3 P.M.—Thomas Moody is still alive, but all hopes of his recovery have been abandoned.
> Since my dispatch of yesterday, another wound has been discovered in Mr. Lee's back, which renders his recovery extremely doubtful.
> Detectives, having the subject in charge, are busily engaged in working up the affair, with fair prospects of the detection and arrest of the guilty parties. It is understood that Mr. Moody's statement of the affair has been reduced to writing, under the belief that

he cannot survive, and that he recognized several of the men of the party of assailants.

The greatest excitement prevails, and a determination expressed that such a deed of violence shall not go unpunished. Ten thousand dollars has been raised to prosecute the guilty parties, and a greater sum than this, if necessary, could be collected for the purpose.

The entire community is terribly excited, and almost wild to get the assassins in their possession. It is believed that the counsels of the more prudent will prevail, but this is not certain, as threats of lynching are repeated on almost every hand."

The headline in the next edition of the *New Albany Ledger* read:

"The Lawrence County Outrage
A Well Planned Scheme of Murder and Arson...
Probable Unjust Suspicions.
Condition of Moody and Lee.

The attempt of unknown assassins to murder the Moody family near Orleans Sunday morning is one of the most dastardly outrages that has been committed in Southern Indiana for years. The vile miscreants evidently went to the house for the purpose of murder and designed to cover up their crime by the destruction of the building and the bodies of their victims... The parties who committed the act had other motives than robbery. There can be little doubt that the object was to destroy the entire family by murder and arson, and had their scheme been fully accomplished, we very much doubt whether any one would have suspected foul play.

> The facts gathered by telegraph, and from other sources, fully warrant the belief that the crime was thoroughly planned before hand by some one well posted in the object to be accomplished. There is every evidence that the assassins were well armed with deadly weapons, as eighteen buckshot were found lodged in the rails of the fence over which Mr. Thomas Moody was climbing when he was shot. That the murder of the three [actually four] Moodys, Mrs. Toliver and Mr. Lee was not accomplished, is no fault of the assassins. It was evidently their intention to destroy them all by murder, or in the flames that they expected to follow their incendiary acts."

The article went on to summarize the history of "the law suits and bad blood" between the Moody and Toliver families, noting that:

> "(T)he two families made their feelings towards each other very bitter, and it is said each party have made open threats against the other. This fact being well known in the community where the families reside, has caused some to connect the Tolivers with the attempted assassination, but there is no evidence against them, so far as we can learn, and they still remain at their homes, the suspicion is probably groundless.
>
> From a gentleman who came in from Orleans this morning, we learn that Mr. Thomas Moody is getting better and hopes are entertained for his recovery. Mr. Lee is not getting along so well. The excitement is still high in the vicinity of the deed, and every effort is being made to discover a clue to the perpetrators."

On June 27 the *Louisville Daily Commercial* began their coverage by listing a series of "savage crimes" that had taken place in the neighboring state of Indiana, then warned "...what we are about to relate is even more savage, more devilish and damnable than any of their bloody predecessors." The story continued:

> "In the county of Lawrence, two and-half miles north of the little town of Orleans, Orange county, and near the dividing line between the two counties, lived four brothers, all of them single men, and well advanced in years. With them lived their widowed sister, Mrs. Tolliver, and a farm-hand named Lee. Throughout the two counties the family was well known as one of industrious farmers; the men rather positive in their character and probably a little bitter in their animosities. They however lived in peace with their neighbors and were well respected. Some have thought that there existed in that neighborhood a vendetti spirit, for there have been hangings and much violence not many miles away. But however well or ill founded this supposition may be, it is certain that the Moody brothers had enemies who had determined upon their destruction at one fell swoop, and in a manner so barbarous and utterly cruel as to make the blood run cold even in its recital."

The only new information in their account of the actual attack was that one of the brothers had managed to rescue Polly, while "another brother escaped, unobserved, and fled from house to house in the neighborhood, alarming the people." The story concluded:

> "The savage villains who perpetrated this most diabolical crime succeeded in getting away before the arrival at the scene of the tragedy of the excited and thoroughly infuriated people. The excitement among the citizens in consequence of this terrible crime is intense beyond description, and if the assassins are arrested there is no doubt that the State of Indiana will have another chapter of mob infamy added to her history. It is believed

> the perpetrators of the crime will be found and secured, as such revelations have been made by the Moody brothers as leaves but little doubt as to their identity. Parties are now scouring the country in search of them, and we will not be surprised if we are called upon tomorrow to record more hanging without the law, and more of those disgraceful and law-defying acts that have of late years made several of the counties of the Second Indiana district famous for terrible tragedies."

The *Cambridge City (IN) Tribune* noted in its coverage that "the Moody's were highly respectable and inoffensive people." One week following the attack the *Bedford Independent* reported:

> "Since our last issue much has been brought to light bearing upon the dark spots of this intricate case, all of which it would not serve the public weal, though it might gratify the public taste ever so much, to make public at this particular time. But we may safely say that enough has been made known, dug up and found out to convict at least a portion of the perpetrators, and every day only serves as so many links connecting one fact to another in the development of the whole, and when all this is ready, the officers 'will go for' the alleged guilty parties and take them in for safe keeping. It now appears that Mrs. Tolliver [Polly] is the most injured of the three, by reason of her burns, and that her sufferings are intense. Mr. Moody and Lee are getting along very nicely, though the bullet in the latter's back has not been found, and may prove fatal any day."

A summary of the feud published five years later by the *Indiana State Sentinel* included some additional details, although the source was not identified:

"... between 12 and 1 o'clock, the hired hand awoke to find a jug of burning benzine beside his bed. With extraordinary presence of mind he leaped to his feet and smothered the flame by placing his hand over the mouth of the jug; but as he did so he was shot through the hips from without. Immediately other jugs of burning benzine were thrown in, and hand grenades filled with nails, bullets, scraps of iron and lead, followed. Fortunately only one of these infernal contrivances exploded, and the jugs, falling upon the bed, did not burst, as it was evidently intended that they should. But the bed was fired by the burning fluid, and the destruction of the house was prevented only by the heroic action of the widow, who seized the burning bed and pushed it into the wide, old fashioned fireplace, where it was consumed without doing further damage. In the meantime, Thomas Moody, who had been wounded by some of the flying missiles, rushed out of the house, and attempted to escape, but being in his night clothes, he furnished a too conspicuous mark for the fiends who were seeking his life, and just as he was crossing the fence surrounding the house he received a load of buckshot, and fell over on the opposite side, stunned and bleeding. Supposing him dead, the assassins did not pursue him, and having partially recovered, he crawled and dragged himself, fainting, to a neighbor's and gave the alarm. The neighbor hastily mounted a horse, rode to Orleans, a mile and a half distant, summoned a physician, and alarmed the citizens. Immediately a rocket was fired by a confederate in the town, which ascending to an immense height, gave warning to the assassins at the Moody house that there was danger. The people soon assembled at the house, but the fiends had fled."

For the next few weeks many newspaper writers and public officials tip-toed around the most obvious suspects, pointing out that there was no known evidence to link the Tolivers or anyone else with the crime. But the Toliver-Jones faction had been very vocal about their hatred for the Moody family, including public and private threats of revenge. It was also noticed that when neighbors rushed to help put out the fire and care for the injured, none of the nearby Tolivers had appeared.

A short account on the front page of the *New York Times* appeared on June 27, 1871, under the headline "**A BAND OF FIENDS**". This story mistakenly located Orleans in Lawrence County (rather than Orange) and misspelled Polly's name as "Mrs. Talliver" – mistakes that would be repeated later in both the *New York Sun* and *New York Tribune*. On June 29 the *Times* provided additional coverage of the "**The Indiana Outrage**" on their front page with a reprint of the *Louisville Commercial's* account from two days earlier, followed by an additional update on July 3. The *Times* offered a possible alternate motive on July 6:

> "There are persons in Lawrence County, Indiana, who believe that the recent outrageous attack on the house of the Moody family… was not the result of a family quarrel, but was an attempt at revenge against Mr. THOMAS MOODY for the part he took during the war in securing the punishment of some deserters who had made a murderous assault on one of his friends."

No additional information could be found regarding the Civil War incident, but there is no indication that this theory was ever taken seriously by local authorities. On June 27 the attack was on the front pages of the *Chicago Tribune*, *Philadelphia Inquirer*, *Memphis Daily Appeal*, *The Tennessean* from Nashville, and the *Baltimore Sun* ("**Despicable Incendiarism and Assassination in Indiana**"). By June 28, three days after the attack, the news from Orleans, Indiana, had reached the west coast with a front-page story in the *San Francisco Chronicle* ("**Horrible Atrocity**"). On July 6 the *Halifax Citizen* reported the story in Canada, followed by an Ontario newspaper two days later.

The first known trans-Atlantic coverage appeared on July 10 in London's *Guardian* ("**Attempt To Assassinate a Family**"). Over the next four days reports about the incident in Lawrence County appeared in the *Exeter Flying Post, London Standard, Liverpool Mercury,* and *Birmingham Daily Post.* On July 15 the *Manchester Weekly Times and Examiner* reprinted the story published in the *Louisville Commercial* nearly three weeks earlier. On the same day reports of the attack were printed in the *Lancaster Gazette* and *Leeds Mercury,* followed closely by the *London Magnet,* the *Western Mail* in Cardiff, Wales, and the *Royal Cornwall Gazette, Falmouth Packet* and *General Advertise*r from Truro.

As the story spread newspapers seemed to compete for the most lurid or misleading copy. A possible winner was *The Sun* in New York City, where a short item on the front page on June 27 was titled "**A Satanic Band in Indiana**". The *Harrisburg (PA) Telegraph* headlined their story "**Kentucky Fun**", although the only reference to Kentucky was a Louisville dateline. The *Steuben Republican* of Angola, Indiana, prefaced their report with "Here is an account of an attempted assassination, that for pure hellishness, beates even the red skins of the forest."

The Ku Klux Klan had been mentioned, without any supporting evidence, in the *New Albany Ledger's* headline the day after the attack. On June 29 *The New York Sun* reprinted a report of the attack from the *Cincinnati Enquirer* under the headline "**KU-KLUX IN INDIANA**", but again there was no explanation of why the Moody family would have been targeted by the Klan. While the original Klan had terrorized parts of the South from 1865-71, it had largely died out even in those areas by this time and would not re-emerge in Indiana until fifty years later. The *New York Tribune* ran a similar story under the headline "**KU-KLUX IMITATORS IN INDIANA**". There were bands of vigilantes in Indiana at the time, referred to locally as "vigilants" or "regulators", ostensibly formed to bring criminals to justice. These included the State Horse Thief Detective Association, local groups known as White Caps that were similar to the Klan, and the Jackson County Vigilance Committee (or Scarlet Mask Society) formed in 1868 to eliminate the notorious Reno Brothers Gang which had originated in Seymour, about fifty miles east of Orleans. That committee was remarkably efficient in their effort, wiping out the Renos after lynching ten gang members.

The press evidently linked a local property dispute to the Klan because of congressional hearings that were underway in Washington regarding Klan violence during Reconstruction. The *London Standard* added:

> "Meanwhile, though the Southern States are perfectly tranquil, lawlessness has been manifested in some of the "loyal" States very much after the manner of the Ku-Klux in its worst excesses, real or imaginary. On the 25th instant, in the model State of Indiana, the home of Vice President [Schuyler] Colfax, a party of unknown men in disguise attacked the house of a family named Moody, living near the town of Orleans..."

In fact, there is no evidence that anyone involved was ever accused of being affiliated with the Klan, White Caps, or any other terrorist group. Nobody in Lawrence or Orange counties blamed outsiders for the attack. The Toliver-Jones faction had made no secret of their intention to kill Tom Moody during several private conversations that would later be recounted under oath. While the Moodys hired detectives and lawyers, the Toliver and Jones men were busy trying to establish alibis, as citizens of the two counties divided into bitterly opposed camps.

Chapter Three:
Now Shoot Him!

EVEN THOUGH CIRCUMSTANTIAL EVIDENCE STRONGLY implicated the Toliver-Jones faction in the attack on the Moody farm, more conclusive proof would be required to support indictments for attempted murder. Tom Moody was reported to have hired a detective from Ottawa, Illinois, to investigate. Later he added New Albany detectives Ben F. Bounds and Thomas Akers.

Simp Toliver appealed his slander judgment to the Indiana Supreme Court in 1871, alleging in part that one or more of the jurors had said "to their fellows in the jury room, that the defendant was 'a wealthy man', which was untrue." On September 7, 1872, the Supreme Court's denied his appeal in a decision that concluded:

> "The defendant made oath that he had been informed and believed that such a statement had been made in the jury room. This was no evidence upon which to set aside the verdict. We see no reason for reversing the judgment. The judgment is affirmed, with costs."

The court also overruled his petition for a rehearing.
The four Moody brothers and their sister, Polly Toliver, made

a sensible decision to move away from their charred farmhouse to a safer location. They kept the farm property but relocated to a large house in Orleans. The home was located on lots 247 and 248 at the northeast corner of Washington and Third Streets, just west of Congress Square. It was said that they rarely left the house after dark, but Tom remained active during the day. In 1872 he was chosen to represent Orleans as a delegate to the Indiana Democratic congressional convention. On the last day of 1874 he completed the purchase of an additional 20 acres of land in Orange County east of Orleans.

In 1873, after spending a reported ten thousand dollars on detectives and legal fees, the Moody family finally concluded that there was sufficient evidence for their case to proceed to court. More legal posturing and procedural motions, however, resulted in a further series of delays. On July 23, 1873, a writer who styled himself as "Jerry Slapjack" wrote in the "Orleans And Items" column of the *Paoli Weekly News*: "Many of our citizens are attending court at Bedford this week on the Toliver-Moody case." But it would be another eight and a half months before the trial would get underway. Three sons of William Toliver – Joseph, Simpson, and Parks – along with brothers-in-law Bent Jones and James Murray, were finally charged with arson and "assault and battery with intent to kill".

On March 24, 1874, while he was awaiting trial, U.S. patent No. 148,832 was awarded to A.B. Jones for a new, improved type of coffee-roaster. He immediately assigned one-half of his rights to Clifton W. Hamilton, also of Mitchell. This is the first of Bent's inventions known to have been patented, but it would not be the last.

Finally, after two continuances and "considerable cross-firing by attorneys", Judge George A. Bicknell denied the state's request for yet another delay due to the absence of "nine important witnesses" for the prosecution. The trial in Lawrence County circuit court at Bedford began at two o'clock on April 9, 1874. Judge Bicknell had graduated from the University of Pennsylvania in 1831 and completed law school at Yale before practicing briefly in

New York City. He moved to Indiana in 1846 and settled in New Albany before becoming judge of the second judicial circuit court of Indiana in 1852. In his portraits Bicknell appears somber with unruly hair and a penetrating gaze that suggests a no-nonsense personality. He certainly was not an indecisive man, as soon became evident.

That day's edition of the *Louisville Courier-Journal* reported that "(a)bout all the local attorneys are employed in the case, beside Hon. D.W. Voorhees, of Terre Haute, in the prosecution, and Major Jonathan W. Gordon, of Indianapolis, in the defense. About one hundred witnesses are subpoenaed on a side. Two detectives from New Albany have been working on the case for about a year past, and everything points to an exciting trial. Both parties are in good circumstances and can furnish the sinews of war."

Each defendant would be tried separately, at their request, and the prosecution chose to begin with Dr. Parks Toliver on the charge of arson. The *Courier-Journal* correspondent described him:

> "He is a young man of about 28 years, lately having had M.D. added to his name, and is now practicing his profession in Mitchell in this county. One looking over the audience for the party on trial would hardly pick him out as the man. He has borne a good character in his neighborhood, and, up to the difficulty with the Moodys, had never had his name used in anything disreputable."

The regular jury panel and a special panel of twenty-five men were used before twelve "good and lawful men" were selected, although it only took about an hour to seat the jury. The *Courier-Journal* complimented the sheriff, Captain Issac Newkirk, formerly of the Fourth Indiana Cavalry, for "displaying good sense by selecting persons removed from the tragedy." After the jury was sworn, one of the prosecutors, Major John W. Tucker, a Union veteran who had fought at Shiloh and during the siege of Vicksburg, made his opening statement. Witnesses were called and sworn in, then the court adjourned until the next morning.

Bob Moody

The prosecution's first witness was Polly Moody Toliver, testifying against her stepson, Parks. She began by explaining to the court that she had gone back to live with her four brothers – or, in her words, "the boys" – on account of an "unpleasantness" between herself and her step-children. Then Polly recounted the surprise night-time attack on the Moody home:

> "The first I knew of trouble was when I was awakened by something which was thrown on my bed, and which burst and made a loud report; jumping out of bed, another one was thrown in, which ignited and flamed up so as to set the bed afire and burn me badly; I ran over to the opposite side of the room, and the firing, etc., was kept up; I went into the room where my brothers were, and found the wall and door facing were on fire; these torpedoes were filled with nails and scraps of iron."

When she reached the room where Thomas slept, she saw that his bed was on fire. Then she noticed "some strange jugs in the room." Shrapnel had gone "in every direction, bursting the glass out of the windows, parts sticking in ceiling, walls, etc., beside quite a number of bullet marks on the wall." Polly told the jury that she had suffered severe burns to her foot and ankle that kept her bedridden for about two weeks. Her brother Thomas, she said, had been incapacitated for about a month. She estimated that about twenty shots had been fired into her room in addition to the firebombs and confirmed that none of the Toliver family had been among the neighbors who responded to the alarm.

Zachariah Burton, a respected resident of the area since 1826, testified that he had been among the crowd at the estate sale of William Toliver's property in 1870 and had witnessed the violent attack on Tom Moody. He "ran up and saw Moody on his hands and knees and one hand raised warding off the licks; also heard Joseph Toliver abusing the Moody's and saw Milton P. [Parks] Toliver striking around with a board." Local residents William McNabb and Samuel Finley also testified that they had witnessed the fight. On that day Bent Jones had been 32 years old; Joe Toliver was 29; the current defendant, Parks Toliver, was 22. Tom Moody was about two weeks away from his 56th birthday.

William Wallace told the jury that he "went early the morning after the attack and found tracks down through the corn-field, going towards where the Tolivers lived, and saw a great quantity of tracks coming from that direction towards the Moody's; also saw blood where Tom had crossed the fence after his escape."

Isom Hall, whose property was adjacent to the north side of the Moody farm, testified that he "was the first one in the house the next morning; found the jugs in the room; saw nails, slugs, etc., sticking in the wall, also where the floor and door-facing were burned." Some of the nails, he said, had been shot through a butter churn. Hall said that Thomas Moody came to his house covered with blood and told him that "all the rest of the family was killed." Hall saw "tracks of three persons going down through the corn field, toward the Tolliver's; also a track coming from that way toward the Moody's, which looked like they had been made the preceding night."

Next to take the stand was William Moody, the oldest family member in the house during the attack:

> "Heard some one coming into the house and then the person ran out and shooting began; I was in the east room and the boys in the west one; heard something fall and in a moment it burst; three torpedoes were thrown in my room, and, judging from the sound, there was two or three other torpedoes thrown into the other room; I was not injured; there was a jug found in my room the next morning, and another one I saw outside; they were gallon jugs; one of them had a white spot near the handle; they were clay jugs..."

Local apple grower Ransom Burton, Zachariah's eldest son, swore that he had heard Bent Jones say, after the estate sale but before the firebombing, "that if he was in the Tolliver boys' place he would get a gun and waylay Tom Moody and shoot him." The prosecution attempted to provide testimony from Samuel Hostetter that "Bent Jones told him that he had proposed to Tom Moody to fight and one get killed and the survivor to finish up the business", but Judge Bicknell ruled that the statement was inadmissible since it had been made after the attack.

James Elrod told the court that he had heard Bent Jones tell Tom Moody, in Mitchell, that "if he (Moody) would take his hands out of his pocket he would beat his old head to pieces." According to Elrod, Tom Moody replied that "he did not want to have any fuss with him." Michael Lindsey testified that he had heard Simpson Toliver make threats at the estate sale, but he didn't remember to whom.

The *Courier-Journal* correspondent, who signed his report only as "D.", but was almost certainly Daniel Spencer, concluded his coverage of the morning's testimony with an odd account that may or may not have been relevant. He wrote that Major Tucker, the prosecuting attorney, took the stand and testified that he:

> "(w)as at Mitchell the night of the attack, and left there about 11 o'clock, in a buggy, in company with Dr. Elrod, of Orleans. When about two miles from Mitchell, in a place where ghosts are supposed to abound, I saw some parties 'deployed' in front, at which his hair stood on end like the quills on the historical porcupine. He reined in his steed, and as he drew near the parties 'huddled' together on one side of the road to let the Major pass. The only weapon he had was a notarial seal, which was duly drawn ready for the emergency. There were about twelve in the crowd, and thinks one was a negro. Did not know them. Got into Orleans about 12 o'clock."

Shortly after noon court was adjourned for the mid-day meal and when the trail reconvened at 2:00 p.m. Dr. Laughlin of Orleans was the first witness. He had been called to treat Thomas Moody and Robert Lee. He described their wounds and confirmed that

Joe and Parks Toliver jointly owned a drug store in Orleans at that time. Another physician, Dr. Richard Single, testified that he had been at the estate sale and that Bent Jones told him:

> "... that he could skin his (Tom Moody's) d----d old bald pate, and, when told it might kill him, said he did not want to do that. He made some further statements in reference to a conversation held at his office between Joe Tolliver and Tom Moody, in which Joe threatened to "kick the d----d old s-n of a b---h," referring to Tom Moody."

Major F.A. Sears saw Parks Toliver throw a half brick at Tom Moody during the fight at the estate sale, but Tom threw his head back and dodged it. Sears had been at the Moody house the morning after the attack and saw the jugs that had been used. Then he added a critical bit of evidence, swearing that he:

> "... saw the wife of one of the defendants and her sister a short time previous to the attack in a buggy, with jugs similar to those containing the benzine, passing his store in Orleans going toward the Tolliver's and were coming from the direction of their drug store."

Major David Kelly was next, recalling that he had urged Bent Jones to seek a compromise over the property dispute. Bent replied "that if the Tolliver boys had the spunk that he had, and that if the property belonged to his mother, Tom Moody would have to walk over his dead body to get it." James C. Carlton, a "practical druggist" in Bedford, confirmed that the jugs in the Moody house smelled of benzine and then the prosecution produced important physical evidence:

> "... a letter in the handwriting of defendant, Milton P. Tolliver, was introduced, ordering 4 gallons of benzine of 74 degrees from Indianapolis, 24th of April, 1871."

The final witness of the day was Tom Moody. According to the *Courier-Journal* reporter:

> "He is a stout, well-preserved, bald-headed bachelor of 56 years; goes neatly dressed in home-spun clothes, and is cleanly shaved. Any one by a casual look would see that he is a man of wonderful resolution, and who knows nothing of defeat or failure. He had been on the 24th to Orleans to a grand Masonic celebration, and only went home after night."

He was sleeping in the west room when he heard the first explosion. He jumped up and ran out of the south door to the sound of more explosions and gunfire. About ten feet from the house he passed three men standing together. He thought they were Simpson, Joseph, and Wiley Tolliver. He turned toward the west and heard one of the men say, "There goes the G-d d----d old s-n of a b---h; shoot him." Tom testified that he recognized the voice as "a Tolliver". Not knowing the extent of his injuries, he hid beneath an apple tree until it was safe to cross to Isom Hall's house for help. It had taken him about an hour to make that journey due to loss of blood.

Tom was then asked about his recollections of the vicious attack at the estate sale. He said that Joe Tolliver had told him to leave because "it was the request of certain parties that he leave the premises." He decided to stay and that prompted the assault by the defendants. More trouble was to follow:

> "About two weeks afterward he had a difficulty with [Bent] Jones at the Faulkner House, in this place [Bedford]. Jones said he had got Polly's head in a halter, and that he (Jones) never had been beat, and never could be, and that the State of Indiana could not beat him. Joseph Tolliver was present, and began abusing too, when the landlord made them quit."

Moody claimed that he had tried to work out a compromise

with Jones in Orleans that resulted in Bent threatening him and walking out the door. Soon after, at Mitchell, Jones told Moody that if he "would take his hands out of his pockets and lay down his weapons, he would tear his gray eyes out." Simpson walked up and added that "he would split his old bald head open."

There was then a "severe cross-examination by Major Gordon, extending nearly two hours, but eliciting but little new, or causing him to vary his statements in any material point." Judge Bicknell then adjourned the trial for the day.

Tom Moody was recalled to the witness stand briefly when the trial resumed on Saturday morning, April 11. He was questioned about statements he was said to have made when it was thought that his wounds would be fatal "as to the employment of detectives, etc." He stated that he had hired "Akers and Bounds" as detectives but denied that he had attempted to bribe a witness.

One of the detectives, Benjamin F. Bounds of New Albany, testified that he had seen screws at Bent Jones's woodworking mill that resembled those found among the shrapnel at the Moody home.

Other witnesses recalled various arguments and threats made against the Moody family. Then the state rested its case.

The only evidence presented by Major Jonathan W. Gordon for the defense was a portion of the testimony of Tom Moody. Tucker objected on the grounds that the entire testimony should be entered but was overruled. At that point Judge Bicknell:

> "...made a statement to the effect that the State had not made out its case, and that it was the greatest failure he ever saw, taking into consideration the labor and expense attending it. The defense rested, and the Court, Judge G.A. Bicknell, directed the jury to return a verdict of 'not guilty'."

The judge's autocratic direction to the jury came as a stunning rebuke to the prosecution and the Moody family. If their case for an arson conviction against one defendant had been so summarily dismissed, it was unlikely that any of the accused could be convicted of "assault and battery with intent to kill". Major Tucker, representing the state of Indiana, tried to negotiate with Judge Bicknell, offering to dismiss some of the remaining charges in exchange for a continuance on others. This motion was denied and eventually all charges against all defendants were *nolle prossed* – a legal term meaning "we shall no longer prosecute". In other words, the three Toliver brothers, James Murray, and Bent Jones were all free to go.

On April 14, 1874, the *Indianapolis State Sentinel* printed a summary of the trial submitted by "an Occasional Correspondent":

> "Although this was a state case it was really Moody vs. Tolliver, Montague vs. Capulet. Thomas Moody furnished the means for a vigorous prosecution and was the principal witness for the state. It is said time heals all wounds, but the animosity existing between the above highly respectable, and once wealthy, citizens of Lawrence county has increased with time and is likely to be transmitted from sire to son."

The writer gave a brief account of the trouble that began with the unexpected death of William Toliver and hard feelings following the estate sale and slander suits, noting that "the parties were always belligerent, and upon meeting on trains, at hotels and public sales, their hands were up on their revolvers, and only by timely interference was bloodshed prevented." He wrote that the 1871 firebombing of the Moody farmhouse "was no less than a carefully prepared and a carefully executed plot to exterminate the first named family at one fell swoop, and attempt to perform the service of cremation while the victims were still alive." The correspondent concluded that the attackers "retreated without being recognized, leaving no traces or clue from whence they came or whither they had gone, and are to this day, and probably will be for all time, unknown." His explanation of Judge Bicknell's decision to force all charges to be dropped included mention of some of the highly incriminating circumstantial evidence:

> "All evidence given upon the trial has not been enough to excite a reasonable suspicion. That the screws were found at the factory where [Bent] Jones worked similar to the ones upon the floor after the house was raided, and that screws were found scattered over the floor of the Tolliver kitchen, on the 25th of June. A written order from Tolliver Bros., who were druggists, to a Louisville firm for 40 gallons of benzine, was introduced, dated April, 1871... Major Gordon, of counsel for the defendant, stated he could show, if permitted, that the defendant was in the company of grey-headed men on the night of the 24th of June, and felt abundantly able to erase the least suspicion of their guilt."

It should be noted that the *Courier-Journal* correspondent had earlier reported an order of four gallons of benzine from a source in Indianapolis, while the *State Sentinel* account of summation mentions forty gallons ordered from Louisville, both in the same month. There could have been two separate orders, or it is possible that one of the reporters misheard the testimony. Regardless, at a time when local law enforcement did not include trained detectives, with no state or federal agencies to provide assistance, and decades before the appearance of basic forensic science, any case that lacked a confession or eyewitness testimony had to rely heavily on circumstantial evidence. In this case such evidence was plentiful.

However, the location of the trial and the political forces in play were hardly insignificant. If the Moody farmhouse had been just one-third of a mile farther south the trial would have been held in Orange County, where sentiment was heavily in their favor. Because it was just north of the Lawrence County line the jury pool likely contained citizens either loyal to the Tolliver-Jones faction or those who were intimidated by them. The fact that Bent

Jones was a formidable Democratic leader in that county would not have escaped the attention of Judge Bicknell, who had major political ambitions. He would be elected as a Democrat to the first of two terms in the U.S. Congress just three years later but was an unsuccessful candidate for re-nomination in 1880.

The feud could have ended there and then. With the benefit of hindsight, that might have been the best outcome for all parties concerned. But this was far from the end of the Moody-Tolliver Feud. The Moodys were, indeed, "obstinate in their convictions" and the Tolivers felt they had been "robbed by the law". Bent Jones made it clear to anyone who would listen that they were determined to retaliate with deadly force. It would take them less than a year.

Chapter Four:
Cowardly Assassination

Tom Moody had missed playing cards while he was being careful to avoid an ambush. After more than three and a half years of threats, but no additional violence, he finally decided to take a chance by attending a card game at a shoemaker's shop in the Orleans business district on Tuesday night, March 2, 1875. At about 8:30 p.m. he left the shop and began the short walk back to the family home on Washington Street. As he crossed the street and stopped to open the gate, someone hiding behind a hedge at the west side of E.H. Taylor's cabinet shop fired both barrels of a double-barreled shotgun. The next day's edition of the *New Albany Daily Ledger-Standard* proclaimed "**LATEST NEWS**" in the form of a "special telegram" from a correspondent identified only as "Morse":

```
    "The Town of Orleans the
  Scene of Great Excitement.
       A Citizen Shot Down While
         Opening his Yard Gate.
  Riddled with Buckshot and Mortally Wounded.
         No Clue to the Perpetrator
              of the Bloody Deed.
      Death of the Victim this Forenoon.
  The People Terribly Excited and in Earnest.
```

> Orleans, Ind., March 3 – Our quiet little village was thrown into a wild state of excitement at 8 o'clock last night, by the double report of a shot gun, and the cry of murder, in the western part of town. A great number of our citizens rushed to the spot indicated by the noise, and it was immediately ascertained that Thomas Moody had been assassinated."

The correspondent explained that Moody had been "shot down in his own door-yard." Doctors found that he was:

> "nearly riddled with buck shot, they having entered his side, back and hips. His arm was literally shot to pieces, and one or two shots through his bowels. The doctors say he cannot recover.
>
> Your readers will remember the great Moody tragedy of three years ago [actually four], when this same Thomas Moody was shot through the breast and back. No clue to the perpetrators as yet. Great excitement prevails."

A later "**Second Dispatch**" from "Morse" announced that Tom Moody had died at 11 o'clock on March 3. He added that "The citizens have petitioned the Board of County Commissioners, now in session, to offer a suitable reward for the arrest and conviction of the murderer. The wildest excitement prevails. A big effort will be made to ferret the thing out. There is a good opening for a good detective."

Two days later another front-page story in the *Ledger-Standard* offered additional information:

"THE ORLEANS ASSASSINATION
Additional Particulars of the Cowardly and Murderous Assault on Mr. Moody.
He Passes Close to the Secreted Assassin a Moment Before the Shooting.

> The Excitement on the Increase in
> Orleans and Orange County.
>
> Orleans, a small but thriving village on the line of the Louisville, New Albany and Chicago Railway, about fifty miles from this city, was the scene, Tuesday night, of one of the bloodiest and most cowardly assassinations that has ever occurred in the history of the crimes committed in Southern Indiana. About 8 ½ o'clock, Tuesday night, the citizens of this quiet town were aroused and alarmed by the double discharge of a shot gun, the noise coming from the direction of the residence of Thos. Moody, an aged and highly respected citizen, and scores of excited men, on rushing to the place from whence the noise proceeded, found Mr. M. lying bleeding and prostrate on the ground, surrounded by his three brothers, who had come from the house, on hearing the report of the gun and the cries of the unfortunate victim for aid. The wounded man was carried into the house, when it was found that he had evidently been shot with a double-barreled shot gun, heavily loaded with buck-shot, as his body was filled with the shot. Four were found in the gate and six in the door, one of which penetrated through the door and sank into the stairway."

Joseph Moody had died a few months earlier. Testimony would later establish that the three "brothers" were William, John, and Polly – the widow of William Toliver. The *Ledger-Standard* account continues:

> "Mr. M. stated that he had been down to the central portion of the town, and on his return home had passed down the street on the side opposite to his residence, crossing the street directly opposite this gateway. When he reached the gate, and just as he was opening it, the first discharge was fired, the four buck-shot taking effect in his right hip,

and completely mashing it. He then turned around and faced the cowardly assassin, who was concealed behind a fence, some thirty paces distant, and hidden from observation by the shadow of a stable, when the second discharge occurred, the load taking effect in his abdomen, and two shots striking his left arm, breaking that member. He fell to the ground, and the cowardly and bloodthirsty miscreant made his escape.

From Mr. Moody's statement he must, on his way home, have passed within two feet of his hidden foe, unconscious of the fact that death lurked in such proximity to him. A very few minutes after the tragedy occurred, several of the citizens of the town observed three or four sky rockets blaze forth about two miles from the town, which are supposed to be connected with the mysterious affair in some manner."

Tom Moody lingered in "the most excruciating pain" until he died at eleven o'clock the following morning. A coroner's jury was empaneled and returned a verdict of "shooting by some party unknown." The *Ledger-Standard* noted that:

"The murdered man was held in the very highest respect by his fellow citizens, who are very much infuriated over the bloody occurrence, and will leave no effort undone to hunt down and bring to justice the perpetrator of this cowardly assassination. It is thought that the assassin came from Illinois, and was hired to commit the deed of blood, by some parties with whom the Moody family have had a feud of many years standing."

The newspaper then launched into a lengthy account of the Moody-Tolliver feud, including the firebombing of 1871 — noting that "suspicions pointed to a family living in the neighborhood, named Tolliver, as the ringleaders in the dastardly outrage" —

and summarizing the subsequent court cases. At the end of that explanation appeared the following:

"THE LATEST"

> "'Morse' the vigilant and attentive LEDGER-STANDARD correspondent, at Orleans, telegraphed us this morning that the Commissioners of Orange county, have offered a reward of $1,000 for the arrest and conviction of the murderer of Thomas Moody, at that place on Tuesday night. They have also called on Governor Hendricks to offer a reward of at least an equal amount on behalf of the State... The Coroner's jury have not closed their examination and are using every means at their command to ferret out the dastardly assassination. The excitement at Orleans and in the surrounding country is rapidly increasing, and every effort will be made by the authorities and the people to bring the guilty party to justice... The post mortem examination of the remains of Mr. Moody reveals the fact that seven buckshot took effect in his person."

On March 9, one week following the shooting, the *Daily Ledger-Standard* printed a remarkable letter. The writer had been upset by the paper's implication that Tom Moody's killer might have been associated with the Tolliver family. Perhaps concerned by the possibility of his own trial for slander – or possibly more lethal retaliation — the editor began with a lengthy preface:

> "We give place to a communication from a gentleman at Mitchell, Lawrence county, reviewing the TOLLIVER-MOODY difficulties, and defending the TOLLIVERS against the insinuations that they were connected with the killing of THOS. MOODY at Orleans, either by their own hands, or that of hired assassins. The information that we gave the public came from reliable sources, but we are not disposed

to do injustice to any one in the affair. Nor do we believe the codes of justice are to be attained by inciting a prejudice against any person. Of the character of the parties we have no personal knowledge, and can, therefore, only depend on those who are presumed to be conversant with the whole matter, and who are living in the vicinity. A great outrage has been perpetrated in the assassination of Mr. MOODY, we care not how bad a man he may have been, and the authorities of Orange county owe it to the good name of her people to ferret the matter to the bottom, if possible. The prompt action of the County Commissioners in offering a reward for the arrest of the assassin will meet the approval of the public, and it is hoped will result in success. The Southern part of Indiana has already suffered too much from deeds of violence to permit any further infractions of the law without rigorous measures being taken to bring the guilty to punishment. The great mass of the people of Orange county are among the most orderly, peaceable, and industrious citizens of the State, and they no doubt feel that they have been outraged by a most dastardly crime, and their fair fame blackened by the worst of criminals, the cowardly assassin."

The letter itself – an exceptional example of placing blame on a victim who had been dead for less than a week – followed, with this headline:

"LETTER FROM MITCHELL
Vindication of the Tollivers by a
Citizen of Lawrence County
(Occasional Correspondent of
the LEDGER-STANDARD)

MITCHELL, IND., March 8, 1875.

'EDS. LEDGER-STANDARD – In your issue of the 4th inst. appears an article in regard to the assassination of Thomas Moody, of Orleans, Orange county, on the night of March 3rd [sic], which leaves an erroneous impression upon the minds of your readers in the remote parts of the State. We say in the remote parts, for every one in this county and vicinity will know that your article is erroneous, and decidedly imaginary. What authority have you for the supposition that the assassin came from Illinois, and that he was hired by any of the Tollivers? Had Thomas Moody no enemies except this one family, and just because they have had some difficulty with the Moody family in the past, must they be accused of as dastardly a crime as this?

We dislike very much to refer to Mr. M. now, since his death, but justice compels us to defend the Tolliver family from such an accusation as this. There was not a more vindictive man in this part of the State than Mr. Moody. It can easily be seen by the records of the courts of Lawrence and Orange counties how many men he has brought suit against for the sole purpose of revenge, and being wealthy, Mr. M. was able to employ the best counsel the country afforded, and in this way have a great advantage over the poorer ones, who should chance to incur his enmity.

In regard to the origin of the trouble between Mr. M. and the Tolliver family: Mr. M.'s sister had married the father of the Tollivers, and father-in-law of A.B. Jones, and after the death of their father, there was a dispute between the Moodys and the Tollivers in the settlement of the estate, and the Tollivers, to save a law suit, offered time and again to settle the difficulty by arbitration, allowing the Moodys to choose three of the arbitrators and himself two, thus giving them the advantage; but still the Moodys would not agree to this.

Afterwards, at a sale of property belonging to the Tolliver estate, Mr. Thom. Moody and A.B. Jones had a personal difficulty, in which Mr. M. was badly worsted. For revenge, Mr. M. instituted suit against Simpson Tolliver for slander, and obtained a judgment for $1,400, and after succeeding thus far, he boasted that he would ruin the heirs of Wm. Tolliver, or spend every cent he had; and in order to do so he brought suit against A.B. Jones for damages in the sum of $5,000, and succeeded in obtaining a judgment for $75, paying the costs of suit himself, which amounted to nearly $500.

Some time after this, there was an attack upon Mr. Moody's house, and himself and several of the family wounded, and in consequence of the troubles between the Moody and Tolliver families, his first thought was to try and fasten this crime upon some member of the Tolliver family, and to make sure of some one of them, they employed several skilled detectives to work up a case against them, and, after spending time and money, they finally succeeded in obtaining an indictment against Joseph, Simpson, Parks Tolliver, A.B. Jones and James Murray. The case came to trial, and, after hearing the evidence for the prosecution, Judge Bicknell refused to hear any evidence on the part of the defendants, and instructed the Prosecuting Attorney to dismiss the case.

As we said before, we hate to bring up a man's character after he is dead, but justice to the Tolliver family compels us to answer the charges made against them, and we do not think Thos. Moody is any a more a saint now than when living, and it will not be sacrilege to mention his name. Every good citizen will denounce this cowardly murder, but at the same time there is almost as great an outrage perpetrated upon the Tolliver family, when they are accused of committing such an enormous crime as this, and that too without the least shadow of evidence against any one of them, as the verdict of the coroner's jury will show. Shall the Tolliver family be held responsible for every thing that happens to the Moodys, simply because they had a difficulty at a former time; How much the voters of this township believe the charges made by Thomas Moody against these Tollivers and Jones can easily be shown by the tally sheet at the last election, A.B. Jones being elected to the responsible office of Township Trustee, overcoming a large majority in favor of his competitor. Voters of Marion township, would you vote for a man if you thought he was guilty of such a crime as this; I venture to say you would not. Then why is it that they shall be accused, and that, too, openly, and the accusation scattered abroad over the State in the columns of a daily paper? We have conversed with a great many of the citizens of Orleans and vicinity, and also of Lawrence county, and all say there is nothing to indicate that any of the Tollivers or relatives had any knowledge whatever of this affair. Upon the contrary, they were all in Mitchell upon the night in question, and as there is no evidence, we can not account for this accusation except upon the vindictiveness of the Moodys toward them, as they well knew there was nothing to indicate that any of the Tollivers were engaged in this crime. Their only show was to trump up the story of a hired assassin. All we ask of the people is for them to consider this affair in its proper light. Take then, the characters of the parties interested. Who was Thos. Moody, and what was his character? It is not our intention to say what his character was, as the people in this section of the country know well the character he bore, and many of them to their sorrow. All we wish is to correct the statements made in your issue

> of the 4th inst., and the publication of this
> article.
>
> JUSTICE"

It was true that Jones had been elected as an independent candidate for township trustee in 1874, beating Democrat James Brown by seven votes. However, there was sufficient controversy about the election to cause the *Mitchell Enterprise* to note that "Some one says the ballot boxes all had the itch the other day." There were accusations that some ballots did not contain the names of every candidate. Bent persuaded the printer to publicly take the blame for any errors.

The identity of "JUSTICE" was never revealed publicly. The editor wrote only that it was "a gentleman from Mitchell". Regardless of his motive, the credibility of this defense would soon be tested in court.

Several local and national newspapers had also implicated the Toliver-Jones faction, but without a similar rebuttal. The *Chicago Tribune, Minneapolis Star Tribune,* and the *Memphis Daily Appeal* all carried a story, based on reporting by the *New Albany Ledger-Standard*, which stated "It is supposed that on Tuesday night last either some of the Tollivers or some one hired by them assassinated Thomas Moody." The *Boston Post* reported that "it is thought that the assassin came from Illinois, and was hired to commit the deed by the Tollivers." And the *Indianapolis Evening News* flatly declared that "Thomas Moody of Orleans, Orange county, was murdered last Tuesday night by a brother-in-law named Tolliver or some of the family. The murder was the result of a family quarrel which had lasted for years."

The *Bedford Star*, in its March 6 edition, included on the front page a blunt assessment of the situation:

> "We learn that Mr. Moody told one or two persons
> the name of the individual who he thought shot
> him, but they, for obvious reasons, withhold
> it from the public. The history of the previous

> attempt, made some years ago, to assassinate Moody when living near Mitchell, are still fresh in the memories of the people. It seems that he has been pursued ever since with the same bloodthirsty vindictiveness, and finally has fallen a victim... It is to be hoped that the guilty wretch may be caught, and meet with the only punishment that will satisfy the people and the law – hanging."

In addition to the $1000 reward offered by Orange County, William and John Moody posted $3000 and Governor Thomas A. Hendricks came through with $600 from the state of Indiana in an official proclamation on March 15. That amounted to a total reward fund of $4600. The matter of reward money was critical at a time when there were no state or federal bureaus of investigation, no modern forensic science, little concept of proper standards for collecting and protecting evidence, and limited communication between law enforcement agencies. If there was reward money offered by the family and friends of the victim, "detectives" could be expected to appear in an attempt solve the case and claim the cash. A substantial reward might interest legitimate investigators from established agencies such as Pinkerton, but often the most enthusiastic investigators were self-appointed and unregulated amateurs. That seems to have been true in this instance, as reported elsewhere in the March 6 edition of the *Bedford Star*:

> "Since the murder of Moody in Orleans, the other night, that interesting village has been turning out first-class detectives by the dozen. Two of them visited Bedford on Thursday, and in less than two hours after their arrival one of them got drunk and attempted to shoot a stranger, while the other told every body in town, in a confidential manner, what he was up to – working up the murder, etc. The only thing he "worked up" while here was his supper, and it required the assistance of a quart of whiskey and half keg of beer to enable him to do that."

The immediate result was disappointing. On April 7, slightly more than a month after the murder, the *Paoli Weekly News* reported:

> "The coroners jury, summoned to investigate the murder of Thomas Moody, at Orleans, on the night of March 2, is still in session at that place. So far as we have been able to learn, nothing has been developed and it now seems very probable that the perpetrator of the dastardly, cowardly murder will escape detection. Every known means should be resorted to, to bring the assassin to justice. Every interest of society demands his detection and swift, sure punishment."

Chapter Five:
Seven Feet of Rope

Press coverage of the feud was brief and sporadic for several months, but both families were busy behind the scenes. Some of the so-called detectives may have been wasting the Moody's time and money, but others were unearthing critical evidence and persuading some of those who knew the truth about Tom's murder to come forward. The Toliver and Jones men, meanwhile, were actively establishing alibis and recruiting friendly witnesses. It soon became obvious that A.B. "Bent" Jones had assumed the leading role in perpetuating the Toliver side of the feud. Parks and Tom Toliver would be tried for murder and both Jones brothers were married to Toliver daughters, but otherwise the family's participation in future incidents was limited.

Meanwhile, there were auspicious incidents indicating how divided the supporters on each side had become. On February 2, 1876, the *Bedford Star* reported "The extensive plaining mill of Jones & Toliver, of Mitchell, was burned on last Tuesday, Loss, $15,000." That translates to about $362,000 in 2020 dollars. One month later the same paper noted that preparations were being made to rebuild the mill. On April 15, the *Star* praised Bent for his public service:

> "A.B. Jones, the popular trustee of Marion township, was in town this week. Mr. Jones has done more for the schools of his township

probably than any other trustee in the county, and at the same time has not increased the taxation. It would be well for those on this side of the river to pattern a little after Mr. J., and pay more attention to educational interests."

This endorsement came as Jones was beginning to campaign for a higher elective office. In less than two months it would prove to be premature.

On June 3, 1876, the *Bedford Star* reported a startling breakthrough in the investigation:

"Considerable excitement was occasioned in Mitchell on last Wednesday over the arrest of A.B. Jones, on the charge of being an accessory in the murder of Thomas Moody, of Orleans... He was taken to Paoli and placed in prison. The preliminary examination will take place, we learn, to-day. It is said that ever since the murder of Moody detectives have been engaged in working up the matter. Mr. Jones' friends are confident that he will be able to show to the satisfaction of the community that he is innocent. It is reported that four or five other parties are to be, if they are not already, arrested, some of whom live in Kentucky and Illinois."

The *Bedford Lawrence Mail* would later report that Bent Jones had been a candidate for the Democratic nomination for sheriff of Lawrence County at the time of his arrest for murder. Indiana Supreme Court documents mention testimony that "he had two revolvers in his boot leg" when taken into custody.

The *New Albany Daily Ledger-Standard* announced that the wheels of justice had begun to turn in its June 12 edition:

"MURDER WILL OUT
The Moody Murder Case at Orleans Being Unraveled.

> A Hoosier Detective Puts in His
> Work in an Effective Manner.
> Resulting in the Arrest and
> Examination of Four Persons.
> All of Whom are Held to Answer
> in the Circuit Court.
> Discovery of the Murderous Weapon
> in a Pond Near the Town."

The newspaper's "correspondent at Paoli" reported that "The case of the State against Alonzo B. Jones, charged as an accessory to the murder of Thomas Moody... was commenced at the Court House last Saturday." It reported that an earlier grand jury had deliberated for several weeks before "they adjourned without finding any clue to the assassin." However, "a detective by the name of Harry Beecher Ward, of Laurel, Franklin county, Indiana, came to Orleans and began to work up the case." Ward had befriended Bent Jones, having convinced him that he was building a case against Jeff Huffstetter. Eventually Jones told him that the shotgun used to kill Tom Moody had been conveniently deposited in a pond on property owned by Huffstetter northwest of Orleans. He also "disclosed the names of parties who were directly or indirectly implicated in the murder. This, with other evidence, induced Mr. Ward to have the following persons arrested: A.B. Jones, Eli Lowery, Colman D. Smart, and a Mrs. Patterson." The *Ledger-Standard* correspondent correctly predicted that "in all probability there will be several long and tedious law suits before it is finally disposed of."

On June 16, the *Bedford Star* provided an update:

> "The preliminary examination of A.B. Jones at Paoli, on a charge of being an accessory in the murder of Thomas Moody at Orleans about a year ago, came to an end on last Saturday. It occupied over eight days, and only the witnesses for the State were examined. At the close of their testimony application was made for bail, and the Justice fixed the amount at $20,000. It was promptly given, David Sheeks,

> Esq., of Marion township, signing the bond. Since that time Dr. Cole Smart has been bailed, his bond being $5,000. Lowry and Mr. Patterson still remain in prison. Mrs. Patterson is only charged with being an accessory after the fact, having come to a knowledge of the murder and not making it known. Court meets at Paoli next Monday, when the matter will go before the grand jury at once."

Bent Jones, who had been so earnestly defended by "JUSTICE" in the *New Albany Ledger-Standard*, would now face a grand jury on the charge of being an accessory to murder. His $20,000 bail was equivalent to roughly $479,000 in 2020 dollars. David Sheeks, who signed the bond, was said to be the largest landowner in Lawrence County (with about 4,000 acres of property) and was one of its wealthiest citizens. This was especially fortunate since he eventually fathered 22 children during three marriages.

"Lowry" was Eli Lowry (or Lowery), a young man who had lived in Mitchell for three or four years and worked at Bent Jones's sawmill and woodworking plant. He boarded with Joseph and Alice Patterson, who were also implicated. Lowry's actual age is uncertain. Newspaper stories claimed he was twenty-four years old when he was arrested, although one reporter commented on how much younger he appeared. The best evidence indicates that he was probably born in 1856, the same birth year as Tom Toliver. That would mean he was about nineteen years old when Tom Moody was murdered and only twenty or so when he was locked up in Paoli.

Dr. Cole Smart's role in the murder (if any) is murky at best. Both the *Indianapolis News* and *Indianapolis People* reported that "Dr. Cole *Stewart*, [emphasis added] of Lagrange, Kentucky, has been arrested for the murder of Thomas Moody at Orleans. He is now in the jail at Paoli." That name was incorrect. La Grange, Kentucky, is in Oldham County, just outside Louisville. The *Louisville Courier-Journal* referred to him as "Cole D. Smart". A Coleman D. Smart had married Emeline H. Clark in Lawrence

County in 1859. They appear as residents of Marion Township in the 1860 federal census. In both 1865 and 1866 there were federal excise taxes assessed against Coleman Smart of Bryantsville, about eight miles from Mitchell, as a "retail liquor dealer." On June 3, 1876, the *Ledger-Standard* reported that detectives "D. Mills, of Mitchell, and C.H. Keeth, of Orleans" had arrived at the Franklin House in New Albany:

> "...having Dr. Cole Smart, of LaGrange, Kentucky, in charge, who is accused of being accessory to [murder]. Dr. Smart was living in Orleans at the time of the murder, but shortly after removed to Kentucky, where he has since resided. He has always borne a good reputation, and does not look like a murderer, at least there is none of the brutal ferocity in his countenance, that one would be led to expect in the face of the liberate [sic] life taken."

Charges against Smart were eventually dropped when Eli Lowry's testimony failed to implicate him directly in the murder. Although he was exonerated in the Moody case, another member of his immediate family would later be convicted of a different murder. On July 27, 1889, the *New Albany Ledger* would report:

> "Henry Smart, who is to be hanged at Louisville on the 31st of this month, for murder committed a year or so ago, was raised at Mitchell, Ind. He is about 23 years old and is a son of Cole Smart, and left there in 1877 with the family. His father and step-mother now reside at Vincennes. Young Smart recently embraced the Catholic faith and is preparing to meet his death that soon awaits him."

Meanwhile, Eli Lowry was uncomfortable with the situation he found himself in and would soon make a futile attempt to disappear from the scene. He would eventually provide detailed testimony that is the most authentic (if assuredly self-serving) account of the events surrounding the murder.

On June 23 the grand jury indicted five men on charges of murder in the first degree. One week later the *Bedford Star* reported:

> "A.B. Jones, Lee Jones, Eli Lowery, Dr. Park Tolliver and Thomas Tolliver, are all confined in the Paoli jail under indictments for the murder of Thomas Moody. We learn that the case will not be tried this term of the Orange Circuit court. Major Gordon having asked for and had granted by Judge Pearson, a continuance until next term, which will be in October next. Bail has been refused the parties by the court."

On the same page of that edition of the *Star* were two other notes of interest:

> "Major Gordon, the great criminal lawyer of Indianapolis, has been employed by A.B. Jones and others to defend them in the circuit court at Paoli."

This was the same Major J.W. Gordon who had led the successful defense of the Toliver-Jones men in their 1874 trial for the attack on the Moody home. And:

> "Dr. J.T. Biggs, of Mitchell, has been appointed Trustee of Marion township in place of A.B. Jones, the former occupant of the office."

The expensive bail for Bent Jones had been revoked after less than three weeks of freedom. His political career had ended and his criminal career had officially begun.

News of the murder indictments attracted new national press attention. On July 3 the *St. Louis Globe Democrat* printed a story attributed to the *Indianapolis State Sentinel*, about troubling new developments for residents of Southern Indiana:

"INDIANA LAWLESSNESS
A Reign of Terror in Orange and Lawrence Counties.
Horrible Murders by a Mob – Danger of Another Outbreak.

"MITCHELL, Ind., June 29 – The County of Orange and south part of Lawrence County, including the town of Mitchell, are just now undergoing a storm of excitement, owing to some alleged recent developments in the history of certain great crimes committed in the neighborhood of Orleans, five miles south of this place, during the last six or eight years. In fact there seems to have been in years past a perfect mania on the subject here – a criminal mania, and a mania even more criminal to punish those affected with it. Bad men have made life and property unsafe by committing crimes against both; and then, by inflicting death on petty offenders by lynch law, have murdered the law itself – the only protection of both that can ever be safely relied on."

This was followed by a gruesome account of the lynching of "two petty thieves" who were hanged "at the bridge over Lost River, between Orleans and Paoli" by a mob of about seventy-five men. According to this story:

"The mob which committed these atrocities... most of whom still reside in the neighborhood... have pretty well concealed their guilt [but] many of them are known. The state of public opinion, however, and the fear of being murdered, have CLOSED EVERY MOUTH... Private feuds have filled the whole community with apprehension and

> fear. None feel safe. Perhaps the feeling of insecurity but feebly expresses the fact, for some of THE MOST FIENDISH OFFENSES known to the dark annals of crime have occurred in this immediate neighborhood within the last few years. Some of these, which have taken place in the families of the Moodys and Tollivers, are peculiar in their character."

This was followed by a generally accurate, if somewhat histrionic, summary of events leading up to the murder of Thomas Moody. The *Globe Democrat* also mentioned two recent fires of suspicious origin that might have been set in retribution:

> "[Following the murder], by crime or misfortune, the planing mill of A.B. Jones, in the town of Mitchell, was burned to the ground, involving a loss of nearly all he possessed, and the house of Simpson Tolliver met with a similar fate. No author of these crimes, if they were such, has ever been discovered."

It is unlikely that any of the surviving elderly Moody family members were running around torching homes and businesses, but there was a growing movement among local "vigilants" to provide rough justice to the Toliver-Jones faction for a variety of alleged crimes. More pertinent, however, was news almost buried in the final paragraph:

> "...Lowry pleaded guilty and was sentenced to imprisonment for life at Jeffersonville. The others remain in the JAIL AT PAOLI. The popular excitement has risen with these events to the highest possible pitch, and the mob spirit, immediately after the conviction of Lowry, was rife in the streets of Paoli. Men were heard to declare with great oaths that all that now remained to complete justice in respect to the other four was to give each of them seven feet of rope... A large meeting of the citizens of this place is now [June 29]

assembled at Moore's corner, and speeches of
a very violent character are being made by
men of position and influence… and although
these orators avowedly deprecate an appeal
to violence, yet no man of intelligence… can
fail to perceive that the direct tendency is
to precipitate an APPEAL TO JUDGE LYNCH."
```

Edited versions of this story appeared in the *New York Sun* on July 6 and in the *San Francisco Chronicle* on July 18.

Young Eli Lowry, believing that the other four defendants were setting him up to take the blame, had turned "state's evidence" and agreed to testify against them in a plea deal to avoid hanging – even though the alternative he accepted was a life sentence at the Indiana Prison South. The *Cambridge City Tribune* added: "It is hinted that other murders will come to light before the investigation has been closed." Lowry appeared to be more concerned that associates of the Toliver-Jones group would lynch him to prevent his testimony than of being strung up by supporters of the Moody family.

Lowry and his cohorts in crime all had reason to fear retribution from what was known euphemistically as "Judge Lynch". Ten days later the Paoli jail was the site of one of the most bizarre episodes in Orange County history.
```

Chapter Six:
A Rude Awakening

In 1876 the Paoli jail and sheriff's residence were in the same two-story building, with a long hallway running through it. On Sunday morning, July 9, 34-year-old Sheriff W.P. Shively was asleep in his upstairs room when, about thirty minutes after midnight, he heard a voice. Sitting up in bed, he saw several men with revolvers pointed at him. The *New Albany Daily Ledger-Standard* provided its readers with a typically vivid account:

> "When Mr. S. inquired what they wanted, he was told to keep still or he would be shot. Under the circumstances, he thought it advisable to remain quiet. They then demanded the keys to the jail, which he refused to deliver, but as the keys were lying on a stand, the vigilants perceived them, and one of them picked up the keys, and they went down stairs, one of them remaining to guard Mr. S."

The intruders also took two Colt revolvers, three double-barreled shotguns, and a pillow soaked in coal oil.

Instead of individual cells, the Paoli jail consisted of one large room, about 26 by 30 feet, with narrow grated windows about seven and one-half feet above the floor. The main outside door was made of solid iron, but the inside one had metal bars. The vigilantes used a key to open the main door and began firing through the bars of the second door into the darkened room. Lee Jones, according to the newspaper, received a slight flesh wound on his right arm above the elbow. As the intruders moved forward, the accuracy of their aim and will to proceed quickly diminished when the prisoners returned gunfire! Finding themselves under attack, efforts to unlock the second door were abandoned. Bent Jones later admitted that friends had smuggled two pistols into the jail from outside by attaching them to a pole that was raised to the level of the grated windows, where they were retrieved by the prisoners.

Sheriff Shively remained under armed guard, but the sound of gunfire roused the neighborhood. Several residents quickly armed themselves and headed for the jail. The *Ledger-Standard* report continued:

> "The hall doors had been unlocked by the mob, so when the citizens came in at one door, the mob went out of the other. The man who had been left to guard Mr. S. remained until all of his band had left the house before he started, but warned Mr. S. not to make any noise, else he would shoot him. Under the circumstances, Mr. S. decided that discretion was the better part of valor, so he submitted, and remained passive."

When the sheriff finally decided it was safe to leave his room he went downstairs and found the building filled with armed citizens. The intruders were all gone, but since they had never unlocked the inner door the prisoners – Bent Jones and his brother, Lee, along with Parks Toliver and his youngest brother, Tom – were armed but still in confinement. According to the *Ledger-Standard* reporter:

> "When Mr. S. got down there, he found Lee Jones, crying 'murder!' at the top of his voice, and he could not be quieted for some time. He evidently thought retribution had come, and that he would meet the fate that had

> been inflicted upon a fellow man, by his hand. As soon as Mr. S. could inquire into the matter a little and ascertain what had been done, he discovered that the party consisted of twenty-one men, that they came there silently, and awakened no one in the village until the firing commenced... The whole occurrence did not occupy more than ten minutes, so the mob, if they had so desired, could not have taken the prisoners out and hung them, before the citizens arrived, but they could have shot them, if they could have seen to have done the work."

Sheriff Shively's deputy also had a rude awakening, according to the paper:

> "As soon as the mob left the house, Henry Davidson, Deputy Sheriff, put in an appearance at the jail. He stated that shortly after 12 o'clock he heard shooting at the jail, and fearing what proved to be the case, he hurriedly dressed himself and started for the jail. He didn't go there, however, as at his own door he was met by an armed posse of men who told him to stay at home, for if he attempted to assist the Sheriff, he would be shot. Mr. Davidson had no desire to immortalize himself, so he remained at home."

There were differing opinions regarding the identity of the mob and their actual intentions:

> "Mr. Shively does not believe that they were residents of Orange county, as they took no pains to conceal their faces, and none of them were recognized... The feeling against the Joneses and the Tollivers is very strong in Orange county, but the Sheriff states that all are in favor of giving them a fair trial. The attorneys of the prisoners have been making attempts to secure a change of venue, and this

has had the effect of making the feeling against the prisoners still stronger. The friends of the prisoners say that the attempt to mob them, showed conclusively that a fair trial can not be had in Orange county, while there are those who say that the mob was a piece of chicanery; that they were friends of the murderers, and that it was gotten up to secure a change of venue, and that they did not intend to hurt them. This story does not seem at all plausible, as the shots were fired with the evident intention of doing some damage, while the manner in which the prisoners responded to the fire, showed they were badly scared and would liked to have killed somebody."

The importance of primary sources such as those cited above cannot be overstated. Newspaper stories written while memories were fresh, or statements given under oath in court offer the most authentic and reliable accounts. Over the years stories tended to change to the point that they are often far from the truth. A good example appeared eleven years later, when the *Indianapolis Journal* printed the recollections of George Buskirk, a member of one of the most prominent local families:

"DEFENDED HIMSELF AGAINST A MOB.
How Bent Jones, the Murderer, Dispersed a Crowd That Tried to Lynch Him.

"Speaking of the Moody, Jones and Tolliver families, of Orange county, reminds me that I had several close calls for my life when they were reigning down there," said George Buskirk, probate county clerk, yesterday, to a Journal reporter. "I was deputy clerk of Orange county during the reign of terror, and until after the three were sent to the penitentiary for life. For a while after the

> arrest of the gang it looked like they would escape conviction, and a mob was organized to come to Mitchell, break into the jail and hang them. One night I was sitting in my office writing, when one of the detectives who had worked up the case against the outlaws came to me and told me I had better blow out my light and leave the court-house. He refused to give any reason for so doing, and I refused to go. Toward midnight the town was filled with a mob that made straight for the court-house to secure the criminals. By some means the friends of the prisoners had heard of the coming of the mob, and after nightfall had, by means of a long pole and a bucket, had handed several loaded revolvers up to the windows of Bent Jones's cell. He secured the weapons, and when the mob neared the court-house he opened fire on them. I began to fear my life was in danger, and in getting out of the building narrowly escaped alive. Several advances were made on the building, but every time the sure aim of Jones drove back the mob. Finally two men were shot and the mob dispersed. The wounded men, I think, both recovered. My brother prepared the indictment on which the men were arrested, and among their last threats before they were taken to Jeffersonville were to kill him if they ever got out. I recently visited the penitentiary, and talked with all of them. They are greatly changed, but still the kind of men who, I believe, would, with the exception of Lowery, become terrors if they should be pardoned. They should never be released."

The most obvious error is that the jail was in Paoli rather than Mitchell, which is in Lawrence County. At that time the Paoli jail was not located in the county courthouse, but in a separate building located near the site of the current Paoli Public Library. There was no record of any of the mob members being wounded; the only reported casualty was a slight gunshot wound to the arm of Lee Jones. Other details in Buskirk's account may be true and it is entirely possible that the reporter did not take good notes. Whatever the reason, garbled and "mis-remembered" accounts of this and other incidents would appear often in subsequent years.

Attorneys for the prisoners immediately sent a telegram to Indiana Governor Hendricks, asking for his help in ensuring their safety. The governor ordered that they be taken to the Floyd County jail in New Albany for safekeeping. The prisoners, accompanied by a group that included Sheriff Shively and Deputy Sheriff Davidson, arrived there Monday night on the seven o'clock train. The *Ledger-Standard* referred to them as "the murderers of Tom Moody", although they would not stand trial for several months. Eli Lowry's confession had evidently left little doubt in many minds about their guilt.

Sheriff Shively would live less than nine months after the mob attack in Paoli. He died of "congestive chill" on April 5, 1877, at the age of 35. He left a wife and, according to the *Daily Ledger-Standard*, "two or three children."

Chapter Seven:
The Other Side

The arrival of the Toliver and Jones prisoners in New Albany on July 10 caused considerable local apprehension - and for good reason. The *Ledger-Standard* reminded its readers about the capture of the Reno Gang just seven years earlier. A band of 65 men, thought to be members of the Scarlet Mask Society, arrived in New Albany by train and marched from the station to the jail, where they beat and shot the sheriff until his wife turned over the keys. Three of the Reno brothers and one of their gang members were dragged from their cells and promptly lynched. No one was ever charged or officially investigated for those lynchings. Sheriff Lyman S. Davis made sure his new prisoners were locked in securely, then "intrenched himself in the jail, intending to give any such party a warm reception."

The following morning the prisoners from Paoli were ready to talk:

> "A LEDGER-STANDARD reporter visited the jail this morning, for the purpose of interviewing the prisoners. He found Bent Jones anxious to see a reporter, and in fact, all wanted to see one, to give their side of the story about the mob. The reporter and Bent Jones took chairs and sat in the rear end of the corridor, while the Tolliver brothers and Lee Jones surrounded them. Bent made a statement,

which is published substantially as it fell from his lips. His companions prompted him every time he wandered from the thread of his discourse, and all seemed to have the same story. Of the truth or falsity of their story, we have nothing to say, but leave it to the reader to judge for himself.

JONES' STATEMENT

About a week ago we were warned that we would be mobbed and probably hung. It is a bad place out there, and hangings by lynch law are not unfrequent, so we felt uneasy about our positions. Friends of ours passed two revolvers in to us, a week ago last Thursday. These we concealed in an old stove pipe, in case we were attacked. On Saturday, Sheriff Shively visited Orleans, and instructed his deputy not to admit any person to the jail during his absence. Before he went he searched our room thoroughly, but did not find our arms. When he returned in the evening, he gave us our suppers, but did not give us any water, as he usually did, and he did not put the chain across the outside door, and only partially locked the door at all. From this we supposed that he would be down again during the evening and give us some water and lock the doors securely.

We desired to have the doors made as strong as possible, for we were afraid of being lynched. This evening he did not come near us. Shortly after twelve o'clock I was awakened by hearing some person come in the house and go up stairs. I awakened Lee, and we both distinctly heard a conversation going on in Shively's room. A hole had been burned through one of the joists, and by placing my ear to that, I could distinctly hear Mrs. Shively begging that our lives be spared, while Shively would not agree to anything. Six men then went out through the hall and went up stairs, but remained only about five minutes. They came down but soon went up again, and the third time they came down, Shively was with them. We were now thoroughly alarmed, for we thought:

OUR DOOM WAS SEALED.

Before they came down we heard the Sheriff telling the men how the guns were loaded, where they could find candles in a drawer, and where a can of coal oil was. Heard him tell them to saturate a pillow and tell them it would make a good light. I left the position I was in, and intended to get one of the revolvers to defend myself, Lee using the other. Shively unlocked the door and we all distinctly heard him say, "Don't be a bit uneasy, the boys are unarmed, as I searched the room to-day." As he said this he threw the door open and called for "Bent". I did not answer him, and I suppose he thought me asleep. Just then two shots were fired, one in the direction of my bed, which certainly would have killed me had I been lying on it. Lee then got to the door as soon as possible and fired two shots into the crowd, upon which the door was immediately closed and locked, before I had a chance to shoot. There are six windows to the jail, and men on the outside placed lights at every one of these, so as to illuminate our room that we might be shot. Myself and the Tolliver boys were to put these lights out, but the assault was so sudden that we were unable to do it. Had we not returned the fire, I think we would have all been killed."

That concluded Bent Jones's statement, but the *Ledger-Standard* reporter added:

"The Joneses and Tolivers say they will swear to the above statement, and they say that in the party the Sheriff was the only man from Paoli, while he recognized several others

> from different places. They blame Mr. Shively for it all, while according to his statement he was powerless to resist, and his seems the more plausible story.
>
> Jones said that about five minutes after the mob left, Shively came down, but did not open the door, as they told him they would surely shoot him if he did. Bent Jones was very communicative, and seemed anxious to impress upon the reporter the guilt of the Sheriff.
>
> When asked for his opinion of Lowery, he said they were all under instructions from their attorneys not to make any statements, and were it not for that, he would cheerfully give the reporter his entire knowledge of the affair. He said he could tell of conversations he had heard between Lowery and others while in jail, and that there was 'a heap of money' backing the prosecution against them."

There are no known photographs of the alleged murderers or their victim - only a drawing of Eli Lowry that would appear in a newspaper during a later trial. However, newspapers of that time often provided colorful characterizations to give their readers a more vivid impression. This reporter offered a personal look at the Jones and Toliver brothers:

> BENT JONES is a man apparently about forty years of age, of medium stature, and rather heavy set. His hair is nearly black and is worn rather short, and this morning it had the appearance of having been surprised by a shock of electricity, as it stood out nearly straight from his head. He wore a neat suit of light linen clothes, and was in his shirt sleeves. His eyes are hard, and at first have a rather pleasing expression, but on a closer scrutiny the fire of passion and adamantine determination are discernible in their depths. His mouth is expressive of nothing but firmness, and the relentless manner in which the lips close, show the man who once

an enemy is an enemy for life. His chin and upper lip are covered with a sandy beard and moustache. He is of good address and pleasing talker, being careful of his statements, but in his remarks about the Sheriff, the spirit of vindictiveness, with which he is credited, showed plainly. He sat beside the reporter and conversed in an easy and graceful manner, rehearsing the late scene as if it had been a very ordinary occurrence. The desperate man does not show it in his countenance, but he has an excellent command of his features, his face being about as expressive as if it were carved in marble.

LEE JONES is a younger man than Bent. and his feelings show more plainly on his fairer countenance. His hair is lighter than Bent's, and his eyes are gray, being the only gray eyes in the party. He looks like a bad man, as does Bent, but he looks as if his knowledge of crime might not be as extensive as his brother's and the pangs of conscience were gnawing at his heart strings. His right arm was bandaged, where he was wounded, and he kept moving uneasily about the jail.

PARKS TOLIVER is really a fine looking man, tall and slender, with black hair, eyes and whiskers. He appeared nervous, and kept constantly in motion, frequently prompting Bent as he was making his statement. He does not look like a man reared in crime, but like a man who could be led into crime, and when once there, would hang like a dog to a root.

TOM TOLIVER is a young man, nineteen years of age, and is really a good looking young man. He appears to have been a tool used by the older men in crime, having been whirled into the vortex that Bent Jones had made, and when once in it was impossible to get out. He assented to every statement made by the others, and seemed to take his incarceration philosophically and stoically, moving about in a nonchalant manner, smoking a good cigar. He gave the reporter two of the buck shot that had been flattened against the walls, when they were fired upon."

Below these pen portraits was a transcript of the telegram from Governor Hendricks to Sheriff Davis, seeking assurance that the lives of the prisoners would be protected and asking "whether or not you will be able to afford them such protection as will insure their complete immunity from danger from lawless organizations." Following that was the sheriff's reply, which included his observation that "I am informed by the Sheriff of Orange county that there is not so much danger of the prisoners being mobbed as of their being released by their friends." He added, "I think that I will be able to afford them such protection..." and concluded by writing "Should I need any more assistance I will inform your Excellency by telegraph."

This lengthy newspaper account ends with a paragraph titled:

"REMARKS:

In conclusion it might be well to state that the room in which the prisoners were confined at Paoli, is in the jail part of the building, and on the first floor, while Mr. Shively's room is up stairs and on the other side of the hall, and it would be impossible for any one confined in the jail to hear what was going on in Mr. Shively's room. Mr. S. could hardly hear the shots which were fired in the jail, and the idea that Bent Jones could hear Mr. S. talking in his room, is simply ridiculous. They have evidently got their stories well learned, and will be prepared to swear to anything. Jones

> says he is a Township Trustee, and that his word is as good as anybody's. His reliability is attested by the fact that several of his witnesses have been indicted for perjury, and they even confessed that Jones forced them to perjure themselves. As for Mr. Shively, he is too well known as a gentleman of honor, for the vile stories of these Joneses to even tarnish his fair name, and it will no doubt add to his popularity as an efficient and conscientious officer. The Jones brothers will not help their cases any by circulating such reports and while they injure themselves, they do not injure Mr. S. Fears are entertained that they will yet meet violence, for the feeling is so strong against them. The police can be depended on, and there is no doubt that the jail will be well guarded, but the lessons of the Reno tragedy should be a warning to their keepers, and a strong guard should be placed about the jail."

On July 20 a *Daily Ledger Standard* reporter met "a gentleman from Orange county" who told him that "while the feeling there against the Jones and Tolliver brothers is very strong, there is no danger of any Vigilants from that county."

One can only imagine the reaction of Major Gordon and the rest of the Toliver-Jones legal defense team when they read this interview. Bent Jones must have realized that he had probably made a bad situation worse because he was soon claiming to have been misquoted. It its July 29, 1876, edition the *Bedford Star* included a front-page rebuttal reprinted from the *New Albany Independent*:

"THE OTHER SIDE
Bent Jones' story of the Paoli Jail Mob.

Soon after the Joneses and Tollivers were removed to the New Albany jail a reporter of the Ledger-Standard, of that city, called on them and held an interview with Bent Jones, which was published in the next day's paper. Jones declares that what he said was garbled and twisted by this reporter until it is not at all anything like the truth, and furnishes the Independent, another paper of that city, the following statement which he avers is a true story in regard to the mob at Paoli:

Mr. Editor:

On last Monday morning I was called upon by one of the Ledger reporters and asked to give a true statement and tell all that I knowed concerning the attempt to murder myself, Lee Jones, M.P. Tolliver and Thos. Tolliver, while in Paoli Jail last Saturday night, which I readily gave the gentleman, and gave it to him correct and in full, with the exception of some conversation heard, and giving the names of some of the parties whom we recognized and which I will also decline giving at this time.

But to my astonishment when I looked over the paper I found no correct copy of my statement there, and for that reason I now write it myself and ask you to please publish it. When I was first dragged from my business and incarcerated in jail, I told my friends and attorneys that it was all done by my enemies and for no other purpose than to murder me, and that my most bitter enemies would be the only witnesses against me, and one of the most prominent citizens of Paoli on the next morning told me that he thought there was danger, and that he feared Mr. Wm. P. Shively would be led into it with money, but that I could not believe, for several days I watched his maneuvers very closely and asked him to be sure and lock both doors tight and put the chain across every night,

> which he faithfully did do every night after we were indicted, except on the night of the attempt to murder us, when he selected some of my most bitter enemies to guard the jail, which caused me strongly to suspect something wrong. I then employed guards myself, and paid as high one night as four hundred dollars for two guards, and asked him to get Mr. John Simpson the County Clerk to select them."

Jones then explained that he had asked Sheriff Shively to provide them with firearms and that "some of the most prominent citizens asked him to arm us, but he plainly refused..." He admitted that when the sheriff deemed it unwise to distribute handguns and ammunition to four prisoners under arrest for murder, "my next move was to procure arms privately and conceal them in the jail..." His account of the night of July 8 closely resembled his statement as printed in the *Ledger-Standard*, claiming that the doors had not been properly secured and insisting that he heard a conversation between Shively and another man through a hole in the ceiling. Bent claimed that both he and his brother had been wounded in the gunfire. He threatened that "We plainly recognized four of the party, and are satisfied of several more of them, and will give their names and the particulars in due time." Jones was not disputing the statement he had provided to the newspaper as much as he was taking issue with the reporter's own conclusions:

> "I see in the Ledger that we surely stated that it was supposed by some that it was our own friends raising a holaboloo in order to give us a change of venue, and that we had been trying to get a change. Now I say that we have never asked for a change, and I think it preposterous to talk of our friends shooting us in the dark to give us a change. Shively is a candidate for sheriff in his county, and, of course, his guilt will be smuggled, as long as possible, but there are too many good citizens who are satisfied of his guilt for him

to ever come to Albany and blow it off through the papers...

All of the above statement I am willing to swear to at any time, and can give many other good reasons to show the truthfulness of it.

> (signed) Alonzo B. Jones, for short, Benton or Bent Jones."

One week later another complaint was printed in the *Bedford Star*:

> "Bent Jones, in a letter to a gentleman of this place, claims that a spy of the Orange county vigilants was caught sneaking about the jail by the police of New Albany the other day and ordered to leave, which he did instanter. Jones says that although the Ledger Standard was made aware of this, it remained silent in regard to the matter."

Regardless of Bent Jones's denial that he and his co-defendants wanted a change of venue, their attorneys were successful in getting the trials moved to Bloomington in Monroe County. A story in the *Indianapolis Journal* reported that the prisoners were transferred from New Albany back to the Paoli jail on November 2 to prepare for their trials. The *Bedford Star* wrote that it happened "after dark, being taken in carriages over the turnpike." The *Star* also reported "It seems that the Floyd county board of commissioners are kicking against paying the jailor's charges for the boarding of the Jones and Tolliver brothers."

Chapter Eight:
Certain to Swing

The July 28, 1876, edition of the *Hickman (KY) Courier* carried an inaccurate story that harkened back to the overblown "Ku Klux Klan" headlines that followed the 1871 night-time attack on the Moody farmhouse:

"VIGILANTS IN INDIANA
If in the South it Would be 'Rebel Work'.

The papers are full of the accounts of a mob, or vigilant committee, at Mitchellsville, Indiana. A squad of disguised men, entered the town, tore the establishment of one Jones, a grocery man, down, and shot him, in defiance of law and the officers of the law.

A correspondent writing to the papers says:

THE MITCHELL PEOPLE OUTRAGED.

'The people of Mitchell finally became so outraged at the crimes of Jones, that they could bear them no longer; and on Sunday

> morning about 1 o'clock, they took the law into their own hands, determined to be rid of so vile a monster. I assure you that the Moody-Tolliver case only bore an incidental relation to the acts of the mob. It was not specially on account of Jones' connection with the Joneses and Tollivers, now under indictment and arrest for the murder of Thomas Moody and the attempted assassination of the entire Moody family... but it was for other and more public crimes that he suffered.
>
> There is no denying that the deepest excitement and indignation pervades Orange county, in consequence of the many outrages perpetrated by red handed outlaws within its borders during the past eight or ten years.'"

This was followed by several examples of organized criminal activity in the region over the previous decade or so. Hickman is in extreme northwest Kentucky, near the Mississippi River. The editor's assumption seemed to be that his readers would know about the Moody-Tolliver feud, but would not be aware of the other recent "outrages". The report concluded:

> "... the end is not yet; nor will it come, until the county is completely rid of the desperadoes who have so long infested it. This we have from the best authority. If they can be got hold of by the vigilants, Joneses and Tollivers are certain to swing."

The town of Mitchell was obviously mis-identified, but the "monster" in this incident was not Bent Jones, who was in jail on the day it happened. The vigilante group's target was Bent's friend and associate Abram "Abe" Jones (no relation), who owned a saloon (not a grocery) in Mitchell. Early on the morning of July 23, 1876, a mob which he estimated to number "75 to 100" men had approached his business and shot him. The wound was apparently not too serious, but the situation was sufficiently alarming for Abe and his family to leave town on September 1.

Major J.W. Gordon was the Republican candidate for election as state Attorney General in 1876. He was being strongly criticized in Orange County for his continuing role in defense of the Toliver-Jones men and was suspected of being the author of published letters defending the accused killers of Tom Moody. General William T. Spicely, a resident of Orleans who had played a role in the Union siege of Vicksburg and was one of the most distinguished citizens in the region, had recently written a private letter to Colonel George W. Friedley expressing his concern that Gordon "will lose numbers of republican votes" unless Gordon would moderate his views. He added, "If there are any on our ticket who wish to plough with strange heifers, let them go and we will supply ourselves with men who will take care of *all people* both in and out of office." A Republican party official loaned a copy of the letter to Gordon. On July 22 the *Indianapolis News* printed a long reply subtitled:

> "Major J.W. Gordon Speaks His Mind About the Attacks Made on Him as a Candidate for Defending Alleged Criminals from Mob Violence – A Manly and Scathing Effort, Worthy of Its Author."

In its introduction the newspaper said Gordon was "being threatened with political assassination in Orange County on account of his attempt to prevent the execution of lynch law." Amidst his defense of the right of all defendants to proper legal counsel – especially when their lives might be in danger prior to judgment – Gordon included some details that, if true, would be of interest to those preparing for the pending murder cases:

> "What was matter of defense for Jones, Murray, and the Tolivers in the criminal prosecutions at Bedford, I learned from witnesses who would have testified if the case of the state had not broken down. I have read Thomas Moody's dying declaration, made at the time he was first shot, and know that in it he stated that

> he did not know or could not identify his assailants or any of them. I do not pretend to give his words; I know that on the trial of Dr. Tolliver he did testify that he knew some of his assailants, and therefore I know there was a contradiction between his dying declaration and his testimony."

This refers to the 1874 trial in Bedford when Gordon successfully represented the defendants against charges related to the 1871 firebombing. Thomas Moody's first "dying declaration" was made after he had been told that he would almost certainly not recover from wounds suffered during that attack. He did survive and lived until his actual murder nearly four years later – at which time he was said to have made another declaration. Also:

> "It is true to-day that Thomas Moody was shot to death in Orleans, at his own door. The question is, who did it? Whoever did is an assassin and a murderer... When they are thus found out all good men will say 'amen' to their punishment. None more heartily than I... There was allusion to the burning of Jones's mill and Tolliver's barn. Of course I was not there when they were burned, but was informed that some one had poured coal oil on the mill, so as to insure its loss before it was fired. There can be no doubt, I reckon, that the barn was maliciously burned. I am told that the loss has been adjusted and paid up by the insurance company."

The indignant Major Gordon stated that "I have nothing to take back, and no apologies to make for anything I have said or done." He might have had second thoughts on August 3 when the *Mitchell Commercial* claimed that Spicely's letter had been obtained "by unfair means, if not by plain false pretense" and that Gordon had "in violation of every rule of honor published it." Gordon replied that he thought the letter was meant for publication and that he did not know it was written as personal correspondence between two friends. Major Gordon was not elected in October, losing to the Democratic incumbent.

The *San Francisco Chronicle* carried a summary of the Moody-Tolliver feud in its November 26, 1876, edition. It concluded: "Altogether, the case is unequaled in interest and mystery in the West."

Attorneys for all four defendants filed writs of habeas corpus, requiring a judicial hearing to determine if the state had adequate grounds to hold them in confinement without bond. The judge would be Eliphalet D. Pearson of Bedford, a former newspaper editor and successful attorney who was described as "an outspoken Republican." Pearson had been elected Judge of the Tenth Judicial Circuit in 1873. The hearing was delayed by the absence of some key prosecution witnesses, the late arrival of lead prosecutor and recently defeated candidate Major J.W. Gordon, and by Judge Pearson's need to attend to other judicial duties in Bedford.

On December 14 the *Indianapolis Journal* noted that Eli Lowery would be brought from the state prison in Jeffersonville to Bloomington, where he would testify. The paper said, "It is believed that the order for Lowery's presence in that county was secured purposely by those whom his evidence will condemn, and that they will attempt to put him out of the way." For whatever reason, Lowry never took the witness stand.

The habeas corpus hearings for Bent Jones, Lee Jones, Tom Toliver, and Parks Toliver finally got underway in Bloomington on Saturday, December 16. On the following Monday the court heard testimony from one of the detectives investigating the murder, but the reporter for the *Indianapolis Sentinel* wrote that his testimony was "not very important." Then a woman named Clara Harvey testified that she had heard Bent Jones tell various persons, when angry, that he would kill them "as dead as he had killed Tom Moody."

Next on the witness stand was Harry Beecher Ward, who had become the most visibly active detective working on the case. Ward said he had traveled to Mitchell and Orleans specifically to investigate the murder and that he had done little else since

February of the previous year. He wasted no time in staking a claim to the reward fund, stating that he and Tegarden would deserve the credit and the cash. He said that he had met Bent Jones for the first time on May 2, when he volunteered to deliver a packet of letters belonging to Jones that had been found "between Mitchell and White River". Ward then told Bent, confidentially, that he was working on the Moody murder case. He convinced Jones that he had made considerable progress and that his conclusion was that Jeff Huffstetter, rather than any of the Toliver and Jones men, was the guilty party. Ward claimed that he could produce enough evidence to indict Huffstetter with Bent's help. Jones replied that "Jeff Huffstetter was guilty as hell" and that he would help Ward prosecute him.

The suspect falsely accused by Ward to gain the cooperation of Bent Jones was 39-year-old David Jefferson Huffstetter of Orleans. Years earlier he had been in a dispute with Tom Moody about opening a road. During the slander trial of 1871 Huffstetter had been subpoenaed to testify in Jones's defense. Later he and Jones were opponents "upon the trial of a cause in the Masonic Lodge, before the Masonic body, at Mitchell, in which Huffstetter had preferred charges against [Jones] of striking and kicking him". Now Bent was prepared to frame him for murder.

Jones told the detective that he could get Eli Lowry to swear that Huffstetter was guilty. He said that "Lowery had got scared about something and gone, but he could get him back". Jones said that Huffstetter had told Abe Jones where the gun that killed Tom Moody was hidden and that he could find out the location.

Ward testified that a few days later he received a letter, followed by a telegram, from Bent Jones asking for another meeting. When Ward arrived in Mitchell, Jones took him to a private room at the Albert House. Bent claimed that he had learned where the shotgun was hidden, but he was worried that Ward might be trying to entrap him. The *Sentinel* then reported that Bent Jones had suggested that a contribution of two or three thousand dollars to his upcoming campaign for sheriff of Lawrence County might help inspire his confidence about the detective's intentions.

With no further reference to the money, Ward testified that Bent Jones then drew a map showing some landscape features that included two ponds near Orleans. Jones then claimed that Eli Lowry had told him that the gun was in one of those ponds and that, after his first meeting with Ward, Bent had gone looking for it. He discovered that he couldn't drag the ponds in daylight without being seen from Huffstetter's house, so he returned at midnight and raked the ponds with no success. The next night (apparently May 18) Jones returned with Robert E. Perkins, who found the gun buried in the mud. He said it was "very rusty, and the varnish scaling on the barrels, and looked like it had been in the pond some time." A gun identified by Ward as the one recovered from the pond was then entered as evidence.

The next time Ward saw Bent Jones was the day before Jones was arrested. Ward told Jones then that "the gun arrangement wouldn't work", but Jones replied that he could get forty men to swear against Huffstetter and that they would say anything that he wanted. Jones said that if they could get Jeff Huffstetter indicted for murder "old Huffstetter" would pay "four or five thousand dollars" to keep Jeff from going to prison. This referred to Jeff's father, the highly regarded Major David S. Huffstetter.

On cross-examination Ward said that he had been the marshal in Greensburg, Indiana, in 1875 and had seen the reward poster for Moody's murderers. Curiously, brief sentences about the Moody reward money and Marshal Ward had appeared adjacent to each other in the March 24, 1875, edition of the *Greensburg Standard*:

> "The reward offered for the arrest and conviction of the murderer of Thos. Moody, of Orleans, on March 2, amounts to $4,000.
> We waited anxiously, Saturday morning, to see Marshal Ward sit down in the street, just to tie his shoe, but he made the trip."

Shortly thereafter Ward decided to go to Orleans and "try to get it". Ward told the court that he came to town to canvass for the

Indiana State Atlas, a job that helped pay his expenses and gave him an excuse to ask questions.

The defense then brought to the witness stand nine men who each swore that they had seen the defendants in Mitchell at the time the murder was taking place five miles away in Orleans. At least two of these witnesses, James Head and Moses Clinton, would later be associated with criminal activities thought to be directed by Bent Jones. Another was Abe Jones, the man who had allegedly told Bent where the gun was hidden. Abe told the court that he had been shot and seriously wounded when a mob attacked his saloon. He suggested that the motive was to prevent him and others from providing alibis for the defendants.

The next witnesses were Joseph and Alice Patterson. Joseph testified that Eli Lowry was a boarder at their house in Mitchell when the murder took place. He swore that the last time he saw Lowry was at dinner that day and that he did not know if Eli had slept in the house that night. At the time "dinner" was the word used for the meal we now commonly call "lunch". Patterson testified that Lowry later demanded that he swear before the grand jury that Eli had also eaten supper (the evening meal) at his house on the night of the murder and to also swear that Patterson and Lowry had walked into town together that night, where they saw the other defendants. According to Joseph Patterson, Bent Jones later warned him on three separate occasions that if he didn't swear in support of Lowry's story, he would be killed. Joseph did as he was told and was promptly indicted by the grand jury for perjury. He claimed that, even after he was arrested, Bent Jones told him not to worry because he would have twenty-five men swear in court that Lowry was with Patterson in Mitchell that night.

Alice Patterson had been indicted by the grand jury as an accessory to the murder after the fact. Here is the *Sentinel's* summary of her testimony:

> "... said that she had stated before the grand jury that Lowery was at her house for supper,

> when in fact he was not; that she did not see him on the day of the murder after 2 o'clock, and until the next day at breakfast; she said she had rode from Paoli to Mitchell in a buggy with a Mr. Sheeks after I testified before the grand jury; that he asked her on that occasion if she could trust Eli Lowery with a secret and she had answered no, and he then said Bent Jones had about come to that conclusion himself; that he believed Eli was going to tell and might try to tell me, that if we did not listen to him; that she asked him if he thought Eli was guilty and he said yes he was guilty and knew the whole party, and that if he confessed it Lee Jones was gone to h__l. She said he wanted her to write a letter to Lowery and tell him not to tell anything, and for her not to go back on what she had said; that she had testified falsely before the grand jury because Bent Jones told her if she plead guilty he would kill her; that he had a pistol in his boot, and would set near her so he would have a fair chance."

The man in the buggy was wealthy Lawrence County landowner David Sheeks, who had posted the $20,000 bail for Bent Jones.

Admitting that she had perjured herself before the grand jury by providing an alibi for Lowry, Alice testified that Eli had also threatened her:

> "He said, if we would not testify to this, the consequence would be that we would not be safe to step out in the yard after dark; the house would be blown up and all of us in it; he said that time and again. He said he himself was afraid of Jones."

The final two days of the proceedings were summarized by the correspondent of the *Indianapolis State Sentinel* in a report datelined from Bloomington on December 20, but which did not appear until the paper's December 27 edition. He began by demonstrating merciful consideration for his readers:

> "A mass of impeaching and rebutting evidence has been introduced in this Jones-Tolliver investigation, which would be uninteresting to the general reader, and will not be reported. The statements of three of the defendants, Tom Tolliver, Parks Tolliver and Lee Jones, are also uninteresting, as details as to how a man did not commit a murder always are. They put in a general denial. As Bent Jones is the supposed leader of, and, according to Lowery, made the plans for, the conspirators, his testimony will be sufficient."

This is an early indication of the frustration several trial correspondents felt due to the legal ostentation and mind-numbing duration of most court proceedings connected to this case. When the verdict was later appealed to the Indiana Supreme Court the official court reporter furnished a 3,300-page transcript. Another source said that the bound trial record was fifty-four inches thick. It was difficult then – and now – for a writer to cut through the theatrics of would-be platform orators to get to the heart of the matter.

When Bent Jones took the stand it was quickly obvious that his strategy was consistent with that of his co-defendants: deny, deny, deny. He denied that he had ever had any conversation with Eli Lowry regarding the death of Tom Moody; said that he did not speak with Lowry or recall seeing him on the day that Moody was killed; and claimed that "I never offered him any money at any time to kill him." He related in detail his movements in Mitchell on the day of the murder and named people who would swear to have seen him. Jones said he spent time at a couple of saloons that afternoon, then went to David Lee's house and stayed there until about 8 o'clock. After that, while the murder was taking place in Orleans, Bent said he went back to Abe Jones's saloon where he "talked and played the fiddle for about half an hour" before going home. According to Jones, "I was not nearer Orleans that night than the railroad crossing at Mitchell. I had no arrangement with any person to kill Tom Moody."

Jones testified that he took the passenger train from Mitchell to Bedford the next day and that was where he first heard about Tom Moody's murder. When he arrived back in Mitchell he was told that "there was a good deal of excitement" in Orleans and got back on the train headed in that direction. He claimed to spend most of his time at Spicely's store before taking a railroad handcar back to Mitchell with "a number of persons", arriving there after dark.

Bent told the court that "I am not much acquainted with Captain Ward". At their first meeting in Mitchell, he said, Ward asked Jones for a private conversation "and then kind of stepped back and said: 'But Jeff Huffstetter, the d----d s-n of a b---h', was there and he couldn't talk." He testified that, during their next meeting, Ward said he wanted to convict Jeff Huffstetter of killing Moody, but Jones claimed that he excused himself.

Under cross-examination Jones was handed a paper and was asked whether he had written it:

> "After carefully reading it he said he did; that he didn't know how long since, it was his handwrite [sic]; that he believed he wrote it in Bloomington since he has been in jail. The paper proved to be a memorandum of some witnesses' testimony, and the prisoner stated he had made such a memorandum of the testimony of every witness, and gave them to his wife. The counsel for the state said a witness was caught memorizing the one produced."

The *Bedford Star* later reported Judge Pearson's verdict:

> "The long and tedious habeas corpus case of the Joneses and Tolivers came to an end last Wednesday at Bloomington, about half-past one o'clock in the afternoon. Notwithstanding the herculean efforts of the prisoners' counsel,

among whom were Prof. McNutt and Judge Lamb, of Indianapolis, Judge Pearson decided that Bent Jones, Lee Jones and Parks Toliver's cases were not bailable. In the case of Thomas Toliver, the youngest of the four, and who at the time of the murders was but a boy of seventeen or eighteen years of age, the bond was fixed by the court at $20,000. He has not yet given bond, however, and is still in jail with the others. Bent Jones proved an alibi by one witness, Abe Jones, the saloon-keeper, who swore that at the time of the killing Bent was in Mitchell, but the evidence of the prosecution was too strong for it to amount to anything."

There was an additional note in the same edition of the *Star*:

"A dispatch from Bloomington to the Louisville Courier-Journal says that on the last night of the Jones-Toliver habeas corpus case, Bent Jones was so fearful of assassination he had the court house windows blinded. It also says that an appeal will be taken to the Supreme Court of the State immediately, when that body will set as a Circuit Court and determine whether bail shall or shall not be granted. The decision of Judge Pearson, it is said, gives satisfaction to the majority of the people of Bloomington."

In the case of *Ex Parte Jones et al.*, the Indiana Supreme Court quickly upheld Judge Pearson's ruling. The justices noted that "(t)he evidence in this cause is exceedingly long and voluminous." They affirmed Pearson's judgment "at the costs of the appellants." The Toliver and Jones brothers had exhausted their legal options and would now face trial on murder charges. The State of Indiana would begin by prosecuting their case against Bent Jones.

Chapter Nine:
Oh, I Am Murdered!

On December 21, 1876, the *Bloomington Courier* published "Sketches of the Accused in the Moody Murder Case". It is interesting to compare their courtroom demeanor with the jailhouse characterizations written five months earlier by the *New Albany Ledger-Standard* reporter:

"Bent Jones

> This prisoner appears to be the oldest of the four, and he takes the lead in managing the case with the attorneys. He gazes intently into the face of every witness and listens to the worst evidence against him with as much indifference as if he were only a spectator in the court room. He is very pale, but it is caused by long imprisonment. His wife is with him constantly in the room and seems far more concerned in the case than he. On Friday night his son, a lad about 15 years of age [Allen Jones], testified for the defense. His evidence was given in a straightforward manner without once looking toward his father who sat directly in front of him.

Lee Jones

Is a brother to Bent, and it was he whom Lowry said fired the fatal shot which killed Moody. He takes no active part in the case but passes the time in court by mixing up with his acquaintances beside the bar and chatting pleasantly with them. He does not seem to be the hardened man that some of the evidence would make one believe him to be.

Dr. Parks Tolliver

He is the most gentlemanly appearing one of the four. His gentle demeanor is the subject of much comment and he is the last man anyone would pick out from among the crowd as one [several illegible words] weight of the charge hangs heavily upon him and that he is much broken down in spirit, although he converses with his friends freely and at times cheerfully.

Thomas Tolliver

Is a brother to the doctor and is only 19 years of age, although his appearance indicates him to be several years older. It is said that he has been in the habit of drinking freely, but his countenance does not denote such to be the case. He told a straight story on the witness stand Friday night and conducted himself in a very gentlemanly manner.

The following sketch of Lowry, who pleaded guilty to the murder, is taken from the *Mitchell Commercial*:

> Eli is considerably changed in appearance, he is smooth shaved, the light mustache he formerly wore being off, gives him the appearance, with

his smoothly combed hair, of a girl of 17 though he is now in his 25th year. He gave testimony in a cool and unembarrassed manner telling all the details of the horrid murder in as easy a manner as a school girl would speak of her geography lesson... He spoke to us of the kind treatment he receives in the prison and of his anxiety to make a scholar of himself, saying that he put in all spare (four or five illegible words)."

If Eli Lowery appeared more like "a girl of 17" than a 25-year-old man, it was because census records and other documents indicate the likelihood that both he and Tom Toliver were twenty years old at that time.

One month after the habeas corpus verdict, there was surprising news of another arrest. In its January 25, 1877, edition the *New Albany Daily Ledger-Standard* broke the story with an exclusive report. One of the sub-headlines proclaimed:

"Justice About to Overtake the Really Guilty
(Special to the LEDGER-STANDARD)

Mitchell, Ind., Jan. 25 - A renewed interest was aroused in the Moody murder affair yesterday by the arrest of a man named James Murray, a brother-in-law to Jones and the Tollivers, now confined for the assassination of old man Moody. Murray is charged with a connection with the conspiracy and with being one of the parties engaged in the murder. After his arrest he gave bail in the sum of $10,000 to appear and answer to the charge. Mr. Ralf. Burton, of Princeton, has been retained for his defense. This arrest has created a sensation, from the fact that Murray has not heretofore been suspected. It is not prudent to give the particulars which led to this arrest, since it might defeat the plans which have been adopted to probe the whole matter to the bottom. It seems probable now that the detectives employed in working up the case will reach the really guilty parties and bring them to justice. So far as developed, this case is one of the most hellish that has ever disgraced the Southern part of Indiana, being simply a plot to destroy a man who possessed a property that the conspirators hoped to grasp by the murder of Moody."

Murray, like both Bent and Lee Jones, was a brother-in-law to the Tolivers, having married their eldest sister, Mahala.

A *Ledger-Standard* correspondent identified only as "N." filed a story on February 9, 1877, headlined "**MORE MOODY MURDER**" that first called attention to difficulty in finding a judge to try the separate murder cases, nothing that "It is a job not at all coveted by the judges up this way...". Then he added:

"A TOUCHING SCENE IN COURT.
Before I close, let me record a touching scene witnessed in court here on yesterday. One of the defendants, Lee Jones, is accustomed to have his little girl in court – a bright-eyed little miss of some 3 years in age – and a child of an exceedingly affectionate disposition. She is a rarely beautiful
EMBODIMENT OF INNOCENCY.
It has been her want [sic] heretofore to hover about her father, and with many a coy manifestation of love, beguile his thoughts away from other subjects to herself. And there is no sort of doubt that Lee's love for the child is fully as tender and as unfeigned. Yesterday
THE TWO MET IN THE COURT ROOM
Here, after a separation of two months, the one from his dark, dark cell, the other fresh from her toys and books and birds. Entering the bar, and espying her papa, there was noticed

a spasmodic twitching of the muscles of the fair young face, and then, raising her arms for a loving embrace, she ran to her father and threw herself upon his lap and began **WEEPING VIOLENTLY.**
Her sobbing voice was lifted by her feelings above the dull argument of learned counsel, or the hum-drum of judicial dedision [sic], on a cold, formal demurrer, and there were many hearts among the spectators whose sympathies went out to the suffering child – went out, aye – even unto **ACTIVE, PAINFUL AGONY.**
Then, clambering up into his lap, the bereaved child threw her arms about the neck of the one who used to fondle with her in her baby life, at home – for Lee has always had an uncommon fondness for home, and his household gods [sic], so the story goes. She cried herself into the **FORGETFULNESS OF SLEEP.**
During this scene I was curiously watching, after a time spent in recovering myself, the faces of those most and deeply enlisted on the side of the prosecution. William Moody, a brother of the deceased, and a big-hearted, child-like man, himself was **ALMOST EFFECTED TO TEARS,**
And turned away, refusing longer to look upon so harrowing a spectacle. Robert Tegarden, the detective who was by my side, when I said to him,
    "BOB, YOU SEEM TO BE EFFECTED?"
Replied, "Yes, if that was before a jury I would feel like deciding the thing as a set-up job, but as it is,
    "OH, JUST LET ME OUT, PLEASE."
There were tears under his voice, and I knew wherefore Bob had gone to the front yard. N."

At the risk of diminishing a good Victorian-era melodrama,

it is likely that the "bright-eyed little miss" was actually a boy. There are no records to indicate that Lee and Louisa Jones had a girl, while later accounts in multiple sources mention "a bright boy of three or four years" who wept in his father's arms when Lee's sentence was read in court. The 1880 federal census shows six-year-old William Jones living in Mitchell with his mother and Tom Toliver. No sister is listed. It is possible that there was also a girl of about the same age who did not survive or was living elsewhere, but during this period male and female infants often wore similar clothing.

In the "Monroe Co. Mush" column in the February 12 edition of the *Ledger Standard* "N." wrote:

"HOW BUSY THE JUDGES SEEM.

Judges Robinson and Allison have, the second time each, expressed themselves as being too busy to even swap work with Judge Pearson in the Jones-Toliver case, and there is now no telling when the case will be tried, nor by whom. There ought to be some legislation on the subject. Judge Pearson says the appropriation for such contingencies is exhausted. I am
INCUBATING AN IDEA
or plan, by which such causes are to be tried over similar troubles. Suppose, for instance, that a statute be enacted whereby any inmate of a county jail may hold special terms of court for the hearing and determining of such cases. Of course, no such inmate should be selected who is very particularly interested in the results of the same. The great advantage of my plan, it is obvious, is this: The parties applied to could not well or consistently decline, on the ground of being too busy, and besides, ordinarily, we should know where to find anyone whose services were thus needed. It is in a crude shape, as yet, but give me time and I think I can fix it up so that the

> present regime shall be improved a bit at
> least. N."

The delays appear to have also shortened tempers among the defendants. On February 14 the *Indiana State Sentinel* reported that "a few days ago" there had been a fight between Bent Jones and Parks Toliver, "the Moody muderers[sic]", in the Monroe County jail in Bloomington. They were subsequently moved to separate cells.

On April 27 eleven prisoners attempted to escape that same jail:

> "They had sawed off the first bar leading to the ventilator with a steel shank out of a shoe, and were continuing their efforts, when a sister of Sheriff Alexander discovered them and called Capt. Allen to her assistance. He promptly notified the citizens who responded to the call and thus prevented the escapade.
>
> Among the prisoners were the Joneses and Tollivers, who are charged with the murder of old man Moody in Orange county... They say they had no hand in the attempt to escape of the prisoners, but assign no reason why they did not attempt to give alarm."

Sheriff Williamson M. Alexander told the press that the escape might well have succeeded if they had been discovered five or ten minutes later. The prisoners were all placed in close confinement in separate cells and were fed on bread and water as a punishment "for their interested labors."

Just as the trial of Bent Jones was scheduled to begin there was another potential delay. Circuit Judge E.D. Pearson had stepped aside and was replaced on the bench by Circuit Judge John C. Robinson. The *New Albany Daily Ledger-Standard* correspondent, writing as "D.O.S.", added that Robinson "in addition to being a ripe lawyer and a great jurist, ... is also a scholarly Christian gentleman." The lead counsel for the defense was 39-year-old Professor C.F. McNutt. He had been a member of the Indiana

University law school faculty until the law department had recently closed due to spending cuts by the General Assembly. It would not reopen for twelve years. Four days before the trial was to begin the McNutt family suffered a shocking tragedy:

> "... just as Prof. McNutt was about to remove his family to St. Louis, Mo., at which place he will practice his profession in the hereafter... his eldest daughter, a lovely child of some nine summers, his almost idolized "Beryl" was stricken with disease. She lingered till last Friday night, when, surrounded by many loving and weeping friends, her poor young spirit took its flight."

McNutt told Judge Robinson that he was aware of "the public calamity of nearly 500 witnesses dancing attendance on the sessions of the Court, at a busy season of the year, and at vast expense to Orange county." According to the *Daily Ledger Standard*, "McNutt, with the tears streaming from his swollen eyes in a torrent, offered to return to his clients his magnificent fees, rather than, in his opinion, be guilty of a cruel species of malpractice by assuming responsibilities so solemn while his faculties were thus impaired by his great grief." Judge Robinson reminded the distraught attorney that he, too, had recently suffered the loss of a child and that "his wounds had been administered unto by employment". With that, he refused McNutt's offer to remove himself from the trial.

The case of the *State of Indiana v. Alonzo Benton Jones* finally went to trial in Bloomington on May 15, 1877. "D.O.S." noted:

> "I presume it is not necessary to give a history of [the case], since it has a national reputation, being pretty generally known throughout the country as the Jones-Tolliver-Moody assassination, presumably one of the most celebrated cases in the history of Western jurisprudence."

"D.O.S." has now been identified as Bloomington resident Daniel Oliver Spencer, Jr. He was the reporter assigned to the case by the *Ledger-Standard* but also provided coverage for other newspapers, including the *Louisville Courier-Journal*. Spencer – known to his friends as "Dank" – was a colorful character. He was a Union army veteran and law school graduate but when work was slow he painted houses. He also had a highly publicized reputation as a popular "mind-reader", both on stage and for private clients. In 1869 Spencer had been convicted of manslaughter for killing a man in a bar fight and was sentenced to ten years in prison. He was freed when the verdict was reversed on appeal. Later he would serve time at the Indiana Prison South after being found guilty of the attempted murder of a woman who was visiting his dying wife. In an open letter to the public Spencer blamed this assault on "a brain inflamed and maddened by intoxicants." Dank drank. Immediately upon his release from prison, where he became something of a benevolent jailhouse lawyer, he had a job waiting for him as a newspaper editor. D.O. Spencer became a respected and much-loved citizen who knew many of the most prominent people in Indiana and Kentucky. His later career included working as the official Monroe County court stenographer.

Spencer marveled at the "vast battalion of witnesses". Estimates ranged from three hundred to over five hundred subpoenaed persons "either here or close enough at hand to avoid any vexatious delays." The *Bloomington (IN) Courier* used a similar comparison when it later reported that "The case was tried here on a change of venue from Orange county, and an army of witnesses were summoned, many of them having to walk to this place, as they were too poor to pay their railroad fare." This included a few witnesses who had "stayed" or had "been put up" in the county jail according to Monroe County courthouse records.

The *Ledger-Standard* reporter began his trial coverage with an updated personal depiction of Bent Jones and his family:

> "The prisoner is looking extremely well, considering his long confinement... Dressed in a suit of blue cloth, he presents a pleasing aspect, so far as his wearing apparel goes... The prisoner is accompanied by his wife and a son. This son is quite intelligent looking, and is taking a deep interest in everything pertaining to the matter so vitally effecting his father. The boy is about nine years of age, so that he is too young in years and experience to school himself from showing his manifest fears that some harm may befall his father. The co-defendants, to wit, Lee Jones, Dr. M.P. Tolliver, and Thomas Tolliver, have not yet appeared in Judge Robinson's court since the trial of the accused began. The other co-defendant... is Eli Lowery. He is now in the State's prison for life, on a plea of guilty."

The boy would have been ten-year-old John Wesley Jones, who would remain loyal to his father as an adult. The *Indianapolis State Sentinel* added, "Bent Jones has stood his confinement well, and looks healthy and flush, but his manner seems rather more nervous and anxious than on the former investigation, being constantly on the alert and watching the movements of the attorneys and other parties with the utmost vigilance."

Before the twelve jurors were sworn in, Judge Robinson "... informed them that they would be, in a sense, prisoners for the next two weeks; would have their physical and mental powers severely taxed, and, as individuals, had met with a misfortune in being selected to try this case, but that it was a duty they owed to the state..." Thanks to the *State Sentinel* we even know the juror's names: Christian Davidson, Henry Mercer, Mark Smith, Henry Smith, James T. Kirk, James B. Bender, Joseph Pennington, William Shields, Moses Fields, Mitchell Mathers, David Miller, and Jesse Hinds.

The defense team asked the court if they would be furnished

means to bring Abe Jones to Bloomington. He was "an important witness... whom, it was just learned, was in Nebraska." This man was not related to Bent and Lee Jones, but he had provided them an alibi by claiming that Bent ("and perhaps others of the defendants") had been in Abe's saloon in Mitchell when Tom Moody was murdered in Orleans. Shortly afterward Abe was shot and wounded when his saloon was attacked at night by a mob. Hearing that he had moved to Evansville, an officer was sent there with a subpoena, but Jones could not be found. According to an account in the *State Sentinel*:

> "His sister, who is principal of the high school in Evansville, and who bears an excellent reputation, told the officer she knew where her brother could be found; had furnished him money to get away, but that she would not tell his whereabouts, because she did not intend him to have anything further to do with this case or the parties concerned."

The judge decided that if Abe Jones would agree to voluntarily appear, he would be reimbursed for his roundtrip expenses, but that no money would be advanced.

The first witness on May 16 was Thomas Moody's older brother, William, who was living with Tom, John, and Polly at the house in Orleans. He testified that the last time he saw his brother before the murder was between nine and ten o'clock on the morning on March 2, 1875, when Tom finished writing a letter and took it to the post office. He did not come home again during the day. William continued:

> "... a few minutes before eight o'clock that night he heard two reports of a gun in quick succession, and immediately after heard his brother exclaim, "Oh, I am murdered"; that on opening the door he was found trying to make his way into the house, whereupon his brother John and sister Polly dragged him into the

house and laid him upon a bed where he lingered until about 11 o'clock the next day and died. That an examination of the premises in the morning revealed the marks of 12 balls or buckshot on the palings of the fence and six in the house; that the wounds on the body of Thomas seemed to have been made from the same kind of balls, one of which passed through his hip and one through his right arm."

William also detailed the 1871 firebombing attack on the Moody farmhouse during which Thomas had been shot. He told the court that "several law suits between the Moodys on the one side and the Joneses and Tollivers on the other, which had grown out of the administration of old man Tolliver's estate" were the cause of the "animosity between Thomas and the Joneses and Tollivers." William Moody told the court, "When we first went there [Orleans] we lived at McDonald's; we rented a portion of that house, slept up stairs and fastened the doors up, and when we moved down where we live now we fastened all the doors, and generally stayed in after dark." William testified that he could not remember a time when his brother Tom was out after dark "excepting the night he was shot, and on occasions when he was away on business, and was gone from home all night."

General William T. Spicely was called as a witness to explain the layout of streets in Orleans. Then Joshua Younger took the stand and testified that he was a carpenter working for Bent Jones from 1871 until the spring of 1876. Younger swore that on two occasions Jones had tried to hire him to kill Tom Moody. The first offer was for $1,000 in cash. Later, Younger was offered the same amount to be paid partly in cash and partly in lumber. Jones assured Younger that "there would be no danger of detection as he had plenty of men to get him out, and would stick by him." According to this witness, Bent Jones said:

"... that Moody had robbed him through the law, and nothing but his life would satisfy him.

> That on one occasion Jones said he was going to kill the d----d old s-n of a b---h himself, and wanted his head for a soap gourd, his bones to make buttons and his hide for a razor strap and for whangs to sew his belts. That after Moody's death Jones said to him that he had got Moody killed for a d-n sight less than he had offered him (Younger); that the d-n old s-n of a b---h was dead and in hell, and now he (Jones) was easy".

A "soap gourd" would be similar to a shaving mug. "Whang" is an antiquated term for "a thong, especially of leather." During cross-examination an attorney for the defense asked the witness if he was not mad because Bent Jones had caught him stealing paint at the factory and had fired him. Younger said that was not true and appealed to the court for protection from such questioning, but the judge ruled that it was a proper question.

A headline in the *Ledger-Standard* later crowed: "**A Number of Witnesses Ground in the Legal Mill.**" During the morning session the prosecution brought to the witness stand sixteen different men and women, including prominent citizens, most of whom testified to Bent Jones making "threats before and admissions after" the killing of Moody. Among them was Andy Noe, a gunsmith in Mitchell, who told the court that he had repaired a double-barreled shotgun a short time before the murder that had been brought to him by Eli Lowry, who said that the gun belonged to Bent Jones, who later paid for the work. Noe added that "… Jones had said after the killing that Moody was killed by a genuine stub and twist gun, which had been thoroughly tested, and that the man who had stood behind it when the deed was done knew what it would do." The term "stub and twist" refers to the type of metal and the method of manufacturing used to create what was regarded as a superior gun barrel.

The next witness testified from about two o'clock in the afternoon until adjournment at six, then again the next day from mid-morning until half past nine o'clock at night. He was Eli Lowry, the young man who had turned "state's evidence" to avoid the hangman's noose. It took him fifteen hours or so to tell his story, but he had quite a story to tell.

Chapter Ten:
He Hollered Willfully

Eli Lowry had already admitted his participation in the murder and accepted a life sentence. There was the possibility of an eventual parole or pardon – a chance that might be enhanced by his cooperation. There was obvious motivation for him to downplay his involvement – but he also knew that he would face cross-examination by some of the most accomplished lawyers in the state.

His testimony began by confirming that he had lived in Mitchell for about four years, most recently with the Pattersons, and worked "off and on" for Bent Jones making peach baskets. He knew all the other defendants, but "had no acquaintance with Tom Moody but knew him when I saw him". Lowry swore that Jones had offered him money at least twice if he would kill Moody. One day while they were in "Bent's log yard" in Mitchell, Jones told him that he "could make a nice little pile of money" in return for the murder, but Lowry declined the offer. Later, while they stood "in the sash house door", Bent made a similar offer. Lowry said he told Jones, "My God, Bent, you had better let that man alone." Jones's reply was, "No, I'll blow his G-d d--n head off!"

According to Lowry, there had been an earlier plot to kill Tom Moody at a "political jollification" in Orleans during the fall of 1874. Jones later told Eli that Tom Moody had started walking toward the event when he spotted Bent in the crowd and returned home.

On the morning of March 2, 1875, Eli ran into Bent Jones on Main Street in Mitchell, where Jones told him that they were going to kill Moody that night and that Lowry had to come with them. He then said that "Doc Tolliver wanted to see me." When he arrived at the doctor's office, Parks took a double handful of buckshot out of a drawer and told him to deliver it to the sawmill. Lee Jones was at the mill, cleaning some guns. They loaded the guns with some of the shot and tested them by firing at a tree in the mill yard. Then:

> "After the shooting we went into the sash house and reloaded the guns. Lee did the loading; he rolled the balls in something he poured out of a bottle, that he said was poison. It looked like castor oil. It turned the balls white though. He poured all the stuff out of a little vial on the desk, and poured the shot out in the poison, or rolled them out in it."

After the guns were reloaded, Lee "took them upstairs in the sash house and hid them. Bent came down with a half pint of whiskey and Lee wanted a drink, and Bent wouldn't give it to him, but took one himself."

After Lee Jones stopped at his house for a pair of socks "to go over his boots", he and Lowry headed toward Orleans together, stopping at Jim Murray's house for supper, where Lee told Murray he was going to kill Tom Moody that night and that if they were successful he would "shoot the gun off in front of Murry's house, on the railroad, as he come back." Then, after walking through woods and pastures, they met Bent Jones, Parks Toliver, and Tom Toliver outside Orleans, "between Huffstetter's and Campbell's" near the railroad tracks. According to his testimony:

> "We all took a drink and Bent said to me, 'Eli, you go with Lee; he will do the work.' I told him I couldn't – was not well – and he

> then turned to Parks: 'You will go, you are not afraid?' Parks and Lee then took the guns and started off towards Orleans… After they left it was not long before we heard a gun fire twice, and not long after that until Parks and Lee come back. When they come up, Lee said: 'We got the damned old son of a bitch at last!' Bent said, 'Are you sure?' and Parks replied: 'Yes; he hollered willfully.'"

Lee Jones told the others they had hidden behind a two-story building across the street from the Moody house until they heard Tom coming. They knew it was him "by the way he cleared his throat." Lee did the shooting, then they ran out the back way "through an old grave yard and through a stock field; that a dog bothered them when they were running." On their way back to Mitchell, Lee fired a gun twice – at an outhouse behind the school and at a telegraph pole as the pre-arranged signal to Jim Murray that the deed had been done. Upon their arrival in Mitchell the guns were hidden in a livery stable owned by one of the Toliver brothers. Then all five men met at Abe Jones's saloon for drinks. Lowry noticed that Bent and Abe walked to a quiet corner of the saloon and whispered to each other for five or ten minutes. Having been seen long enough to establish a possible alibi, Bent ordered everyone to go home and to bed. He had to escort his brother, Lee, who "was pretty full, talking loud and cursing, and I think broke a little tree down in front of Mr. Lemon's house…" A different account said the little tree was in front of "Mr. Lincoln's house". There were both Lincolns and Lemons living in Mitchell at the time.

The next morning Lowry went back to Abe Jones's saloon, where he saw Bent Jones "jumping up and cracking his heels and saying, 'By God, Tom Moody is dead.'" Later that morning Eli Lowry, Simpson Toliver, Lee Jones, Parks Toliver, and others "borrowed" a railroad handcar and rode to Orleans for a lunch of cheese and crackers at Condor's. They all spent time at Spicely's store before heading back to Mitchell. That evening Lowry saw

Bent Jones "offer a $300 reward for Moody's scalp." Lee Jones told Eli that his brother and Jim Murray had agreed to pay him $50 each for the murder. Bent Jones later claimed that Murray never paid his share.

Lowry swore that he had not been promised any money for his participation in the murder:

> "All that was said or done about it, Bent asked me one day if I didn't want a nice suit of clothing. I told him I didn't care; would not object. He said for me to come and go round Sheeks & Wood's store and he would get one for me. I went with him and he told them to let me have a good suit of clothes if it cost $50 [approximately $1165 in 2020 dollars], and then went away. I told them I did not want a suit, but would take other things, and took a pair of pants, box of collars, necktie and things for my boarding house, I think to the amount of $20 [about $466 in 2020 dollars]. I have talked about the murder with Bent several times; he always said it was the best managed murder scrape he ever heard of."

Before he was arrested, Bent Jones told Lowry, according to his testimony, exactly what he should swear under oath before the grand jury:

> "That Jeff Huffstetler [sic] tried to hire me to kill Moody twice; that I took supper at Patterson's the night of the murder, and played cards in Abe Jones's saloon with certain parties, and for me to tell Patterson to swear that I ate supper at his house that night."

An obvious question concerning the plan to kill Tom Moody remains unanswered. Did the assassins have advance knowledge that Tom would be attending a card game in town on that specific night? Several accounts emphasized that after the firebombing Moody rarely left home after dark. At least one newspaper claimed that the night of his murder was the first time he had ventured out in darkness since moving to the house in Orleans. A later account stated: "... they lived in a house with the doors and windows barricaded and remained inside the house after night." William Moody had testified that he could not recall a night when Tom was outside the house after dark other than when he was on an overnight trip. Perhaps it was a coincidence. Lowry testified that Lee Jones claimed he had been waiting for Moody to come out of the house when he heard him walking toward them.

Eli Lowry did not explain why they expected Tom Moody to be outside after dark on the night of the murder, but he was able to shed some light on the 1871 firebombing of the Moody farmhouse:

> "I went to Orleans with Bent, after the attack on Moody's house in the country; he told me he was going to get Gen. Spicely and Mr. Hood and get them in to see the Moodys and get the Moodys to pay him $5,000 and give him the land back, and while we were on the road he told me all about the attack on the Moody house... at the forks of the road, where it makes a turn, he showed me a pond which he said contained the can in which they bought the benzine they used that night. He said himself, Abe Jones, Lee Jones, Bill Sheeks and some others who I don't now remember, were in the raid. Said Lee shot Moody that night with a Colt revolver; that they lost some of the loads out of their guns in climbing fences."

This corresponded with testimony from Zachariah Burton that Bent had asked him to approach the Moody family with the same deal, but with the added condition that Polly Moody would pay back rent from the time that she had taken possession of her land and "if they did not do so he would make it cost them $10,000." Jones asked Burton "if he did not wish to live in a civil community." When Zachariah agreed that he did, Jones "said it would not be, and that the poisoning of Bob Hall's horses was nothing to what it would be." Isom Hall told the court that he had been aware of a similar "peace" proposal.

At some point "in the spring" Lowry said Bent Jones told him that he "had better go out West and work with Joe Toliver for my health." Joseph, brother of Parks and Tom, had moved to Illinois. Lowry, Parks Toliver, and another man headed west, but when they had got to Loogootee (28 miles away) they were intercepted by Lee Jones, who informed Lowry that he had been accused of stealing some money from Jefferson Jones. Lee wanted Eli to return home and absolve himself, but Lowry decided to change course and go to work as a farmhand for an uncle in Sullivan County. That is where he was arrested and charged with murder. Lowry said that when he was returned to Paoli for trial, he found Bent Jones already in jail there. Bent said that he would get out on bail the next day and would provide bail money and a good attorney for Eli. After he was released, Bent Jones sat on the jail yard fence and spoke to Lowry through his cell window, telling him that he would be outside within three days. Bent Jones did eventually tender bond for Eli's release.

Professor McNutt challenged Lowry's account during the cross-examination and suggested that his testimony was intended to help earn him a pardon. McNutt asked whether any pistols had been taken to the murder scene. Lowry replied that Parks Toliver had "a very large one" that he had borrowed from an unnamed person, but it was so big that Parks had difficulty carrying it in his pocket. When he and Lee Jones started toward town "to do the killing, Bent cautioned Parks not to lose it in Orleans, because if it should be found everybody would know at once where it come from."

Daniel Spencer wrote in the *New Albany Daily Ledger-Standard* that the prosecution had examined a total of fifty-one witnesses. He added:

> "Of course, the cross-examinations, conducted by Professor McNutt and sometimes by Major Tucker and J.R. Burton, were very damaging to certain of the State's witnesses, but still

> the impression prevails pretty generally at
> Bloomington that the case is much stronger
> against Jones than it was at the time of the
> application for bail last winter."

On Saturday, May 19, several witnesses for the prosecution corroborated Eli Lowry's testimony. The state also introduced fragments of gun wadding found at the murder scene that contained words such as "sash windows" and "size of windows", along with printed columns of figures that indicated they could have been from a price list from Bent Jones's planing mill. Harry B. Ward and Captain Samuel R. Tegarden had been the primary detectives for the prosecution. Ward repeated his earlier testimony about the ruse he had used to ask questions in the community, how he had obtained the trust of Bent Jones by pretending that he was really on the trail of Jeff Huffstetter, and how Jones had helped him find the murder weapon. This time, however, Ward elaborated on the incentive offered to Jones for his help. Ward told the court that "he said he was going to run for Sheriff. I told him that if I could make $3,000 [in reward money], I would not mind giving him $300 to electioneer on." Ward said Jones had also talked about the earlier attack on the Moody farmhouse, claiming that Jeff Huffstetter had held the horses during that raid. Bent also boasted that one day when Tom Moody was taking the train to Bedford, he had forced him off the train in Mitchell and made him go back to Orleans. Later Bent proposed that he and Ward should stage a public quarrel at a hotel in Paoli to convince observers that they were not working together to convict Huffstetter.

The cross-examination by the defense was aimed at casting doubt on the character of Detective Ward:

> "The cross-examination by Judge McNutt was
> exhaustive and exciting, and elicited several
> admissions which show conclusively, to say
> the least, that this detective (Ward) has
> very little care or regard for his family.
> Capt. Ward has, however, worked hard on this
> case, and if the party deemed be guilty, is

entitled to great credit for his industry and daring in his pursuit of the defendant. It was also shown... that Ward, with three others, has a pecuniary interest in the result of this trial."

With no court session on Sunday, Daniel Spencer shared a carriage ride to Owen County, just northwest of Bloomington, with Judge Robinson, whose home was in the town of Spencer. While the judge enjoyed time with his family, the reporter visited other friends at their country estate, which he found "restful and invigorating. And so here in this goodly place, after I have gotten somewhat surfeited with croquet, and skiff riding on a fine, large fish pond, and the like, and shall have enjoyed for a time the excellent music ... by the cunning hands and eloquent tongues of my friends here, I shall write up my report for the LEDGER-STANDARD."

The newspaper reporter and the judge left early Monday morning to resume their roles at the trial in Bloomington, where spectators were waiting to see if Bent Jones would take the witness stand in his own defense. Their return was delayed by one hour due to a storm Sunday night that had blown down trees "making our roads disagreeable and heavy." Other attorneys had also been delayed in returning from their homes in Bedford and Paoli, but the defendant was brought into court on time.

Chapter Eleven:
The Blood of Abel

During Bent Jones's murder trial Daniel Spencer declared that "...this case has been worked up on both sides more searchingly and thoroughly, I venture to say, than any case ever tried before in the State... The character of many persons, and even whole families of heretofore highly respectable citizens of Orange and Lawrence counties are imperiled, and will stand or fall by the results of this intensely interesting, and solemn trial." He added that such a celebrated trial was attracting not just the usual courtroom spectators but, surprisingly, even women:

> "Occasionally ladies come in and sit with us awhile, but do not attend as numerously as they will when they come to know how delighted the court and its officers are when they see good women gracing the bar and court room with their presence."

On the morning of May 21, before the court was called to order, the attention of the reporter from New Albany was drawn to one woman in particular:

> "The prisoner came into court before we arrived and we found him consulting with his witnesses and attorneys with unabated interest and vigor. He possesses wonderful executive

ability, and his zeal and energies are being expended on this cause with sleepless vigilance and extraordinary industry. His wife is still with him, and her fortitude and fidelity are winning for her golden opinions. She is quite as industrious as her husband, and is doing more effectual work for Bent Jones (her husband) than anybody else. Tall and stately of stature, quick and graceful of movement, she possesses every characteristic, seemingly, of a heroine. When not engaged during the sessions of court in looking after witnesses, passing in and out of the court room with noiseless foot falls, she is anxiously looking on as the evidence proceeds, her black, kindling eyes flashing forth a very significant suggestion as to the sentiments with which, for the nonce, her heart may be stirred."

Three days later a correspondent for the *Indiana State Sentinel* echoed that observation:

'Whatever opinion one may form as to the guilt or innocence of the prisoner on trial, Bent Jones, there can be but admiration for the heroic devotion of his wife. She seems never to grow weary or disheartened. At every term of court she is present in the court room, and by her knowledge of the evidence of each witness is enabled to be of the utmost importance to the attorneys for her husband. She marshals the witnesses and prompts the attorneys. She is modest and unassuming, but vigilant and watchful; and if Bent Jones is acquitted of this charge, he can give his faithful wife the everlasting praise for having managed details, without which his attorneys, of the first ability though they are, would have been in a great measure powerless."

The 38-year-old Mrs. Alonzo B. Jones also had a strong interest in the verdicts for her husband's co-defendants. She was the former

Clarissa Toliver, sister of defendants Parks and Tom Toliver, and sister-in-law of Lee Jones.

The defense began by presenting a dozen witnesses to dispute earlier testimony that was damaging to the defendant. Daniel Spencer noted that "several of the foregoing witnesses were badly damaged by the cross-examinations… for the State." One of them, Lucinda Lee, had an especially unpleasant experience:

> "[She] left the witness stand protesting in bitterness and tears that Prosecutor Miers 'oughten ter be allowed to ax her' whether, heretofore, she was the kept mistress of the defendant, and who went back on most of her important evidence on former occasions."

The reaction of the faithful and heroic Mrs. Jones to this line of questioning was not recorded.

Another witness, Fannie Elrod, widow of former Orleans postmaster Moses Elrod, claimed to have seen Eli Lowry near the scene of the murder shortly before it happened. That would contradict Lowry's testimony that only Lee Jones and Parks Toliver were in the vicinity when the shots were fired. When asked how she had recognized him, Mrs. Elrod responded, "I recognized him by his face; how else could I recognize him(?)"

When Major David S. Huffstetter, father of Jeff Huffstetter, was called to the stand he said Bent Jones had told him that he had not killed Tom Moody, "and if he had, he had friends enough to get him out of it." Jones had implied that he had inside information that Jeff would be indicted for the murder. When the defense attorney asked the Major if he had retained counsel to protect his son or helped pay for the prosecution, the elder Huffstetter emphatically replied, "No!"

A witness named Columbus Moore said he had once seen Bent Jones and Parks Toliver together in the bar of the Hughes Hotel in Bedford. Parks, who "appeared to be slightly intoxicated" and was holding a pistol, asked if Tom Moody was upstairs. Moore replied that he was upstairs playing cards. He said Parks became impatient, saying that he was getting "damn tired of waiting." The prosecution claimed that this testimony indicated that a conspiracy to murder was already in place.

Samuel R. Tegarden, whom an *Indiana State Sentinel* reporter declared "to have provided the bulk of the brains in the detective line in this case", testified that he had examined the outhouse that Lee Jones had allegedly shot into as a signal to Jim Murray, and had dug out several pieces of buckshot, which were exhibited to the jury.

Elizabeth Brown told the jury that while Bent Jones was working on her house in Mitchell he told her "that some persons had been around his mill one night and had pounded Eli Lowery, who was watching for him, and that he believed it was some of the Moody gang; that he (Jones) and the Moodys could not live in the same country."

As usual, the *New Albany Daily Ledger-Standard* offered the most entertaining digest of testimony. Spencer began by stating "We are groping our way through a mass of evidence for the defense…" He then listed twenty new defense witnesses. It became clear that there was a lot of conflicting testimony between witnesses for the prosecution and defense, but there were no real surprises. Among the most colorful characters to take the stand were:

```
"Moses    Clinton    (who    supplemented    the
administering  of  the  Clerk's  confirmation  in
the oath with a pious and unctuous 'I do')…"
```

Clinton, owner of a "truss-hoop factory", provided alibis for all four defendants and under cross-examination denied that he had discouraged other potential witnesses from testifying against Bent Jones or encouraged some to "say they were sick" to avoid being called to the stand. The prosecution read Clinton's testimony from the habeas corpus hearing that conflicted with his current story. Clinton denied having testified to the contrary despite the official transcript.

> "Mrs. Mehalia Murry [sic], against whose husband an indictment is now pending in the Orange Circuit Court as an accessory to the crime alleged against defendant now on trial..."

She was not only the wife of James Murray but also the sister of Parks and Tom Toliver and the sister-in-law of Lee and Bent Jones. Mahala appeared to have a selective memory regarding the night in question.

> "Lidy Giles, an intelligent and very comely young brunette, who, although a niece of defendant, A.B. Jones, yet swore to the alibi as to co-defendants Benton Jones, Thomas Tolliver, and Dr. Parks Tolliver in such a way as to be considered singularly pleasing and honest..."

The 18-year-old niece had been living in Uncle Bent's household at the time of the murder. On cross-examination she was shown a paper containing a copy of her testimony. During the habeas corpus hearing Bent had admitted under oath that he had written the document and had given it to his wife to give to Miss Giles. But she testified that she had never seen it before and did not recognize the handwriting.

> "Minerva Danning, a "lewd lady" from your city..."

Regrettably, "D.O.S." did not elaborate on why Ms. Danning (or Dunning in another account) was lewd. She provided an alibi for Parks Toliver, claiming that she picked up a prescription for a sick child at his office in Mitchell shortly before the murder.

> "... and James Murry, indicted as before mentioned..."

Murray steadfastly denied any involvement in the murder. There was a bit of drama when a man named Henry Oldham testified that he had been a grand juror during the term of Orange County court when the true bills were returned, but that he was not present when the case against Bent Jones was presented and did not vote to indict him. A surprised Judge Robinson, understanding that this could result in a mistrial or worse, stopped the proceedings immediately but was persuaded by State's Attorney Miers, who had questioned that grand jury, to allow Oldham to continue his testimony. According to the *State Sentinel* reporter:

```
"... the witness was permitted to proceed, when
it was found, after a half hour's pumping,
that he was about as ignorant of what took
place at that sitting of the grand jury as
Crazy Horse would be supposed to be."
```

Oldham may have been the witness described by Spencer as "a grog-blossomed fellow... a very bad citizen indeed." Crazy Horse, the Lakota warrior known for his role at Little Bighorn, had surrendered to U.S. troops in Nebraska two weeks earlier.

Miss Mattie Pearson, "a niece of His Honor, Judge Pearson, and a young lady of pleasant address and very great intelligence", appeared on the stand "clad in deep mourning apparel, by reason of the death of her mother last January." She swore that Dr. Parks Toliver had been in bed at his home as early as 9 o'clock on the night of the murder. Miss Pearson was his sister-in-law; Parks was married to her sister, Ella Belle Pearson.

Local farmer and livestock trader Daniel Boone (no, not that one) testified that on the night of the murder he had delivered "a car load" of eighteen horses to the Toliver livery stable in Mitchell. He claimed to have seen both Parks and Tom Toliver in town after dark, but his memory faltered under cross-examination to the point that he could not swear to specific times or places.

Almost all the defense witnesses claimed to have seen Bent Jones in one location or another that would have made it unlikely, if not impossible, for him to have been near Orleans at the time of the killing. During cross-examination it would have been difficult for the jury to ignore that many of these alibis conflicted with each other and others (such as Moses Moore) admitted to having been coached or provided written instructions prior to their testimony.

Altogether about thirty witnesses would testify during this portion of the trial, including Allen Jones, the fifteen-year-old son of Bent Jones. The *Ledger-Standard* reported, "Of course they got away with the little fellow on the cross-examination."

Co-defendant Thomas Toliver may have begun his testimony with a lie. When Professor McNutt asked his age, Tom replied "Nineteen years old." Census records, his death certificate, and tombstone all indicate that he was, in fact, twenty-one. Tom testified that he had been sick for three or four weeks just prior to the night of the murder but, when asked to identify his disease, he answered, "I forgot the name of it." He swore that he had supper on the night of the murder with his brother-in-law, Lee Jones, with whom he boarded. After helping Mr. Boone with his horses, he said he had gone to Abe Jones's saloon in Mitchell between eight and nine p.m., where he saw Bent Jones. Tom testified that he was still in the saloon at the time of the killing and did not learn of the murder until after ten o'clock the following morning. He claimed that he had not seen Lee Jones after supper and did not recall seeing his brother, Parks, at all that night. Tom swore that he had not seen Eli Lowry "for over two or three days", that he had no advance knowledge of the murder plan, and that he was nowhere near Orleans when the shooting took place.

Saloon owner Abe Jones was "now in the far West" but counsel and the judge agreed to let his testimony from the earlier habeas corpus proceedings, as recorded by reporter Daniel Spencer, be presented as evidence "as if said witness was present". Professor C.F. McNutt, lead counsel for the defense, read a transcript to the jury.

Abe had confirmed that he was not related to defendants Bent or Lee Jones or to Parks and Tom Toliver, although he was acquainted with them all. He had lived in Mitchell and operated a saloon there for about eight years prior to leaving town on September 1, 1876. He swore that he did not know of Tom Moody's murder until the following morning when he visited George

Alvey's store "to get something, maybe some crackers" for his business and the proprietor told him "I think Thomas Moody was shot." Jones claimed that on the night of the murder he saw Bent Jones and Tom Toliver in his saloon at about 7:30 p.m., then went to the Odd Fellows lodge. On his way he met Lee Jones in the street and they had a brief conversation. Abe said he left the lodge around 8:00 or 8:15. He later admitted that he left then because "there were charges preferred against me that night." Abe Jones said he returned to the saloon, where he spoke with Bent Jones.

Abe then explained that he had moved his family to Evansville "for safety to my life" after he had been shot outside his establishment early in the morning of July 23, 1876. The saloon was closed and he was at home when he heard a commotion outside and saw what he estimated as 75 or 100 men surrounding his saloon "on the corner of Sixth and Mississippi". A report in the *Bedford Star* said that the mob "began to cut with axes on the saloon of Abe Jones, evidently with the intention of destroying it." When Jones was within twenty yards of the saloon he was shot: "... the ball, a very large one, entering one of his thighs near the groin and passing through, causing a wound that will in all probability prove fatal..." A very much alive Abe admitted that he had been shot, but he was not questioned further about the circumstances. The court was also not told of Abe Jones's notorious reputation before that incident according to a dispatch from Paoli reported in the *New Albany Daily Ledger Standard* almost exactly one year earlier:

> "About two weeks ago one Abram Jones, of Mitchell, gave notice to the citizens of Paoli that he intended to make application to the County Board at their June term for license to start a saloon in this place. On this fact becoming known, a petition was at once circulated and signed by 114 voters of the town, calling for a mass meeting at the court house, Monday evening the 15th inst. At the time and place appointed about five hundred people assembled and passed resolutions

pledging themselves to use all honorable means to prevent the said Jones from accomplishing his design. A committee was appointed to wait on Jones at his home in Mitchell and notify him of the action of the meeting, and, if possible, persuade him to change his intention to establish a saloon in our town. Paoli has been without a saloon for the past four years and our good people intend it shall remain so until the next Centennial at least."

This item was dated May 17, 1876, and was signed "OTHELLO." Despite the fervent opposition to his Paoli saloon proposal, Abe had no trouble getting his liquor license renewed in Mitchell. On July 8, the *Bedford Star* reported "Abe Jones, of Mitchell, has secured license for the sale of spiritous liquors. He keeps on hand the best of wines, ale, beer, and pure white wheat whisky."

The moment had finally arrived for the defendant, Alonzo Benton Jones, to testify in his own defense. Bent told the court that he was 38 years old, had been born in Ohio, moved with his family to Washington County, Indiana, when he was four years old, and had lived in Mitchell for almost twenty years. There was questioning about the nature of his sawmill and woodworking business, which had burned down in February of 1876. He confirmed that Eli Lowry had worked for him at various times but flatly denied that he had ever had a conversation with Lowry about killing Thomas Moody. Furthermore, he testified that he had never offered anyone money to kill Moody. Jones spent a lot of time trying to establish his whereabouts on March 2 and mentioned several persons with whom he had spoken in Mitchell, but he could not recall seeing Eli Lowry at any time that day. Bent swore that he had been at Abe Jones's saloon when the murder was committed. The prosecution attorney asked what he was doing there. Bent replied:

"I was just doing what people normally do at saloons, talking. There was a violin there, and someone asked me to play on that. I played, or tried to play one tune, and then some one asked me to play something else, and some of them asked me to sing."

Jones testified that he went directly home and was never anywhere near Orleans. In fact, he insisted that he did not know about the murder until the following day. Bent claimed that he had heard that Moody had been shot before boarding a train the next morning in Mitchell and was told that Tom was dead when he arrived in Bedford.

Testimony concluded late in the day on May 25, 1877. The *New Albany Ledger-Standard*'s correspondent, the indefatigable "Dank" Spencer, named 32 different witnesses who testified. As usual, he added some colorful asides:

> "Gen. Wm. T. Spicely (a witness often introduced and examined by both parties and as often left the witness stand with the highest respect of counsel and court and jury and of spectators)..."

> "J.H. Crim (the depot agent at Mitchell, and the best looking man of the five hundred witnesses)..."

> "E.S. McIntyre (editor of the *Mitchell Commercial* and who testified with singular clearness and precision)..."

The defense called several witnesses in support of Moses Clinton "who swore to an alibi for defendants... and whose general character for truth was impeached by a large number of the best citizens of Mitchell..." Among those were "Rev. Mr. Harper", whom Spencer had overlooked in a previous list of witnesses:

> "I forgot him; forgot him, may be, because he is so diminutive; and because he wanted to do so much and accomplished so little for Clinton. God forbid that I should forget him entirely. The truth is that ordinarily a person

> ought not, after looking upon this sleek, dapper little man of God, forget him. It is difficult for me to believe that the Lord calls such comic-looking fellows into the ministry. Why this grinning, sunken-nosed little divine resembles Eli Lowery, and was pointed out frequently this forenoon to spectators, by waggish persons, who knew better, as the chief prosecuting witness. The atmosphere must have been quite heavy about his ears, or his hearing greatly impaired, when he fancied himself called to the ministry. It cropped out in the evidence that this Moses Clinton and the 'Rev. Mr. Harper'… have been running a little evangelical Protestant church down there in Mitchell when brother Clinton was not otherwise engaged."

The *New Albany Ledger-Standard* reported that impartial court observers "were pretty clearly of the opinion that Judge Robinson has kept the record free from errors", making it doubtful that there could be grounds for an appeal. "D.O.S." gave examples of contradictory testimony from multiple witnesses. Regardless of the verdict, it was obvious that many citizens had been willing, for whatever reason, to perjure themselves. Some, such as the Pattersons, had already admitted perjury during their earlier habeas corpus testimony.

"This has been a wonderful case", wrote Daniel Spencer. He continued:

> "Let me give you an illustration: Of the battalion of witnesses introduced there has not been a dozen of them, all told, and on both sides, who have been treated with civility, with, perhaps, a dozen exceptions. As to all others they are considered bad citizens, by one side or the other: against whom one or more of the crimes and enormities peculiar to mortals has not been leveled [sic]. Some hint or innuendo or direct charge of immorality, embracing every specie of

> crime and misdemeanors. The mildest type of such charges, general [sic] thrown out on the cross-examinations was a mild form of exaggeration; then followed in their order and grade (so far as the affair seems to be arranged by the parties) common lying, the hanging of negroes from bridges, then house burnings, dog and horse 'pisinings'; some more lying, assassinations by night and day, and on land and sea, of slanders not a few, highway robberies, perjuries, pilfering, yet other lies, mobbing of jails and violent assaults on saloons, whoredoms and assignations and adulteries beyond computation, to say nothing of such unpardonable sins as the stealing of kegs of white lead and the like. I believe the Court and parties and jury and bystanders will bear me witness, that everybody in this case has shuddered most at the imputation against one of the witnesses, that said witness had stolen a keg of beer. This is regarded by the parties not as a venal offense, but ranks along side of the hand-grenade attack on the Moody house in 1871."

Spencer closely observed the jurors as they filed past his desk at the end of the day "to see whether I can find on their solemn faces any hints as to what impressions have been made on their minds by the mass of evidence already taken... I look for a sign, but no sign is given me. The jury for the most part look wearied and worn, yet there are a few of their number who have been guilty of such gross inattention and carelessness..." He did, however, detect "one precursor of the probable fate of the defendant" while Dr. Milton Parks Toliver was being questioned:

> "Mr. Hinds, lately of Indianapolis, and a very attentive juror, in ordering the Doctor, who is a co-defendant, to 'set up and talk louder - we can't hear you', did so in tones so chilling as to suggest what his feelings are touching the case."

Closing arguments began on Saturday morning, May 26, and were not expected to be concluded before Tuesday at noon. The first speaker for the prosecution was J.W. Buskirk. He declared:

> "Since the day the Lord declared a curse upon Cain, whereby he was declared to be a vagabond, a fugitive for slaying his brother, one of the highest and most brutal of crimes, this crime, which the defendant committed, has never been excelled in its ferocity and fiendishness, whether committed in a civilized or uncivilized land."

Expanding on the Biblical theme, the reporter wrote that Buskirk told the court that "As the blood of Abel was wont to cry out from the ground for vengeance, so the blood of Thomas Moody was crying to the jury that his death should by the law be avenged." The attorney also refuted allegations against the victim's character, although perhaps less emphatically than the Moodys might have wished:

> "The character of Thomas Moody was now warmly defended against the assaults and aspersions of the defense, in which connection some scorching rebukes were administered. If Moody became somewhat intemperate toward the close of his life, let it be remembered that Benton Jones and his co-defendants, who drove him from his home on his farm to the little village by their murderous attacks, compelling him to remain indoors at night, these murderous assassins are themselves to blame for it, and besides, no matter how intemperate and loose in his morals he might have been the defendant and his co-defendants had no right to murder him."

The weary – and hungry – correspondent from the *New Albany Ledger-Standard* concluded his daily report:

"I very much regret that, by even going without my dinner, I have had less than an hour for this imperfect sketch of his powerful effort. The interest in the trial is increasing, and the excitement here now is intense.

            D.O.S"

Chapter Twelve:
Devilish Delight

A CITIZEN OF THE TWENTY-FIRST CENTURY would probably be astonished and appalled if called to serve on a nineteenth-century American jury. This was the beginning of what would later be known as the Gilded Age. Both the content and duration of legal rhetoric used during a major trial would seem outrageous to modern sensibilities. Passionate and extended eloquence was expected by jurors of the day, as lawyers attempted to appeal equally to their understanding and imagination. It was understood that both the prosecution and defense would use highly emotional language and imaginary recreations to justify the verdict they desired. Closing arguments that included references to classical literature and impromptu poetic recitations today seem especially odd when directed to a jury panel that might well include men (and they were always men) who were poorly educated, if not illiterate. However, all parties concerned would have been disappointed by anything less.

The extensive oratory and theatrics would take a lot of time, of course, but neither the jurors, the accused, nor the spectators in the courtroom seemed to mind. In a world without radio, television, or motion pictures, a prominent trial was both a social event and a highly anticipated form of free live entertainment. Indeed, on May 27 the *New Albany Ledger-Standard* reported that "The audience attending the argument of this case is immense,

The Terror of Indiana

filling the corridors and aisles, and doors and windows, and every available foot of space in and about the court-room. Many persons, I will say hundreds of persons, are here from many towns, farms, and villages of Southern Indiana" as young J. Ralph Burton stood in the Bloomington courtroom to argue in defense of Bent Jones. He began by denouncing the murder of Thomas Moody in the strongest terms but declared that "Alonzo B. Jones... is not the man that committed the murder." Burton then took issue with Buskirk's defense of the victim's character:

> "It matters not if Thomas Moody was as bad a man as ever lived in this country; we yet have no right to comment on it, nor have they the right, under the ruling of the Court, I believe, to assert that he was a good man... Moody is in his grave and when God puts His hand on a man, I always want to take mine off... They say he was 'a good man, a quiet farmer, an excellent old gentleman, who had but one failing' and that one failing to be attributed to Alonzo B. Jones. Well according to the evidence here you learn that Moody had acquired his habits before he left his farm; had acquired his habits long before Alonzo B. Jones was born. Now, the idea... that a man of Jones' age should lead the venerable Thomas Moody into the vices and immoralities of intoxication and gambling... How preposterous!... The evidence is... that in the gaming in the little saloon in Orleans, Moody, to use the language of one of this State's witnesses, 'Most nigh always won.'... did he learn those tricks from a young man twenty-three years, or more, his junior?... I don't want to grapple in the grave of Moody and bring his carcass here for public exhibition. He had a right to live, whatever he may have been, and the man that killed him is a bloody, cowardly and dastardly murderer. But we say Alonzo B. Jones is not guilty of that murder."

J. Ralph Burton was just getting started. His speech would continue for three hours and twenty-five minutes, "and, at its close, Mr. Burton sat down in a state of great physical prostration." Daniel Spencer resorted to summaries of the defense arguments, while inserting pertinent quotations. Burton, who was related to the Toliver family by marriage, painted an idyllic image of that family during the days before William Toliver was killed. He claimed that some of his earliest and most pleasant personal recollections took place in the Toliver home during "those happy, peaceful, prosperous days..." He said it would be ungrateful for him not to mention that he knew "there was never any association between those families, and no sort of relations existing between them until the reason of William Tolliver was dethroned." Indeed, Burton implied that his "departed friend and benefactor" must have been senile when he married Polly Moody. "William Tolliver", he said, "cannot come here to deny that he ever associated with the Moodys during his hours of sanity."

At some point, possibly later, "D.O.S." added a lengthy transcript of the most melodramatic portion of Burton's speech. It is a remarkable example of Gilded Age legal persuasion. Among the persons named are attorneys representing the State, witnesses for the prosecution, detectives, reporters, and local law enforcement officials. The complete text can be found in the May 29, 1877, edition of the *New Albany Ledger-Standard*. This is an edited sample:

> "Suppose, gentlemen of the jury, you ignore this mountain of evidence in favor of the defendant, and upon this rotten case made by the State, bring in a verdict of guilty and assess the death penalty. By that verdict you direct Mart Alexander, within the next two or three months, to erect within your jail yard that gloomiest of all structures, the scaffold... The seats for the audience are arranged, and the guests to that carnival of death have been invited... There, upon a prominence in the center, sits Bob Tegarten [sic], with

his three thousand pieces of silver, the price of Bent Jones' blood; upon one side is Charles Keith, upon the other Colonel Millis; behind the trio is Capt. Ward... Bring in a table, for there comes the reporter – the only one admitted to this party, Dr. E.S. McIntyre. Ah! with what devilish delight will he picture to his readers the death struggle of the defendant. Then the reserved seats in front are being filled by the counsel for the State. Yes, gentlemen, witness the scene you demand to be enacted. There is Bob Myers [sic], John Buskirk, his brother Tom... There is Judge Wilson, and because of his imposing appearance, it has been arranged that the Hon. Geo. W. Friedley shall preside at this, the bare thought of which makes the soul sick. Now bring forward the victim; pinion his arms; put him on the trap; put the black bandage – the signal of death – over his eyes. The audience demand that the last prayer be short. They grow impatient of the delay. One moment of awful agony, the rope is cut and a murder more foul than was that of Thomas Moody has been committed, beneath the very shades of the State University, for Moody was killed in defiance of law, and Benton Jones is murdered in the name of justice. The horrible picture is completed with the last death struggle of this poor defendant."

Burton then recited a stanza from a poem titled "Marco Bozzaris" by Fitz-Greene Halleck, once known as "the American Byron":

"Come to the bridal chamber death,
Come to the mother when she feels for the first time its breath,
Come when the blessed seals which close the pestilence are broke,
And crowded cities wail its stroke..."

"But", said Burton, "when to this grim monster is added the frightful spectre of the scaffold, the heart shrinks from the accumulated horror." He then claimed that Bent Jones would prefer death to life in prison:

> "... we will not make any appeal to you for mercy. Benton Jones would rather step upon the gibbet and face this motley crew I have just described, than to hear the grating doors of the penitentiary close behind him. Benton Jones says to you to be neither cruel, nor merciful; *be just;* BE JUST. Aye upon that high and lofty plane of justice he demands - he does not request - he demands, because it is his right and your duty, a verdict of not guilty."

To many experienced orators this might have seemed an ideal place to end his appeal. But J. Ralph Burton was not finished:

> "The prosecution of this case has a distinct individuality... Milton's Mulock has not a more grim visaged appearance. It is so steeped in blood that:
>
> 'Sin leads on to sin,
> Tear falling pity dwells not in its eye.'
>
> It stands without a likeness in the history of criminal prosecutions. Nothing but the blood of the defendant will appease it."

Burton then attacked the credibility of Eli Lowry:

> "(T)his prosecution comes to you... with a case made by the self-contradictory story of a self-condemned murderer, wrung from him by a vile conspiracy, black as the shades of night, and corroborated alone by perjury; and notwithstanding this story is contradicted

by an alibi, strong as the backbone of a mountain..."

He said that the prosecution was "longing to wallow in blood" and proposed that heaven and hell were breathlessly awaiting the jury's verdict. If Jones's life was taken, Burton said, "the fiends of hell will laugh and the angels of heaven will weep." To the contrary, a verdict of not guilty would "teach innocence to tremble in the presence of guilt" and "the glad heart of that faithful wife will leap to heaven and bless you." Shortly after that Burton rested. Presumably, so did everyone else.

The *Ledger-Standard* correspondent felt that Burton had made a powerful and effective case:

"In discussing the evidence supporting the alibi, he made the defense formidable, and rolled away many a huge stone in the way of the prosecution, over which much stumbling will be done, no doubt, ere the jury shall come into court with a verdict of guilty. His descriptions of some of the scenes and incidents and witnesses were highly appreciated and thoroughly enjoyed by court and the jury, and were received by the crowded auditorium with approving smiles and friendly and flattering merriment. The best evidence of genuine oratory is the effect produced in causing men to act, and I therefore, in justice to Mr. Burton, record the fact that quite a number of persons have assured me that this brilliant speech had unsettled them in their original notions that the prisoner is guilty. He was frequently eloquent, and in a few grand passages was absolutely thrilling."

A much later newspaper summary of the trial added:

"...the surprise came in the argument of J. Ralph Burton, who was looked upon as a dude, owing to his youth and dress and from whom nothing was expected. It turned out, however,

> that he was a gifted elocutionist, and for several hours he held the court room in an argument of marvellous brilliancy."

On May 30, the *Indiana State Sentinel* reported:

> "As the days go by and this Jones-Toliver trial draws nearer to a close the interest becomes more and more intense. All parties are wishing and dreading, as it were, the finale. It is no longer a matter of moment to the prisoners and their immediate families alone. The attorneys on each side have been so long studying and planning this case that they have become personally identified with their respective sides and the public is as radically divided as during a heated political campaign. Street discussions are common, and to enter a group composed of the adherents of one side dissecting and vilifying witnesses of the other is of hourly occurrence. The jury, who must sit and hear this almost inexplicable mass of evidence unprejudiced, can not but feel their unusual responsibility and become almost as solicitous as the prisoners themselves."

Bent Jones may have felt a new sense of optimism as he was escorted back to his jail cell following J. Ralph Burton's virtuoso performance. The claim that Jones would prefer hanging to a life sentence was a calculated risk, but there was new hope that he might be found innocent.

Chapter Thirteen: Scalp Dance

When Bent Jones's murder trial resumed the following day, Daniel Spencer, reporter and raconteur, was not his usual ebullient self. His next report in the *Ledger-Standard* appeared without his customarily colorful introduction and included both occasional missing words and poor punctuation. At times it was difficult to determine which person was speaking. He began abruptly with a speech from prosecutor Robert Miers, who took a folksy and more humble approach in speaking to the jury as he outlined his responsibilities as a representative of the State. He allowed that "If I shall, in my feeble manner, so discharge those duties I shall be content." He was complimentary to Professor McNutt of the defense team, even as he argued against the evidence presented on behalf of Bent Jones. But Miers, too, was capable of an obligatory rhetorical flourish:

> "... truth, like a beautiful white-winged angel, has perched itself on this forum, and is now, in all its beauty and brightness, eradiating the mind of each juror in this box, and in doing so has dissolved the shadows of darkness in which his client has been heretofore turning his wayward feet, leaving that client exposed to a full view."

Miers reminded the jurors that J. Ralph Burton had, in effect, invited them to impose the death penalty if Jones was found guilty of murder. He then began to methodically point out blatant contradictions in the testimony of many defense witnesses, to the point where it was obvious that some of them had to be lying. It was noteworthy, he said, that Bent Jones had issued blanket denials during his relatively short appearance on the witness stand but did not challenge specific testimony from some leading citizens. This included a claim, not denied by Jones, that he had told a witness that:

> "... if the Moodys would deed back the... Tolliver tract of land and pay him five thousand dollars in money, the Moodys might move back to their farm and live in quietude on their farm all the balance of their days, but if they failed to accept his proposition the troubles they had been through were nothing then, even after the raid on the Moody house in 1871, to what would follow."

Miers asked why Jones, whom he described as "the head devil of those inhuman and fiendish monsters who made that midnight raid", had not denied under oath any connection to the farmhouse attack? He then recalled several colorful threats ("every dollar Tom Moody compels me to pay out is only driving another spike around his grave") and other incriminating statements made by Jones that were witnessed by upstanding citizens and recounted under oath. Among them was testimony from "uncle Ransom Burton" that "[Jones] would not law with Tom Moody, but would shoot him like a hound" and "that if he [Jones] was not afraid of the law he would cut [Moody's] heart out and throw it to the hounds."

Daniel Spencer wrote that "Mr. Miers rose to a high degree of eloquence when he... came to describe Eli Lowery, smitten of conscience, and miserable, walking the floor of his lonely cell in the Paoli jail on the night before his wonderful confession." Miers concluded by reminding the jurors that a guilty verdict could result in either a death sentence or life imprisonment and said he would be content "Whether the verdict... says to this defendant, 'adamantine [unbreakable] bonds and chains for life' or "penal sufferings of body and mind upon the gallows tree unto death'."

This speech lasted almost three and one-half hours, beginning "about half past two o'clock and was finished a few minutes before the hour of six." Reality may have begun to reassert itself to Bent Jones as he was once again walked back to his cell.

George W. Friedley was a Bedford attorney and self-described "radical Republican". He was a former Indiana state senator who, as President of the Senate, had filled a vacancy as Lieutenant Governor. Friedley was said to have "an imposing appearance". He was six feet, three and one-half inches tall and described as "well-built and proportioned". On Monday, May 28, he delivered a memorable appeal for the conviction of Alonzo Benton Jones. Daniel Spencer, back to his usual form, judged it to be "one of the most powerful speeches to which it has been my good fortune to listen for a long time. His introductory was captivating and fell on one's ear with the smoothness and attractiveness of a charming romance." According to Spencer's timepiece, Friedley would speak for seven hours and thirty-seven minutes from start to finish. He began with the arrival of Alexander Moody and his family in Indiana:

> "... forty and seven years ago the Moody family settled in the county of Orange, in this state. Their lot was that of almost all persons who settled in Indiana at that time. They were in comparatively poor circumstances, but they were industrious and hard-working, and by their energy and perseverance they made for themselves a home and acquired a considerable amount of money and a large number of acres of land. They also, during those early years, by their good conduct built up reputations which gave them the respect and esteem of all their neighbors. They were quiet, inoffensive and good citizens."

His facts were slightly inaccurate – the Moodys had first settled in *Lawrence* County *fifty*-seven years earlier – but the tone was remarkably cordial. This rustic pastoral theme continued as Friedley introduced their neighbors, the Toliver family:

> "They aided each other in their duties, as neighbors and friends should do, ... Afterward the wife of William Tolliver passed away... after he had lost his first companion, he sought another. There was Polly Moody. She had grown up beside him. He had observed her life from day to day and had seen that it was pure and blameless, so that when he looked for one to take the place of the one departed he found no one so fitted, in every respect, to take the place of the departed one as Polly Moody. He, accordingly, sought her hand in marriage and won it."

This was a radically different view of events than the one presented to the jury less than forty-eight hours earlier by J. Ralph Burton.

Friedley calmly and methodically recited the lengthy series of conflicts, both legal and physical, between the families following William Toliver's death:

> "There was the beginning of a systematic course of intimidation; there was the inception of all those acts of violence and terrorism; there was their programme, and there was the defendant's connection with it, and from that day to this, gentlemen of the jury, that policy of intimidation has been on all occasions adopted and followed out carefully by this defendant and his co-defendants. And so we find today, that who opens his mouth against them, I care not what his standing in society may be, I care not how pure, elevated and blameless his life may have been, nor how high his character may be regarded by his neighbors; no matter who he may be, he

is at once fiercely assailed and denounced by the defense, charged with being an enemy of A.B. Jones or an enemy of the Tollivers, and charged with having entered into a conspiracy to break down, to prosecute and ruin these defendants..."

Friedley proceeded to defend specific community leaders who had been accused of conspiring against the Jones-Toliver defendants. These included Samuel R. Tegarden, John Wesley Burton, and detectives Charles Keith, Ed Millis, and Captain Harry Ward (whom had been characterized by the defense as a "wharf-rat"). Not to be outdone by J. Ralph Burton, who had burst into verse from a poet known in his day as "the American Byron", George W. Friedley included in his closing remarks part of a poem by the *actual* Lord Byron. Titled "A Sketch from Private Life", his excerpt began:

"Oh! Wretch, without a tear, without a thought
Save joy above the ruin thou hast wrought,
The time shall come, nor long remote, when thou
Shalt feel far more than thou inflictest now..."

For added impact, Friedley altered a single line, meant to refer to Bent Jones's eventual grave, to:

"And when thou fain would weary heaven with prayer
Look on Moody's grave and despair.
Down to the dust, and as thou rot'st away
Even worms shall perish on thy poisonous clay..."

Daniel Spencer wrote that "It is pronounced here by many persons who lived at this place for a great number of years the grandest argument ever delivered in Bloomington." He praised the "fine specimens of vigorous, terse, and eloquent language" as Friedley described how Jones's men "shot away the life of old Thomas Moody, and on the day following danced a scalp dance, like barbarous, cruel, savages..." The reporter insisted that "Hundreds of persons sat through the seven hour address without becoming wearied. At no time did the speech seem weak or less interesting and thrilling. It was certainly in every way a masterly argument, and as such will live always here."

Judge Francis Wilson of Bedford, an attorney for the State, began his closing statement on Monday morning, May 30. This continued until "At about six o'clock [that] evening an adjournment was had for an hour and a quarter, when, having meanwhile refreshed the inner man", Wilson returned to address the jury for an additional hour and three-quarters. Daniel Spencer wrote that Wilson "had been earnestly trying to conclude his speech [that] evening, but found himself wholly unable to do so without doing injustice to his cause, and so obtained permission of the court to finish his argument" the following morning. Those long hours and a desire to focus on Judge Robinson's instructions to the jury compelled "D.O.S." to admit that "after a wearisome and honest day's work" he had no time to review his notes and provide an adequate summary of Wilson's speech. He asked the attorney and his friends to forgive him, adding:

> "But the truth on this subject is, however, that nothing short of the entire argument, an address over seven hours in length, would do the gifted author of it justice. I will say this: The speech is regarded by all who had the pleasure of listening to it, as being one of great beauty, eloquence, and power. Judge Robinson pronounced it masterly in logic, forcibleness, eloquence, and beauty and vigor of language. The intense interest manifested by the court, jurymen, and the vast audience, an audience at no time impatient or restless through all those hours, was a compliment the likes of which is seldom paid to any occasion or to any orator."

As the trial drew to an exhausting conclusion, Spencer expressed his admiration of the work done by the clerk, bailiff, and other officers of the court. He withdrew his earlier criticism "made on the want of attention of certain jurors, for their conduct since has been praiseworthy and unobjectionable. I am satisfied now that the jury are now, to a man, striving to conscientiously discharge their solemn and onerous duties. They have had their powers of endurance very severely taxed throughout this great trial, yet I ought to say they have uniformly been patient and good natured." He also praised the courtroom spectators:

> "They have always been respectful and undemonstrative, and have thus shown themselves to be possessed of strict fairmindedness and impartiality, and many other graces peculiar to intelligent and good citizenship."

Finally, he noted that "members of the bar deserve a recognition of their gallantry in surrendering their place within the bar for the occupancy of the ladies."

The *New Albany Ledger-Standard* printed a detailed account of Judge John C. Robinson's charge to the jury, totaling five columns of small type. Items I through XIV defined legal terms and outlined the juror's options, emphasizing that accessories who aide or abet a felonious crime "shall suffer the same penalties and punishments, which are by law prescribed for the punishment of the principal." The judge explained the proper ways for jurors to evaluate specific testimony or allegations. He ruled out any consideration of the brief attempt by Jones's defense team to implicate Jeff Huffstetter or any party other than the defendants. Overall, Judge Robinson managed to present clear and impartial instructions on how to reach a verdict in a trial that was already acknowledged as one of the most complex in recent history.

Years later, when Judge Robinson was practicing law in Indianapolis, in an interview about the Moody murder trial with an *Indianapolis News* reporter identified only as "Snacks", Robinson admitted that he had done all he could to "break down all desires in the breast of the jurymen to inflict the death penalty, for Judge Robinson conscientiously believed (as he yet believes) that a jury has no right to become the vicegerent [deputy] of Almighty God in a matter of life and death, and so made it a point to impress this view as powerfully as he could on the minds of the jurors in his instructions." The *Ledger-Standard*'s printed summary does, indeed, indicate the judge's strong disapproval of the death penalty in his charge to the jury:

> "The Legislature has made it a part of the law of the State that you shall have the right to prescribe the penalty of death for such offence. Just how far such legislation has changed or modified, or to what extent it is in accordance with the eternal laws of the Author of Life, you must determine on your own responsibilities to Him. I do not attempt to determine this for you, and, on the other hand, would not be understood by this charge as giving any personal sanction to this feature which our law-makers have borrowed from the barbarians of the past."

Daniel O. Spencer concluded his report:

> "At nine o'clock and twenty minutes the jury retired to their room, and are now deliberating upon their verdict. The defendant and his co-defendants, and their immediate relatives and friends are now awaiting that verdict with anxious hearts and probably with perturbed minds. Business has been pretty generally abandoned here for the last few days, on account of the attractiveness of this trial, and now that we are so near the supreme moment of interest there is but the one engrossing subject in the public mind."

They would not have to wait long. At 9:30 the following morning, slightly more than twenty-four hours after beginning their deliberations, the jury returned to the courtroom. After they were seated and responded to roll call, jury foreman Fields handed the written verdict to court clerk W.F. Browning, who was instructed by Judge Robinson to read it aloud:

> "We, the jury, do find defendant guilty as charged in the indictment, and assess as his punishment that he be imprisoned in the State Prison for life."

Daniel Spencer witnessed the reaction of Alonzo Benton Jones, newly convicted of first-degree murder:

> "These terrible words, or their counterpart, had been anticipated by the defendant, for just before they were read, and while the Court and the Clerk were examining them, the prisoner refused to comply with Judge Robinson's request, that he stand up and hear the verdict, his faithful friend and counselor, Prof. McNutt, explaining that Mr. Jones was ill and very weak, and begging that he be allowed to remain seated. Then, for the first time, Bent Jones broke down. A deathly pallor overspread his face and his frame was tremulous with deep emotion. He looked utterly broken down and dejected… I suppose we may record the fact that the earthly doom of Alonzo B. Jones is fixed for all time."

The *New Albany Daily Ledger-Standard* scrambled to print a brief story about the verdict in their June 1 edition. It said:

> "While the jury was absent, there was the most intense feeling among the people, especially those from Orange and Lawrence counties, who had been present during the whole proceedings. It was generally believed, in the popular mind, that Bent. Jones was a guilty man, and it is doubtful whether they could have been restrained, had the verdict been favorable to the prisoner, from a summary punishment of Jones."

Bent's younger brother, Lee Jones, would be the next defendant to stand trial, while their brothers-in-law, Parks and Tom Toliver, were waiting with him in the Bloomington jail for their own murder trials. The news from the courtroom must have been ominous for them.

On June 4 the *Ledger-Standard* published a story dated the preceding day, signed merely "S.", that reported on Bent Jones's journey from the trial in Bloomington to the Indiana Prison South in Jeffersonville. By that time there were two state prisons in Indiana, in Jeffersonville and in Michigan City, home of today's single Indiana State Prison. It is almost certain that "S." and "D.O.S." were both Daniel Spencer. He wrote that private business affairs had coincidentally placed him on the same train as Jones and his escort of Sheriff W.M. Alexander, Deputy Robert Strong, and detectives Charles Keith and William Clark of Orleans. There were serious concerns that there might be an effort to remove Jones from the train while in transit, either to rescue him or lynch him. The sheriff had specifically instructed the telegraph operator in Bloomington, John Crafton, not to send any messages indicating the progress of their departure.

The newspaper reported that the farewell of Bent to his kinsmen and co-defendants in the Bloomington jail was "solemn and suggestive. Now, that their main adviser has been brought away, the main solace and encouragement, also, it will be pretty bad on those of the prisoners who are still in jail." A large crowd had gathered at the Bloomington railway station by 2:00 p.m. on Saturday, June 2, to witness the departure. Despite the sheriff's warning, spectators had gathered at almost every railroad station along the way to watch for the prisoner. In Bedford, Mitchell, and Orleans the crowds were especially "immense". There were tense moments in Mitchell when "hundreds of persons" clambered onto the train, insisting on seeing Bent Jones. Most of these were relatives and friends who wished "to speak a word of encouragement and bid him farewell." Also present were his wife, Clarissa, a sister (most likely Mary Giles of Salem), and one of his sons who "gave vent to his grief in violent sobs and outcries". The sister fainted and had to be carried off the train. The reporter wrote that "The prisoner so bore up under all this as to render these scenes less harrowing than they would have been had he been possessed of a feebler control over his emotional nature."

The train arrived late in Jeffersonville due to the "many and vexatious delays". Bent Jones was not delivered to the Indiana Prison South until just before 11:00 p.m. He would not leave that place for a long, long time.

Chapter Fourteen:
The End Is Not Yet

Once Bent Jones was convicted and imprisoned, with his co-defendants still locked inside the jail in Bloomington, citizens of Orange and Lawrence counties who regarded him as the ringleader of a criminal faction felt safe to take the law into their own hands. On June 21, 1877, less than a year after a party of "vigilants" had ridden into Mitchell and shot Abe Jones outside his saloon – and only three weeks after Bent's arrival at a state prison – a mounted vigilante group claiming to number 240 men stormed into downtown Mitchell. Arriving around 11:00 p.m., they hung stuffed effigies (probably two, although some papers reported ten) with warning notes attached, then proceeded to the telegraph office. The operator had stepped out of his office and the vigilantes refused to let him return until he found them some glue to use in pasting up posters around town with the following proclamation:

> "NOTICE.
> TO THE OUTLAWS AND INCENDIARIES OF
> MITCHELL AND MARION TOWNSHIPS
>
> It is now five years since Bent Jones organized his band of murderers, robbers, counterfeiters and house burners with headquarters at

Mitchell. During these five years every honest man has lived in fear of losing his life or his property at the hands of those assassins.

One year ago the leader, Bent Jones, and four of his confederates were arrested, two of whom have been convicted, received sentence and are now incarcerated in the Penitentiary for life, while four others are awaiting trial. A small portion of the gang has left the country, while others are left to commit additional depredations upon people and their property, as is witnessed in the burning of Edward's factory, Mills' barn, the shooting of Barnes' son and many other villainous acts. Among those left will be found Jones' First and Second Lieutenants and two or three of his alibi swearers. There are also a few men whom the people formerly looked upon as good citizens, but their present active support of these outlaws and of their denunciation of every effort to bring them to justice, has led the community to believe there exists some intimate relation of a criminal nature between these men. One man in particular is making himself extremely offensive to honest, law-abiding citizens (who do not think it altogether in the interest of his son, the attorney) by personal insinuation and harangue.

Now be it known to all outlaws and apologists, that we, the Vigilance Committees of Washington, Orange, and Lawrence counties, assembled in the town of Mitchell this Thursday night, June 21, 1877, do hereby give this due and clear notice that you, the above-named outlaws and apologists, will be held strictly and personally accountable for the destruction of all property, burned or otherwise maliciously destroyed. The safety of a community is at stake, and our coming tonight is one of warning; but our next coming will be one of a terrible avenger!

240 Vigilantes"

Those named above the notice included blacksmith Jim Head, identified as:

> "the gambler, perjurer, villain, and Bent Jones' accomplice in the Moody murder. Beware. Your exit from the community is demanded. By strictly complying with the above you may cheat the gallows of its prey, and the devil of one of his imps."

It was signed by "The Committee". There was another warning directed to Moses Clinton, "a tress-hoop maker" that was reported to be similar "only in rather more forcible terms and language." Head and Clinton had been witnesses supporting Bent Jones's alibi at the habeas corpus hearing and during his murder trial. Some references in the manifesto are unclear. There were only three defendants awaiting trial at the time and one of them, James Murray, would soon have charges against him dropped. Details could not be found regarding the specific violence cited ("Edward's factory, Mills' barn, the shooting of Barnes' son...) and the identity of the "extremely offensive" man and his son, the attorney, is unclear. Especially intriguing is the suggestion that James Head was an accomplice in the murder of Tom Moody. He was never charged with that crime and no evidence to support that allegation was given in court.

Southern Indiana once again attracted significant national news coverage, including front-page stories on June 23 in Salt Lake City's *Deseret Evening News* and two days later in the *Daily Fort Worth (TX) Standard*.

The headline in the New Albany *Daily Ledger-Standard* was typically dramatic:

"VIGILANTS
Mitchell and Neighborhood
Thrown Into a Fever
Of Excitement.
Assembling of Washington,

> Orange and Lawrence
> Counties Vigilants.
> Two Hundred and Forty
> Avengers called in Council.
> Warning Given to Outlaws to
> Get up and Dust.
> The Movement Not Favored
> By the Best Citizens
>
> MITCHELL, June 23. — There is an unusual degree of excitement among the people of Lawrence, Washington and Orange counties in regard to the lawlessness which has been displayed in these sections for the past few years. There seems to be an apprehension that the confederates of Bent. Jones will be enabled to escape through some technicality. Nor is this all that disturbs the minds of many good citizens. There is an impression abroad, and may be not without foundation, that there is a band connected with the Joneses and Tollivers that is not safe to the community. To put a check to the lawlessness which has manifested itself hereabout should be the earnest effort of every good man."

However, the un-named writer added:

> "This action is deeply regretted by the best citizens of this place and surrounding country, as since the conviction of Bent. Jones it is believed the whole band of conspirators, cut throats and scoundrels will receive justice through the ordinary channels, and will do the State service for many years at Jeffersonville."

A similar unsigned story in the June 27 edition of the same newspaper provided a follow-up view:

"MITCHELL'S MOB"

Additional Parties Notified by
the Vigilants to Get
Up and Get.
Mrs. Bent Jones Stood Not
Upon the Order of Her
Going, but Went,
Followed by Others Who Had
Been Warned to Flee
From Wrath.
One of the Spotted Remains,
Defying the Cautionary
Proclamation.
Let Mob Law be Suspended.

In obedience to the orders issued by the Vigilants Mrs. Bent Jones, Moses Clinton, and William Golden have shaken the dust of Mitchell from their feet, quietly folded their tents and stole away, bidding the good and bad people of this favored locality a long farewell.

James A. Head has also been notified that his absence was better than his company, but up [to] the present time, regardless of the solemn warning given, and notwithstanding he was hung in effigy on a cross planted in front of his door, he does not seem to scare worth a cent, but remains to see what these self-constituted judges will do in the future."

The reporter speculated that Head might not believe they "are in earnest so far as he is concerned", or "thinks they have not the nerve to carry out their murderous threats", or he might possibly be "fully prepared to die, preferring death and rest in Abraham's bosom." The newspaper condemned those persons "who in their great zeal to do good and rid the country of a set of bad men, commit a crime no less than that of the Joneses and Tollivers... It is astonishing to witness good, pretending christians [sic] justify the proceedings of these lawless Vigilants, who have disgraced Southern Indiana for sometime past."

The *Indianapolis People*, in its June 30 edition, took a differing view of the mob's justification in a report from Mitchell dated June 22:

> "Two hundred and forty vigilantes entered our city last night for the purpose of warning the perpetrators and avenging the outrageous wrongs that have been perpetrated upon this vicinity for the past year by an unprincipled, lawless band of highway robbers. For some time the band was quiet, but lately broke out anew, terrorizing the people by burning considerable property and making loud threats against people and property. Their outlandish depredations called for prompt action on the part of the citizens, hence the formation of the Vigilant Committee, who have posted a proclamation of warning to the desperadoes. Undoubtedly the desperadoes are the immediate friends of Jones, who was sent to the penitentiary from here. The cause of the trouble originated some years ago over a church situated in Dutch Hollow, in which the pastor and one Shephard had a serious difficulty, and the present band are the outcroppings of the old feud."

The *People* concluded with an observation that "There is trouble brewing on the streets now. Several shots have been fired, and it is altogether probable the two above named will be hung before morning, in connection with others, if they are found."

Only one vigilante was identified by name in a story from a correspondent in Mitchell, dated June 26, that appeared three days later in the *Columbus (IN) Democrat*:

> **"The Vigilants Still Plotting.**
>
> The vigilants had a secret council meeting here last evening, in which several of the old members were recognized. Several were here

from Washington [County], among which were Henry Pusick. The ambitions of the mob have not as yet been fully realized, since Jim Head still remains in town. They only seem half-satisfied in having driven off Mose Clinton and Mrs. Jones. It is rumored that Golden has also left Mitchell under fear of violence. The warnings which were posted up over town have all been torn down, probably by some of the friends of Head and Clinton. There is now danger of the trouble developing into a political fight. It is stated, on excellent authority, that every member of this vigilance committee is a republican, and it is known that every man against whom threats have been issued is a Democrat. Several members of an old organization known as the White League have been seen in town, and it is feared that they have come on no peaceful errand. Jim Head still holds the fort, and the end is not yet."

Property violence continued for at least two months after the vigilante's order. On August 25 the *Bedford Star* reported that "the barn burners in Marion township are at work again. Jeff Huffstutter's [sic] was set on fire last Sunday night and destroyed."

If Clarissa Toliver Jones, who had been so admired by reporters at Bent's murder trial, had (as the *Ledger-Standard* headline claimed) "went", she and her targeted colleagues did not stay gone long. By 1880 she was back in Mitchell, listed in that year's census as living with two children in a neighborhood where she was surrounded by friends and family members. Likewise, a 66-year-old carpenter named William Golden appears in the 1880 census, along with his 25-year-old son, also named William, who was a cabinetmaker. The elder Golden died in 1892 and was buried in Mitchell. James A. Head may have never left town. In 1880 he was still working as a blacksmith in Mitchell. He died in 1892 and is buried at the Mitchell City Cemetery, where his tombstone identifies him as a veteran of the 6th Kentucky Infantry. Moses Clinton died in

Greenwood, Indiana, in 1911. He, too, is buried at the Mitchell City Cemetery.

These developments could not have been reassuring to the three men inside the Bloomington jail awaiting their murder trials. Lee Jones, whom Eli Lowry had accused of pulling the trigger, would be next, to be followed by Parks and Tom Toliver. Earlier in the year there were published rumors that the three remaining defendants would try to have their trials moved back to Paoli because "it would save Orange county lots of money." Surely the county budget was the least of their concerns when such a change of venue would return them to a place so hostile that they had been attacked while behind bars.

Lee Jones's trial was originally scheduled for August, but there were the usual seemingly inevitable delays. One motion asked that Circuit Judge E.D. Pearson, who had ruled in the habeas corpus hearings, be replaced. Pearson had stepped aside in favor of Judge Robinson for Bent Jones's murder trial and he was willing to withdraw from the bench again, but fellow judges were not lining up to take his place. On October 6 the *Cincinnati Enquirer* reported: "The trial has been delayed because no Judge could be found to try the case, notwithstanding every effort was made by Judge Pearson to secure one; but the prisoner having concluded that Judge Pearson is a pretty fair Judge, after all, has withdrawn his objections to him, and he will preside over the trial." A jury was empaneled that same day and "locked up in the Court House until Monday afternoon...", according to the *Bloomington Courier*.

Rumors were circulating that strong new evidence would be given to prove an alibi for Lee Jones. A contrary "sub-rosa rumor", reported by the *Enquirer*, was that he would make a confession "which would not only let light in upon the Moody murders, but would clear up several other dark deeds in that portion of the state." Regardless, the *Courier* seemed to like his chances of acquittal:

> "Lee Jones has a better chance of being acquitted than did his brother, Bent, as

> he has not the numerous threats to meet in evidence that the latter had. His faithful and devoted wife is constantly by his side through this his trying hour, and it will be as a new life has been born within her if the verdict is 'Take your husband home with you...' Lee Jones does not look to us like a bad man, and we hope that he will get a full and fair hearing."

Major John W. Tucker, who had successfully defended the Jones-Toliver men in the 1874 firebombing trial, would represent the defense again, along with lead attorney J. Ralph Burton, who had delivered the memorably melodramatic speech at Bent Jones's trial. Lee's family had also managed to secure former Indiana Governor Paris C. Dunning for their legal team. The 71-year-old Dunning, according to the *Courier*, "is not excelled as an alibi lawyer", although his lack of background regarding the case meant that he was probably hired more for his local popularity.

The State's case would be presented by three men who had been effective in securing the conviction of Bent Jones: George W. Friedley, Judge Francis Wilson, and Robert W. Miers. They brought Eli Lowry to Bloomington from the State Prison South to testify against Lee Jones. Likewise, the defense arranged for Bent Jones to appear as a witness for his brother, but he was never put on the witness stand. The *Enquirer* noted that Bent was "...devoid of that nervousness which characterized his actions when on trial here, and his appearance was that of a man who is engaged in some fixed purpose." Thomas and Parks Toliver, while readily available, also did not testify.

Testimony began on Monday, October 8, and lasted six days. Judge Pearson was determined not to let this trial turn into another marathon spectacle. He brokered an agreement between counsel for both sides to allow evidence taken in the Bent Jones's trial to be read to the jury, who were directed to treat that testimony as if the witnesses were present. The judge ruled to "exclude many of the horrid and malignant declarations and threats which were peculiarly characteristic of the trial of Bent Jones, thereby very sensibly abridging the trial." While more than three hundred potential witnesses had been subpoenaed and examined, no more than one-third of them would be called to testify.

J.R. Burton's opening statement was "exhaustive and very able" according to the *Indianapolis Journal*. The defense introduced some new witnesses, including James Page, "the one-armed telegraph operator at Medora", who provided additional alibis for Lee Jones and the other defendants. These witnesses did not fare well during cross-examination. The judge was also keeping a close eye on the cost of the trial to taxpayers. When "the handsome sheriff from Columbus stepped up to his Honor's desk, and, with a bland smile" presented a bill for forty dollars to escort a subpoenaed witness from his city, the judge questioned his choice of routes and reimbursed the sheriff only twelve dollars.

The *Journal* noted that "Lee Jones is always accompanied in court by his faithful wife [Louisa Toliver Jones]. A three-year-old child [William B. Jones was actually five] is also here, manifesting in many a childish way an affectionate fondness for the accused."

All attorneys for both sides were applauded by the press for their speeches, although it was noted that Judge Wilson "was still suffering from the effects of ague, contracted during this trial, and did not, therefore, make as exhaustive an argument as he probably would have done had he been in good health." On Saturday afternoon, October 13, lead attorney J. Ralph Burton gave another stirring closing statement for the defense that "bristled with law and logic." That night his counterpart, George Friedley, closed for the prosecution with a four-hour oration. The Journal reported that "His arguments were unanswerable." Judge Pearson's instructions were given to the jury just before midnight but "notwithstanding the lateness of the hour and the exhausted condition of the jury" everyone seemed to still be awake.

Early on Monday morning the courthouse bells indicated that the jury had reached a decision. At 9:35 a.m. Lee Jones was found guilty of murder in the first degree and, like his brother, was sentenced to life in prison. The *Cincinnati Enquirer* described the reaction:

> "The scene was affecting in the extreme when the verdict was returned and read. The wife and little boy of the prisoner were with him in the Courtroom. The child, a bright boy of three or four years, nestled in his father's arms, and their moans and sobs were calculated to move the hardest heart to pity."

This day, October 15, 1877, was Lee Jones's twenty-fifth birthday.

The *Journal* reported that "The prisoner was deeply affected, and gave vent to a flood of tears." It added:

> "This little boy, now scarcely three years old, joined his parents in his childish way in expressions of grief this morning. The little fellow is quite popular with the ladies of this community. He is uncommonly fond of his father, and absolutely spent a week with him in his prison cell some months ago, coming hither and returning to his home in Mitchell all alone."

It was a different world.

When Lee Jones was asked if he had anything to say, he put the boy down from his lap and told the court:

> "I have not very much to say. I think it is pretty hard, under all circumstances, the way I have been treated, and the way I have been sent to prison for life. Men have come right here and sworn against me, trying to swear my life away, who helped to mob me. I carry marks on myself now that were put on my body while I was in the jail at Paoli, and was helpless there… I shall hope to have happiness in the next world if not in this one. I am innocent

of the killing of Thomas Moody – as innocent as any man in the world."

The defense immediately filed an elaborate appeal for a new trial, but after four hours of deliberation Judge Pearson denied the motion and ordered that the prisoner be sent to join his brother in Jeffersonville at the State Prison South the following day.

While Lee Jones prepared to spend the remainder of his life in prison, attorney J. Ralph Burton returned to his home in Princeton, Indiana. He continued to get glorious reviews. His hometown newspaper, the *Princeton Clarion-Ledger* wrote:

"J.R. Burton, Esq., of this place, returned home last week from Bloomington, where he had been engaged as principal defense in the trial of Lee Jones, for murder. Mr. Burton received the highest approbation for his management of this case."

The *Bloomington Progress* added:

"Mr. J.R. Burton, the principal attorney for Lee Jones, it is a subject of common remark, managed the defense of Lee Jones in a much abler manner than the Bent. Jones case of which he was but junior counsel, was managed. Mr. Burton deserves credit and recognition for his ability and energy."

Neither comment noted that his client had been found guilty and sentenced to life in prison. Burton would move to Kansas the following year. He was elected to represent that state in the United States Senate in 1901 but resigned five years later after being convicted on corruption charges. J. Ralph Burton eventually died in California in 1923.

Shortly after Lee Jones's sentence was imposed the attorneys for Parks and Thomas Toliver requested a change of venue from Bloomington, the scene of two convictions, to their home base in Lawrence County. The State objected unless the new venue would be in Orange County, home of the Moodys. Eventually both motions were denied and the court ruled that the Toliver brothers would also be tried in Bloomington, beginning in August of 1878. Given the history of legal machinations leading up to the previous trials, this must have been regarded as a highly optimistic prediction.

Chapter Fifteen:
Tolliver Takes Tall Timber

On January 7, 1878, Monroe County circuit court convened and the Toliver cases were called. It was then revealed that Circuit Judge Eliphalet D. Pearson had disqualified himself because he was related by marriage to Parks Toliver. Ella Belle Pearson was the daughter of Dr. James Carson Pearson of Orleans. She was only sixteen years old when she married Parks Toliver in 1870. Now, at the age of 23 and with two young sons, Ella Belle Toliver was regarded as one of the most beautiful women in the area. Judge Pearson continued the case for five weeks while he attempted to find another judge to preside, but the *Cincinnati Enquirer* pointed out that "the appropriation made by the last Legislature for extra judicial services throughout the State has been expended, and it is doubtful whether a Judge can be secured." In retrospect, it was good that Judge Pearson had withdrawn himself from the case since Ella Belle would eventually play her own role in the proceedings.

On March 13 all charges against James Murray, the admitted perjurer who had been accused of being an accomplice to the murder of Tom Moody, were dismissed. He was the husband of Mahala Toliver, the eldest sister of the two Toliver brothers awaiting trial. Murray had almost certainly been aware that the murder was about to take place – the killers allegedly fired a gun as a signal to Murray that Tom Moody had been shot – but he would have been powerless to stop it.

The joint trial of Dr. Milton Parks Toliver and his brother, Thomas, began on Wednesday, June 5, in Bloomington, with Judge John C. Robinson, the death penalty opponent who had presided over Bent Jones's conviction, on the bench. That was sooner than expected and it quickly became obvious to observers that the mood surrounding this proceeding was quite different from the theatrical atmosphere of the Jones trials. A reporter for the *Indianapolis Journal* noted: "There is not the interest taken in the trial of this case as was in the Jones brothers. There seems to be a letting up on both sides."

From the beginning there had been more sympathy for the Toliver brothers than the Jones boys. Parks was a doctor and every description of his appearance and demeanor had emphasized that he simply did not look or act like a criminal. Thomas was only 22 years old and, while he already had a reputation as a heavy drinker, was reported to have "conducted himself in a very gentlemanly manner" during the habeas corpus proceedings. Bent Jones had been convicted of instigating the murder of Tom Moody and now vigilantes were accusing him of being the head of a gang that was terrorizing their communities. Lee Jones was also a young man, but he had been identified by Eli Lowry as the person who fired the gun that killed Moody. The men who had planned and committed the murder were now serving life sentences in Jeffersonville. It would be a challenge to convince jurors that the Toliver brothers would be a threat on their own.

Warden A.J. Howard of the Indiana Prison South escorted Eli Lowry and both Jones brothers from Jeffersonville to the circuit court in Bloomington, where they would be available to testify.

On June 12, after only a week of testimony and deliberations, the jury reported that they could not reach a verdict. Judge Robinson declared a mistrial and released Parks and Tom Toliver on bail of $10,000 each. In the June 26 edition of the *Journal* a correspondent in Bloomington reported that "Our county jail is now empty, for the first time in two years. The Toliver boys gave bail a few days ago, and left for their homes in Mitchell."

C.F. McNutt had filed an appeal to the Indiana Supreme Court on behalf of Bent Jones. In April of 1879 that appeal was denied. The decision, written by Justice James Worden, noted that motive is an important element in murder cases, "especially where the identity of the supposed murderer is controverted and required to be established." The court ruled that evidence of a motive had been properly admitted and "the reason that the murder was not committed sooner was that the deceased lived in a guarded manner...". As to Bent's participation in the killing, Worden wrote that "the appellant, if he did not perpetrate the homicide with his own hand, counselled, aided and abetted in the perpetration thereof." The decision also stated that evidence of any guilt on the part of Jeff Huffstetter had been properly rejected. The verdict was sustained and the judgment was affirmed.

Meanwhile, Bent Jones was looking for revenge from inside his prison cell. Soon after he had arrived at the Indiana State Prison South, the *Cincinnati Enquirer* reported the tantalizing news that he was working on a book:

> "We learned from Warden Howard and Colonel Kegwin that Bent Jones is writing a biography of himself, in which he proposes to introduce short sketches of other men and expose certain crimes which he alleges they participated in. Some of these men, he claims, live in Lawrence County, and are prominent citizens of that section of the State."

Nearly two years later work on his autobiography was still underway according to a report from a Salem newspaper reprinted in the *Bedford-Mitchell Banner*:

> "Bent Jones, of Mitchell, the murderer of Tom Moody, who is in the State Prison at Jeffersonville for life, is at work during his leisure hours writing a book, in which he

> purposes [sic] showing up in their true light some of the citizens of Lawrence county w h o live in Mitchell and its vicinity who were his partners in many crimes and who "went back on him" when he was arrested. It was his intention, in the event of his getting a new trial and in the end being acquitted, to not publish the book, but as the Supreme Court the other day took final action in his case, which renders his imprisonment for life a settled matter, he will at once proceed to finish the manuscript and have it printed. He has already written over 250 pages of it. There is no doubt but that Jones knows a great deal about some persons that they would rather he not tell, and this determination on his part will make several of them quite uneasy. – Seymour Democrat."

It would seem that any such book would have caused a local sensation, but no indication could be found that it was ever completed, much less published.

Meanwhile, the Tolivers were awaiting a retrial on charges of first-degree murder. Once again, the issue was finding an available judge. Pearson was not only related by marriage to Parks Toliver, but he was also now involved in trying a significant political corruption case. On August 5 a story in the *Cincinnati Enquirer* headlined "**Tolliver Murder Trial Hangs Fire**" noted that a special term of circuit court had opened that day in Bloomington, with Judge Franklin presiding. The trial had been expected to take place during this special term and both sides had subpoenaed witnesses. However, there was another problem:

> "... but now the objection is raised by the State that Judge Franklin is not a regular Judge, and that defendants would not be bound by judgment, even if consenting to the jurisdiction and trial; and that, moreover, the case was not set down before Judge Franklin by Judge Pearson, the judge to try not having

been named when the change was taken. Under this state of affairs the case must go back to the regular term in September, which will leave the prospect of a trial in the immediate future extremely slim."

The case finally came before special judge Archibald C. Voris of Bedford, a graduate of the Harvard Law School, on September 24. The defense filed for yet another continuance until November and the outgoing prosecutor, John R. East, surprisingly filed a motion to dismiss the case. Judge Voris granted the delay but overruled the dismissal and specified that the trial would begin in Bloomington on the first day of the November term.

The earlier convictions, a hung jury the previous year, and the slow passage of time had resulted in making the Toliver case much less of a sensational news story than the Jones's trials had been. Rather than filing daily updates, most newspapers waited until closing arguments were due to summarize the testimony given. A *Cincinnati Enquirer* report noted that testimony had been concluded on November 22 and that the case was expected to go to the jury sometime before midnight. The most serious accusation against Parks was that he had been standing with Lee Jones when the fatal shots were fired in Orleans. His wife, Ella Belle, and her sister, Mattie, once again swore that Parks was in bed at home when the murder took place. Daniel Boone returned to repeat his testimony that he had been "housing a drove of horses" in Simpson Toliver's livery stable in Mitchell and that he had seen both Tom and Parks Toliver there at the time of the Moody murder. In fact, he claimed that Tom had helped him handle the horses. Not surprisingly, closing arguments ran long and Judge Voris did not deliver his charge to the jury until Tuesday morning. According to the *Enquirer*, both sides – each of which included many of the same attorneys from the earlier trials – claimed to be confident.

Then, just as interest in the case seemed to be waning, came one of the most sensational developments yet. The shocking news was reported in a late-breaking front page telegraphic report by the *New Albany Daily Ledger-Standard* on November 25:

"THE TOLLIVER TRIAL
At Bloomington Ends in a Sensation Not Expected and Tolliver Takes Tall Timber And It Seems That His Plans Were So Well Laid That He Is Likely To Escape."

Parks Toliver had, indeed, escaped while the jury was still deliberating his fate. That much is certain, but to this day it is not clear exactly how he got away. The *New Albany Ledger-Standard* reporter, no doubt in a rush to get the story to press, gave this account:

> "This morning the judge delivered his charge to the jury, a bailiff was appointed to take charge of them, and as they were rising to leave the court room, the defendant Tolliver made a break for liberty. Owing to the temporary confusion in the court room, incident to the close of the trial, and the fact that the officers were engaged in making arrangements for the jury, he obtained a good start and was in fact, almost out of the room before his absence was discovered.
>
> Pursuit was immediately made, but the prisoner either had his plans well laid, or was very fortunate, as he has not yet been overtaken."

More details emerged the following day. The *Columbus (IN) Republic*, in a story datelined November 25, reported:

> "This morning at 9 o'clock, after the Tolliver case had been submitted to the jury, the prisoner, Dr. Parks Tolliver, slipped from under the immediate notice of the deputy sheriff and made his escape, and it seems now that he has made a good job of it. The

The Terror of Indiana

last report is that he was last seen a mile west of town, mounted on his own steed – an iron grey – going westward, declaring that he would never go to the penitentiary alive. The jury is still up in their room, and the question among common folks is whether they can render a legal verdict in the absence of the prisoner."

The *Cincinnati Enquirer,* under the headline **LEFT IN THE LURCH,** added some names and details:

"As soon as the jury had retired to their room the prisoner was put in the custody of the Sheriff, and remarking to that official that he wished to go into the Clerk's office a minute, he received the permission of that official, and went out of the Court-room. But the Sheriff immediately dispatched a bailiff, Mr. Lon Davis, to keep watch on him, and he was in his company and that of a young man named Korns, a relative, just before he made his escape. Davis says he had no suspicion that he would attempt an escape, and left him in the company of Korns.

The conduct of the prisoner has been such as to throw the officers off their guard. He was at one time on "straw bail," and could have made his escape without the danger of immediate pursuit, but failed to do so, and in every way has demeaned himself so as to quiet suspicion.

There is a general impression that the escape was prearranged and would have taken place last night if Judge Vorhis [sic] had charged the jury as it was expected he would, and have placed the prisoner in the custody of the Sheriff; but he held the instructions over it till this morning on account of the lateness of the hour, and therefore, Tolliver's bondsmen were not released till he was placed in the hands of the officers to-day. The proprietor of the National House says he saw a man, who holds close relations to the prisoner, take a horse into the alley back of the hotel last night. It was a bold move on the part of Tolliver to attempt an escape in a country as thickly settled as this, at this season of the year. There is a mystery connected with the escape, which the Prosecuting Attorney, Judge Moritz, says he intends to investigate. In the mean time the jury are in their room deliberating over the case all unmindful of the escape. It was and is the general opinion that the jury will fail to agree, which is strengthened by the fact that they have been out five hours.

As soon as it became certain that Tolliver had escaped Sheriff Alexander sent mounted men out on the roads in the direction he was last seen, among whom was Detective Tegarden; but up to this hour no tidings upon which reliance can be placed has been heard of the prisoner or those in pursuit."

Webster's 1913 Dictionary defines "straw bail" as "worthless bail, as being given by irresponsible persons". The idea seemed to be that Parks Toliver had previously been released on $10,000 bail, relatively low for a man accused of first-degree murder and was deemed to be such a low flight risk that he could be trusted in the custody of a bailiff and a relative while the jury was still deliberating.

There were variations of these accounts, as well. The *Sullivan Democrat* carried a story attributed to the *Sentinel* that changed the young relative's name from Korns to Koonse and claimed that they "walked out of the Court House and up College Avenue... and made his escape." A much later story in the *Bloomington Courier* claimed that Toliver had "escaped from Deputy Sheriff Lon Davis who had accompanied him home to get some clothes... He left the Deputy Sheriff talking to his wife who, by the way, was a very handsome woman, while he stepped into an adjoining room to change his suit ostensibly, but instead he skipped the rear way and emigrated West where he remained for years..."

The next edition of the *Enquirer* carried a similar account under a curiously mis-spelled headline:

"TRICKY TOLLIVAR

```
BLOOMINGTON, IND., November 26 - It seems
Parks Tolliver has completely outwitted the
officers and made good his escape. He has at
least succeeded in securely hiding himself for
the present. The men sent out on the different
roads yesterday morning in the attempt to head
him off returned last night without having seen
or heard any thing of him. It was impossible
yesterday to learn just how he managed his
escape, there being so many reliable reports
of the affair, but by persistent effort the
following, which seems to be the facts, was
learned:
    After Parks Tolliver was placed in the hands
of the Sheriff, and by him given in charge of
his Deputy, as stated in yesterday's dispatch,
he persuaded the Deputy to accompany him to
the boarding-house of his wife, one square
north and one square west from the Court-
house, his brother and codefendant, Tom, his
wife and sister-in-law also going along.
When the party arrived at the house Parks,
remarking that he wanted some clothing, as he
had to stay with the Deputy that night, walked
into the yard, and, instead of going into
the house, passed round into the back yard,
unobserved by the Deputy, and, getting over
the fence, was joined by his brother and they
both walked leisurely up Railroad street,
keeping the house between them and the Deputy,
who was waiting at the front of the house and
talking to the wife and sister-in-law. This
was the last seen of Parks by any one; but Tom
soon returned, and to the Deputy's question
as to where Parks was, replied that he had
```

> gone to the Court-house, he guessed. This seems like gross carelessness to those not acquainted with the facts, but the conduct of the prisoner had been such as was calculated to throw the officers off their guard. Parks and Tom Tolliver have both been on bail for months, and could have escaped long ago, but neither ever seemed to care the least about getting out of the scrape in that way."

This was the point at which the episode began to emit a distinct odor of suspicion. As gentlemanly as Parks and Tom Toliver may have been, they were still charged with first-degree murder. The scene of the escape had moved from the courtroom to the Clerk's office, to a boarding house two blocks away, with a possible accomplice waiting in an alley behind the National Hotel. The young male relative named Korns or Koonse was no longer a participant. The deputy was sufficiently distracted by the attractive Mrs. Toliver and her sister (probably 22-year-old Mattie) to have allowed not one, but *both* defendants to take a leisurely stroll through downtown Bloomington. The *Jeffersonville Daily Evening News* printed an edited version of the "Tricky Tolliver" story (with the name spelled correctly) with no mention of Ella Belle's sister being present.

It also seems odd that Tom Toliver returned instead of joining his brother. Did Parks panic, believing that his alleged presence at the murder scene would result in a conviction even after the earlier hung jury? If so, he was profoundly mistaken:

> "This morning at eleven o'clock Judge Vorhis took the bench and sent for the jury, which had made no verdict, and discharged them, not inquiring whether they were likely to arrive at a verdict or not, but simply on the ground that the escape of the prisoner rendered it impossible for him to receive a verdict, if they should find one. The Judge then directed the Prosecutor to use every means and make every effort to ascertain who, if any one,

assisted in the escape, and take vigorous measures to bring them to punishment.

The case of Tom Tolliver was continued last night and he remanded to the custody of the Sheriff, who placed him in jail. This morning the continuance was set aside, but the prisoner still left in the hands of the Sheriff. A member of the jury, after their discharge, informed your correspondent that they stood seven for conviction of murder in the first degree and five for acquittal, with not much of a prospect for agreeing. Their discharge was the first they knew of the prisoner's escape."

Parks Tolliver was now a wanted man after escaping from a trial that was almost certain to have resulted in a second hung jury. Judge Wilson, observing the trial as a spectator, told the *Enquirer* reporter "that it was a bad move on the part of Parks Tolliver, for the reason that the cases against him and Tom would have been nollied if the jury had failed to agree, it having been the second hung jury." There was a high likelihood that he would have walked out of the courtroom a free man. An 1887 summary of the trial in the *Indianapolis News* emphasized this point:

"By the time his trial was reached public interest in the matter had flagged; the excitement had cooled off; witnesses had become scattered – some of them were dead; recollections had faded; contradictions in statements crept in, and such a degree of confusion and doubt had been created that his acquittal was confidently expected by almost all who heard the trial. Park [sic] was a dashing, handsome, intelligent fellow, and these attributes, together with his gentlemanly and modest bearing during the trial, had so won upon public sympathy that a verdict of acquittal would have received general approbation."

The daring if dim-witted escape of Parks Toliver reactivated national press attention to the murder of Tom Moody and the original Moody-Tolliver feud, although the narrative was garbled and corrupted in many accounts. For example, a story attributed to a special edition of the *Bloomington Gazette* reappeared in newspapers located in Maryland (including the German language *Deutsche Correspondent*), Kansas, Pennsylvania, Nebraska, Tennessee, Arkansas, Delaware, and New York. That account identified the escaped defendant as "David Toliver". This presumably did not help authorities attempting to apprehend Parks Toliver, although there is considerable doubt about how much effort was made to locate him after the initial search parties came back clueless and empty-handed.

Two years later, on December 1, 1881, all charges were dismissed against both Parks Toliver, who was still on the run, and his younger brother, Thomas. Not only was there little appetite for a third trial, but politicians in Orange County were being criticized for the huge amount of tax money spent prosecuting the cases. The reward money, totaling $4600 (over $115,000 in 2020 dollars), was divided between Harry B. Ward, S.R. Tegarden, E.D. Millis, and Charles H. Keeth. With Bent Jones, Lee Jones, and Eli Lowry all serving life sentences, this marked the end of the legal proceedings meant to bring justice to the killers of Tom Moody. But for many of those involved – especially the five men charged with his murder – plenty of drama and trauma was yet to come.

Part Two

THE 1880 U.S. FEDERAL CENSUS was taken on July 9 of that year at the Indiana Prison South in Jeffersonville. These names are clustered near each other on the official return:

Eli Lowry	24 yrs.	Prisoner	Sand Belter
Alonzo B. Jones	39 yrs.	Prisoner	Machinist
Lee Jones	25 yrs.	Prisoner	Carpenter

All three were serving life sentences for the murder of Thomas Moody. Their Toliver co-defendants were (more or less) free men: Parks was still a fugitive from justice, while his 23-year-old brother, Thomas, was living with their sister, Louisa Toliver Jones, and 6-year-old brother-in-law, William, in Mitchell. Louisa and William were the wife and son of Lee Jones. Tom Toliver's "Profession, Occupation, or Trade" was listed in that census as "Sporting Man".

The Indiana Prison South in Jeffersonville, just across the Ohio River from Louisville, was one of two state prisons at the time. The Indiana Prison North in Michigan City was a newer and more regimented facility. Inmates at both were required to work at trades or manufacturing, but an *Indianapolis News* reporter who visited in 1890 wrote:

```
"In 'Jeff' the 'lock-step' has been abolished.
Men can grow beards and hair and not all of
```

> them wear full suits of stripes. They are allowed to converse freely but can not leave their work and gossip with each other. They march to their meals in double rows and talk all they please while eating. They are allowed an hour to whistle, dance and sing and on holidays they are allowed to mix with each other in the yards and have a general good time."

Warden James B. Patten, who had replaced Warden Howard, told the reporter, "I believe the prisoners here are as content as in any prison on earth. I give them good food, and aim in every way to make the institution a reformatory as much as possible." The article noted:

> "There are 550 convicts and fifty of them are serving life sentences… So, too, men are serving sentences for most insignificant offenses. One man is serving a year for stealing a pair of ten-cent socks… There are hundreds of chicken thieves in the prison, the average punishment being one month for each chicken stolen… So, too, do many cranks find their way to 'Jeff'. A young burglar insisted that he wrote the opera of 'Pinafore' and proposed to sue Gilbert and Sullivan for damages..."

Each prisoner admitted to the state prison underwent a thorough physical examination. Since mug shots were not yet common in Indiana, both a general description and specific distinguishing marks were entered in the prison log. Eli Lowry, the first to be processed in 1876, was listed as 24 years old, single, 5 feet 4 inches tall, with a fair complexion, blue eyes, and light hair. His marks included "Mole on each shoulder blade". A note was added in the "Remarks" column: "No Education". That is surprising considering the administrative role he would later be given in the prison office.

In 1877 Bent Jones was described as 29 years old, 5 feet 9 inches tall, with a dark complexion, dark eyes, and black hair. He was still married to Clarissa Toliver, who visited him in prison at least once. His identifying marks included seven scars on various body parts and "the two first fingers on left hand (are?) mashed." It was noted that he could "Read & Write."

The entry for his brother, Lee Jones, included a surprising disability. His general description was 25 years of age, 5 feet 7 inches tall, with a dark complexion, hazel eyes, and dark hair. He was married to Louisa Jones and could both read and write. The inspection revealed three scars – four fewer than big brother Bent – and a "tender place on chin." Then comes this: "Thumb, forefinger and small finger off of left hand."

To a present-day observer it may seem odd that this disability was not mentioned during the trials and didn't appear in any of the newspaper profiles. However, it was probably not too unusual at that time, especially for a man who had been working in sawmills and woodworking plants. After all, Bent also had a couple of "mashed" fingers. Missing a thumb and two fingers would not have prevented him from lifting and firing a shotgun, which does not require the precise aim of a rifle. His attorneys probably realized that would not be an adequate defense for the man accused of firing both barrels of the shotgun that killed Tom Moody. However, it might have been a factor on the last day of Lee Jones's life.

The ages given by all three men were inconsistent with other records. Lowry and Lee Jones were probably younger than the ages listed at their admission, while Bent Jones was almost certainly older.

New research has now disclosed surprising information about the eventual fate of the defendants in the Moody-Tolliver Feud. This extended epilogue provides, for the first time, the remarkable stories of their remaining years.

ELI LOWRY:
UNWILLING TOOL

L OWRY WAS THE ONLY GUILTY party with no family connection to the Tolivers. He had no apparent motive for assisting in the murder of Thomas Moody other than to placate his employer. Eli admitted that he had been a courier for the other defendants and that he had helped test the guns used in the murder but swore under oath that he had claimed to be sick when told to accompany Lee Jones to Orleans. According to his testimony, Lowry's only compensation was about twenty dollars of clothing and accessories paid for by Bent Jones. His quick confession in exchange for a life sentence was prompted by the realization, surely emphasized by the detectives and law enforcement, that he had been "set up" by the others. Once he had escaped the gallows, Lowry then had to worry about being lynched by friends of the Toliver-Jones faction to prevent his testimony.

It would have been reasonable for Lowry and his attorneys to expect some degree of leniency in return for his detailed and damning confession. Instead, he received the same life sentence as the Jones brothers – and would be confined in the same prison as the men he had testified against. When Eli spoke with a *Cincinnati Enquirer* reporter visiting the Indiana Prison South in 1883, he seemed resigned to his fate:

> "Lowry when interviewed, said he had no hope of being paroled; expected to remain in prison all his life. He seemed to realize both the heinousness of his crime and the hopelessness of the situation. The prison officers say he is a good prisoner, giving no trouble, and always to be depended upon. He tells the same story now that he did when arrested. The pond he indicated in his testimony was dragged, and the shotgun recovered."

One of his defense attorneys filed an appeal on the grounds that the judge had acted improperly by sentencing Lowry to a life term without benefit of a jury trial following his confession and then had refused to issue a writ of habeas corpus. On October 30, 1885, the Indiana Supreme Court affirmed the sentence. An opinion written by Justice George Howk held that the court had made an error, but that it did not negatively impact Lowry since "he was given the lighter of the two punishments for the crime to which he acknowledged his guilt..." and that all the Supreme Court could have done was to remand the case for another trial with instructions to the jury to affirm the same sentence. In other words, Lowry should have been offered a jury trial, but that could have resulted in the death penalty, with the only alternative being the same sentence he received from the judge.

Lowry's view on a possible parole had changed by 1889, when he was mentioned in a *Louisville Courier-Journal* story about Jeffersonville prisoners who were, as the headline put it, **PINING FOR LIBERTY.** A sub-headline mentioned him specifically: **Eli Lowry Grows From Youth To Middle Age Within the Walls of the Prison.** He was probably 33 years old. The article continued:

> "Many visitors to the prison have noticed a small, neat-looking man going in and out the guard hall with his quick, noiseless step, his zebra-like suit differing from that of the other inmates on account of its clean appearance. This is Eli Lowry, one of the famous Jones-Tolliver gang, sent up several

> years ago for life from Lawrence county for waylaying Dr. Moody [sic] and murdering him... Lowry has enlisted the sympathies of nearly every committee that has come to the prison for years... Lowry has no man's blood upon his hands, although he was an eye-witness to the tragedy and knew that it was to occur. This was some fifteen years ago, and Lowry was little more than a green country boy, who worked in the saw-mill of Lee and Bent Jones, in Orange [actually Lawrence] county, Ind. The Joneses and Tollivers on one side and Dr. Moody on the other had long been lawing over a tract of land, and it was decided by the Jones-Tolliver side to put Dr. Moody out of the way."

This was followed by a muddled and incorrect account of the feud and trials that followed the murder of "Dr." Moody. The final paragraphs concluded:

> "The last man to be put on trial was Lowry, who frankly testified against himself, and, to the surprise of every one, was given a life sentence. He had expressed himself as being desirous of going to prison for a short term, as he was afraid to be given his liberty, lest the friends of the Joneses might kill him for testifying against them.
>
> Gov. Gray had signaled his intention several times to pardon Lowry before leaving the gubernatorial chair, and the now disappointed convict had formulated many plans as to what he would do on his release."

Meanwhile, remarkably blatant political pressure was being applied by some Indiana legislators on behalf of all convicted murderers. According to the *Paoli Republican* on March 6, 1889:

> "Willard's bill making a life sentence 25 years has passed the House. Allowing for good time a murderer can get out after 15 years and 6 months confinement... The Jones' and Lowery

would be released in a few months. The bill is looked upon by some as a license for murder. It appears that these life men, many of whom have money, after having failed to secure a release in any other manner, are to be turned loose on the people by this lawless Legislature."

That bill did not become law but the fact that it had progressed that far was indicative of the political climate at the time.

When the *Indianapolis News* sent a reporter to visit the Indiana Prison South in 1890, a lengthy account in the October 10 edition concluded with a remarkable section subtitled:

"AN OLD TRAGEDY RECALLED.

The visitor to 'Jeff' is met at the door by a good looking man of medium size, very gentlemanly in his talk and actions, who, but for the striped pantaloons he wears, would not be taken for a convict. He is an usher and the Warden's private messenger, and is trusted above any man in the prison. This is Eli Lowry, who, with two others, Alonzo B. Jones and Lee Jones, has served fourteen years of a life sentence for murder. The crime for which they are suffering was the result of a family feud and was one of the most startling in the criminal annals of Indiana. The history of the Orange County vendetta was thus told to *The News* man by Lowry:

'I am now thirty-five years old, and was born in Washington County. When I was seventeen years old I went to Lawrence County and began work for Bent Jones in a sawmill. Jones was a Democratic politician, and was known as a revengeful man. He married Clarissa Tolliver, a relative of the notorious Kentucky Tollivers. Her mother died and her father, old man Tolliver, married a sister of Tom Moody. Six weeks after the marriage old man

Tolliver was killed by his mules running away. His wife (Moody's sister) thus fell heir to considerable of the old man's property, and this made enemies of the Joneses. A sale of the property was held, and Tom Moody insisted that his sister should have her share. Jones and the other heirs refused to give her anything. Bent Jones knocked down Tom Moody and the crowd beat him nearly to death. This was in 1871 [actually 1870], and thus the feud between the Joneses and Tollivers on one side, and the Moodys on the other commenced. A few nights after the sale [almost nine months] an attempt was made to blow up Moody's house with nitro glycerine, but no one was hurt, though Moody's sister, Mrs. Tolliver, was severely burned. Moody ran out of the house with his gun and was shot through the body. No one ever knew who fired the shot, but it is supposed that Bent Jones did. Moody was afraid to live on his farm and moved to Orleans, in Orange County, for protection. From that time until 1875 the families were constantly engaged in litigations, in which Moody was always the winner, and numerous fights took place between the factions. In 1875 the Joneses laid a plot to murder Moody. The Joneses loaded their guns in the afternoon. I was present and saw them do it, and knew just what they intended doing. They rode to a brother-in-laws and staid until dark and then went to Orleans and hid in a carpenter shop. Moody had been up town – the first time in four years. After dark, and as he entered his gate, Lee Jones shot him in the back from the carpenter shop. He fired both barrels of the gun, and killed Moody instantly. There was a great deal of excitement, and a reward of $4600 was offered for the conviction of the murderers. An Indianapolis detective named Harry Ward came there selling maps, and soon got in with Bent Jones. Jones sent me to his brother-in-law's in Illinois, and while I was gone was trying to throw the blame all on me. I heard I was accused, and started back. In Sullivan County I was arrested. I found the Joneses in jail and trying to put the murder of Moody on me, and then I turned State's evidence and told the whole thing. It was one of the biggest trials ever held in this State, there being 315 witnesses examined. The Joneses and myself were sentenced for life and this ended the feud. I think I have been punished enough and should be set free. I didn't kill Moody –'

'But you had knowledge of it!' interrupted the reporter.

'Yes. But had I revealed anything I would have been murdered. I was compelled to go with them to save my life. Why, Jones gave a horse to the negro who saddled their horses the night they tried to blow up Moody's house, and after he had got away some distance, organized a mob and lynched him for horse-stealing. His sending me to Illinois was only a scheme to work up a job on me. Governor Porter told me in his office that I ought to be pardoned, but he was afraid to release me unless he let out the Joneses, and he dared not do that. I was an unwilling tool in the power of desperate murderers. There is a political influence keeping me here. Many of the people of Orange County want me released and some of the most prominent men in the State have signed a petition for my pardon.'

Lowry is held in high esteem about the prison, and it is the opinion of the officials that he should be granted his liberty. He was but a boy when the crime was committed, and fourteen years behind stone walls is punishment enough for his share in the murder. He keeps up his spirits wonderfully, and has laid by over $100."

A petition for his pardon was, in fact, circulating in Southern Indiana. It had been signed by Judge E.D. Pearson, who had been actively involved in the long legal battles, along with "the prosecuting attorney, county officials and more than two thousand leading citizens of that district."

According to the December 26, 1890, edition of the *Bedford Mail*, Governor Alvin P. Hovey, a former Union general, had visited the prison on December 16, at which time Eli Lowry begged him not to forget his case:

> "'I am contented to wait,' said he 'until you see your way clear to granting me a pardon, but don't go out of office, Governor, without setting me free. I have waited long and patiently, and my punishment has certainly been sufficient for my connection with the crime.' The Governor was touched with the man's quiet, patient demeanor...'"

On Christmas Eve, 1890, the *Indianapolis News* broke the story with a front-page headline:

ELI LOWRY IS FREE.

The *Chicago Inter Ocean* also carried the news that day after having received a special telegram. Governor Hovey had signed the pardon on December 23, but the Secretary of State could not provide the paperwork in time for it to arrive in Jeffersonville by Christmas Day. Instead, the governor's private secretary sent a telegram to Warden Patten. The *Bedford Mail* later reported that Lowry was responsible for receiving all telephone messages sent to the prison from the telegraph office and speculated "... his breath was probably taken away last night when there fell upon his ears the music of the following five words: 'The Governor has pardoned Eli Lowry.'"

The official proclamation was not quite that concise: "Whereas, the Judge and Prosecuting Attorney and Jurors who tried the cause wherein the prisoner was convicted, and many respectable citizens living in the County where the offense was committed, have united in a written recommendation for the pardon of said Eli Lowry and stated therein their reasons for the recommendation... I do hereby grant the said Eli Lowry a Pardon and do, by these presents, release him from confinement under the sentence aforesaid."

This was a perfect "feel good" story for the holiday and it was widely reported as such. On December 26 the *New Albany Ledger* headlined their story:

A CHRISTMAS GIFT
Eli Lowry, Pardoned from the Prison, Steps Out a Free Man on the World's Holiday.

The *Logansport (IN) Pharos-Tribune* overstated the truth a bit:

ELI LOWRY'S CHRISTMAS GIFT
It Was a Pardon for a Crime He Was Forced to Witness.

The *Jeffersonville Daily Evening News* took a more pragmatic approach: "Eli Lowry of Paoli, who served fifteen years in the State Prison, will locate in this city, and engage in business."

On New Year's Eve the *Paoli Republican* reported the news and wrote: "The pardon [will] give general satisfaction in this county." Less than one year later Governor Hovey would die while in office.

If Lowry ever opened a business in Jeffersonville, it did not prosper. A year later, on December 16, 1891, the *Orleans Progress* noted that "Eli Lowry, who is engaged in the mercantile line at Terre Haute, has been visiting friends in and around Orleans this past week." The 1894 Terre Haute city directory did not list an occupation for Eli, but his residence was at 308 South Third. There is evidence, however, that by 1894 he had found a new job in, of all things, law enforcement – and he was already back in trouble.

On January 13 of that year the *Indianapolis News* included this headline:

Bob Moody

NICE STATE OF THINGS.
A Man Isn't Safe in Terre Haute After Dark According to This

The story told of the arrest of Harry Hamill, superintendent of the workhouse, for robbing an intoxicated man of nearly $300 – and Eli Lowry was involved. The superintendent and another man had taken the drunk fellow from Fred Pierce's saloon on South Fourth Street to the Vigo County jail "for safekeeping". Eli, who was variously reported to be the "turnkey", "custodian", or "assistant jailer", had gone ahead of them and sent a fellow jailer away on an errand so the others could rob the man. The paper added:

> "The affair has caused a sensation because it exposes a practice that has been generally supposed to exist about the all-night saloons. Lowery is an ex-convict and was brought into notoriety at the time the Bruce gang of burglars nearly escaped from the jail."

The next day's edition of the *St. Louis Post-Dispatch* added that "Lowery was unable to give bond, he being almost a stranger [in Terre Haute]." It also offered the tantalizing news that "Saloon-keeper King, the man who flashed part of the stolen money in a house of ill-fame, is still in jail". That was Charley King, who was also arrested. The victim was identified as Clay County merchant J.F. Tribble, who was in town to see a doctor about his "heart trouble".

Only a few months earlier 21-year-old Mary Lockard had been convicted of smuggling a bundle of more than twenty burglar saws into the jail. The Bruce gang had almost succeeded in cutting off the cell door when they were discovered. Obvious questions were asked regarding how she was able to get that much contraband into the jail and why the escape attempt had escaped Lowry's attention.

A few days later the *Orleans Progress*, under the headline: **Eli**

Lowery in a Box, explained that Vigo County Sheriff J.W. Stout had met Lowry on his numerous visits to the Indiana Prison South while transporting convicts and had given him a job following the pardon. Governor Claude Matthews visited Terre Haute at the end of the month and was reported to admit that Lowry's latest crime "was calculated to deter the pardoning power from being lenient."

Eli Lowry died in Terre Haute on December 13, 1895 – less than five years after he was pardoned. He had regularly given different ages for himself over the years, but records from the City Health Office listed his age at death as only 38. There was no official cause of death, but newspapers cited both consumption (tuberculosis) and pneumonia. His burial place is unknown.

On Christmas Day of 1895, almost two weeks after his death, the *Fredericksburg (IN) Blue River Gazette,* from Washington County, where Lowry was born, reported his passing ("about forty years old") and added:

> "While a trusty at Prison South he created a sensation by trying to elope with a governess employed by Deputy Warden Parnes. He had supplied her with money he had earned shining shoes and selling cigars, and it was their intention to go where they could conceal their identity and get married."

Perhaps the "unwilling tool" – the inmate "trusted above any man in the prison" – was not quite as innocent as he appeared.

Lee Jones:
A Little Careless

Lee Jones was the man convicted of murdering Thomas Moody in cold blood by emptying both barrels of a shotgun into his back after allegedly adding poison to the buckshot. Lee had married Louisa Toliver in 1871, so he presumably had some inheritance at stake in the feud, but testimony against him suggested that his primary motivation was to please and impress his older, richer, more powerful brother, Bent Jones. Locked away inside the Indiana Prison South at the age of 25, he faced a long lifetime in prison.

An 1885 article in the *Bloomington Saturday Courier* reported:

> "[A] short time after his incarceration in the state prison, Lee Jones, thinking he was about to die, made a confession which corroborated the story told by Lowry. There may be no truth in this report, however."

This brings up an important point. As time passed, newspaper accounts of the Moody-Tolliver Feud became increasingly unreliable. With few resources to rely on other than memory and whatever earlier accounts might have been kept in newspaper morgues, facts were often garbled. Dates were incorrect, names misspelled, relationships reversed, and details added that were never reported during the trials. For example, in 1897 the usually reliable *Indianapolis News* published an account of Thomas Moody's murder that differed completely from eyewitness reports in 1875 and described a scenario that was never mentioned in testimony:

> "[Thomas Moody] was in his home at the time, and was disturbed by some one creating a noise some distance from the house. He got up to see what was the matter, and had just turned the door-knob when a load of shot, discharged from ambush, lodged in his back, it having been fired through a window in the opposite side of the house."

The same story claimed that "Lowrie [sic] was to be pardoned soon after [his sentence], because he had assisted in convicting the others. But, strange as it may seem, he was allowed to remain in prison until a few years ago… It was in evidence that he was present at the time [of Moody's murder]." The evidence presented in court placed Lowry some distance away from the actual shooting, waiting with Tom Toliver and Bent Jones. According to this reporter, Park [sic] Tolliver had eventually settled in Elnora, *Kansas*, [rather than Elnora, Indiana] and Bent Jones "is now said to be living [as] a quiet and law abiding citizen at Mitchell." This story, printed just four days after Lee Jones was killed, added an interesting and apparently accurate note about the weapon he had been convicted of using to commit the murder:

> "The old shot-gun that evidence proved fired the fatal shot, has been handed down through the score of years and is still a relic in the clerk's office at the Monroe county court-house."

This confirmed an earlier note in the June 10, 1891, edition of the *Bloomington Republican Progress*:

> "The shot gun that killed Moody about ten years ago [actually in 1875], is on exhibition at the [Monroe County] clerk's office. It was for a long time hidden in a pond and as a

result it is rust eaten and has a very elderly appearance."

Later accounts also place the shotgun that killed Tom Moody in the Monroe County Clerk's office, although inquiries indicate that it has long since been removed. The gun's present whereabouts are unknown.

In 1877 the *Martinsville (IN) Weekly Gazette* reported:

> "It is estimated that the Jones-Tolliver-Moody case will cost Orange county $30,000 before it is ended. When the trouble began the county was out of debt and had a surplus in her treasury."

Three years later the *Cincinnati Daily Star* offered a more realistic estimate:

> "A claim amounting to $2,496.50, in favor of Monroe County, for expenses incurred in the trial of the murderers of Thomas Moody, was allowed and paid at Paoli last week. These cases have now cost Orange County over $16,000 in actual cash, and the end is not yet."

In 1897 a report in the *Indianapolis News* suggested an even lower total cost:

> "The prosecution cost Orange county over $11,000 and resulted in a feeling that only died by the passing away of the participants in the tragedy."

That "feeling" was evidently one of outrage at the amount of tax money the county had spent on trials in addition to the exorbitant personal legal expenses for the two feuding factions. Even the lowest estimate of "over $11,000" would be more than $268,000 in 2020 dollars.

An equally unreliable example of bad reporting appeared in a 1904 edition of the *Indianapolis Star*:

> "Another famous case in Lawrence county was the Jones-Colliver-Moody case... Lee and Bent Jones and Thomas Lowery, on confession of the latter, were sentenced for life. All were afterward pardoned. Bert Colliver and his brother Tom were also indicted in the case, but escaped conviction."

It is difficult, and often impossible, to evaluate the validity of information reported so long after the actual events, but the *Saturday Courier* story included details – in addition to the alleged "confession" – that would be of interest if they are true. It stated that the wives of both Lee and Bent Jones had obtained divorces "although they were very devoted to their husbands through the trials of their cases." As noted earlier, in the 1880 census Louisa Toliver Jones's brother, co-defendant Tom Toliver, was living with her and her young son in Mitchell. The newspaper reported that Lee was working in the prison plating shop and that he "gets along better than his brother. He lives on hope, and tries to be cheerful."

Surprisingly, there was some basis for hope. Efforts were being made to obtain pardons or parole for Eli Lowry and both Jones brothers. In 1885 these pleas "fell flat", but efforts on their behalf would continue. Bent Jones would later publicly proclaim that he would refuse parole while his younger brother remained behind bars. That was shameless posturing, since no one in authority had offered to release him first, if at all.

On September 10, 1887, Lee Jones would receive terrible news. His wife, Louisa Toliver Jones, had died at the age of 38 while he remained in prison. The *Bloomington Telephone* carried an account provided by the *New Albany Ledger* that gave the heart-rending details:

> "That was a sad sight in the former home of Lee Jones in Mitchell Tuesday. Mrs. Jones is dead, dead from grief, a broken hearted

> woman. By the bier stood her husband, a lifetime convict, who by the lieniency of Gov. Gray was permitted to attend the funeral of his faithful wife whose death was caused by his sentence of life imprisonment. Children, relatives, and friends were gathered around the corpse. The stoutest heart shed tears. Lee Jones was one of the Tolliver, Moody, Jones men whose lawsuits, fights, murders, arsons, etc., were the terror of Lawrence and surrounding counties for years. No matter where the blame might lie, whether Lee Jones was a felon deserving imprisonment or worse, no one who beheld his grief over the remains of his devoted wife, could refuse him sympathy in his sorrow. Mrs. Jones died Sunday night while sitting up with a corpse, it is supposed of heart disease."

Lee Jones would serve nearly six more years in prison before getting the good news he had hoped for. On July 20, 1893, Governor Matthews granted him a conditional pardon after serving almost sixteen years of a life sentence. The petition for his release was impressive. It included the names of Judge E.D. Pearson, who had presided over Lee's conviction, prosecuting attorney R.W. Miers, ten of the jurors who convicted him, fifty-one prominent residents of Orange County, and 284 other un-named citizens. Two reasons were listed as justification for a pardon:

1. "There is doubt of his guilt."
2. "Is asked by all the prominent citizens."

Before Governor Matthews authorized the document, someone had handwritten the word "conditionally" as an insertion to modify the printed "pardon". However, no conditions were specified in the proclamation.

The press gave special credit to S.J. Glover for "some clever work in securing Jones' parole". It should be noted that the terms "pardon" and "parole", while having distinct legal definitions, were often used interchangeably by the press. It was not unusual for a headline to declare a "pardon", only for the same action to be labeled "parole" in the body of the story.

The *Orleans Progress* announced that Lee Jones would return to Mitchell, "the home of his childhood… where he will be permitted to remain so long as he conducts himself as a law-abiding citizen. Let us hope that he may ever do that." A later press report claimed that he was given "an ovation" when he returned to his old home. There were widespread reports that ringleader and big brother Bent Jones was expecting similar news soon.

To his credit, Lee Jones apparently did remain a law-abiding citizen for the remainder of his short life. He found a job as the chief engineer at the Mitchell Electric Light Company, whose plant was located near Fifth Street and Warren, close to the site occupied in 2020 by Lawrence County Farm Supply. In 1894 he married Elizabeth "Lizzie" Toliver – the older sister of his late wife. Lizzie had taken custody of Will Jones, the son of Lee and Louisa, after his mother's death. After Lee was released, he and Lizzie apparently lived together briefly before their marriage.

This happy, if unconventional, family lived quietly until fate delivered a mortal blow to Lee Jones. At about eight o'clock on the night of June 22, 1897, a heavy rumbling noise was heard coming from the direction of the electric plant, accompanied by a city-wide blackout. Citizens ran to investigate; among them was Will Crites, the assistant engineer. He shut down the machinery and discovered the badly mangled body of Lee Jones lying amidst shattered debris on the floor. He had "a terrible wound in his head, and a great ragged splinter thrust through his cheek." The man convicted of firing the shots that killed Thomas Moody was carried on a stretcher to his room a short distance away in South Mitchell, where he died within minutes. He was only 44 years old.

James Bell, Superintendent of the Bedford electric light plant, arrived in Mitchell early the next morning to investigate. He concluded that the exact manner of death could not be known but noted that Jones was in the habit of standing on a chair to oil the machinery and adjust a clutch that governed the machine.

Bell speculated that the chair might have slipped on the greasy floor, causing his clothes to be caught in the clutch. About six square feet of the floor was badly torn up and the chair was across Jones's body, with one chair leg thrown across the room. The contents of his pockets were scattered over the area, suggesting that Jones had been whirled on the shafting to his death. The *Mitchell Commercial*, wrote that "Lee Jones was a careful engineer and said to be one of the best in the State. The excellence of our electric light system was due in great measure to his skill." The *Bedford Daily Mail* added, "Mr. Jones was an industrious man and was thoroughly acquainted with this business, and his loss will be felt." Nevertheless, Superintendent Bell reluctantly concluded that "the probabilities are that Jones was a little careless."

None of the press accounts of the accident mention that Lee was missing the thumb and two fingers on his left hand. Bell's original report has not surfaced and there is no evidence that he considered the missing digits as a contributing factor. Yet it is reasonable to assume that someone who slipped off a chair while working on machinery would have found it more difficult to catch himself and recover without a thumb and a full set of fingers on both hands.

On July 1 the *Mitchell Commercial* covered the funeral:

"LEE JONES' FUNERAL

> The funeral of Lee Jones was attended by a large concourse of friends last Thursday. Rev. Thomas spoke from the text, 'Lo! I come quickly,' in a touching manner. His own father was killed by the cars so the grief and anguish of the bereaved ones he could take upon himself. The pastor urged all to be ready for the change that comes 'in the twinkling of an eye.' The Baptist choir assisted by some members of the M.E. choir rendered some choice selections. The body was buried in the Burton family cemetery south-west of town.

Will Jones, the son, is a member of the Cadet band and they attended in a body, the following named acting as pall bearers: Walter Burton, Wilson Hawk, John Holmes, Sam Holmes, John Humston and Holbert Hart.

In the death of Lee Jones, the city loses one of its most efficient and faithful employees and one too, whose place will be hard, very hard to fill. He took pride in his work and it occupied his whole mind and time. He went from his home to the electric power house and when morning came, he went home, the two forming the circle in which he seemed to live and move and have his being. Whatever may have been Lee Jones' imperfections they are buried with the clod that rests upon his bosom and we shall remember him as one who did his duty in the station assigned him."

The *Bedford Democrat* reported that Parks Tolliver traveled from Elnora to attend the funeral. There is no certain indication that Lee's brother, Bent Jones, by then also a free man, was among the mourners, but the July 1 edition of the *Commercial* also included this note:

"A CARD.

We desire to return our heartfelt thanks to all who so kindly ministered to us in our recent bereavement. To Rev. Thomas, the members of the town Council and the Cadet Band as well as kind friends and neighbors, our hearts will ever turn in grateful remembrance.

Mrs. Lee Jones
Will Jones
Bent Jones"

THOMAS TOLIVER:
THE MOST DANGEROUS MAN

TOM TOLIVER WAS THE LEAST culpable defendant in the murder of Thomas Moody. According to Lowry's testimony, Tom knew when the murder would take place and was waiting with Bent Jones and Eli Lowry when Lee Jones and Parks Toliver returned to confirm that Lee had shot Moody in front of his home. That could have been enough to convict him as an accessory to murder, but judges and juries appear to have taken his youth into account. Thomas was the youngest child of William and Delana Toliver. He was only twelve years old when his widowed father married Polly Moody and the murder of her brother took place when Tom Toliver was eighteen.

Thomas and Parks were tried in 1878, but there was a hung jury. A retrial the following year was halted when Parks escaped from custody while the jury – which later was found to have again failed to reach a verdict – was still in deliberations.

That does not mean that Thomas Toliver was an innocent or admirable man. In the 1880 federal census he was living in Mitchell with his sister, Louisa Toliver Jones, the wife of the imprisoned Lee Jones, and her son. He was not, however, listed as the "head" of the household and, as noted earlier, his occupation was given as "Sporting Man" – a euphemism for "gambler". At that time there were still murder charges pending against him.

All charges against Thomas and Parks Toliver were officially dropped in December of 1881, but less than one year later Tom was involved in an argument that resulted in the murder of Marshal George Easley in Mitchell. Under the headline **Fatal Affray**, the November 20, 1882, edition of the *Columbus Republic* ran a story credited to the *Louisville Courier-Journal*'s correspondent in Mitchell:

> "LOUISVILLE, November 17. — The Courier-Journal's Mitchell, Ind., special says: A shooting affray occurred here this afternoon, in which marshal Geo. Easley was mortally wounded by a gambler named Tom Bell. Two men, named Skip Shomel and Thomas Tolliver, got into a quarrel with Bell in front of McDonald's saloon, and after several blows had been exchanged Bell drew a pistol and fired at Shomel, wounding him slightly in the leg. Marshal Easley rushed up and catching Bell took the pistol away from him and placed him under arrest. Just as he was opening the door, Bell suddenly jerked the officer's pistol out of his pocket and retreating a few steps fired, the ball entering Easley's side just above the abdomen, ranging downward and inflicting a mortal wound. Bell fled after the shooting but was pursued by a number of citizens and several shots were fired at him. He was finally captured and brought back to town, where great difficulty was experienced in preventing the crowd from lynching him. He was removed to Bedford and put in jail for safe keeping. Bell had only lived in the town a few weeks, and came here from Louisville, where he lives."

"Shomel" was actually Julius "Skip" Chomel, another well-known gambler who was also one of the owners and publishers of Washington, Indiana's *Weekly Advertiser and Daily Enterprise*. In 1885 he attempted suicide by shooting himself in the head but, according to the *Indianapolis Journal*, "his aim was bad, and his effort at shuffling off proved a failure."

In 1885 a group of alleged "bond swindlers" headed by R.B. Pollard fled from Indiana to Canada to avoid prosecution, apparently taking with them more than $220,000. The *Indianapolis Journal* reported in November that Thomas Tolliver, an "old crony" of Pollard, had recently returned from a trip to London, Ontario, where he visited with some of "those emigrating gentlemen".

In March of 1887 an Elkhart, Indiana, newspaper reported: "Thos. Tolliver and J.H. Bradley were fined five dollars each for gambling Tuesday. They were out-of-town gams, and think 'Squire Arnold deals the hardest 'brace' they ever played.'"

Three years later the *Loogootee Martin County Tribune* reported that Tom and his friend Julius Chomel "engaged in a rough and tumble fight at Seymour... during the progress of which a stove was knocked down and falling on the latter broke his leg."

Thomas Toliver's character and unique personality were on display in an Indianapolis courtroom in 1891. The details appeared in the *Indianapolis News* on November 10:

"ONE OF THE TOLLIVER GANG
Arrested Here for Gambling; but Permitted To Take Leg Bail.

Yesterday afternoon Thomas Tolliver and Charles Long, card sharps and "skin" gamblers, were arrested by Chief Splan and Detective Doherity. They were charged with loitering. Long claimed to be a yard clerk for the Louisville & Nashville railroad at Evansville, but the evidence was against them and they were shown up to be 'short-card' and confidence men. 'I will fine you $100 and thirty days,' said the Court, 'and suspend the sentence if you get out of town.'

'How long will you give us?' anxiously asked Tolliver.

'Until noon.'

'We will be gone before eleven, beloved,' and the pair started out of the court room

> almost on a run. Tolliver is one of the gang who figured some years ago in the Tolliver-Jones fued [sic] in Orange county… 'He is the worst man and the most dangerous man that has ever been in this court,' remarked Police Judge Buskirk. 'I have known him for years, and a good many people in Orange county believe that he, and not Lowry, should have been sent to prison.'"

An account of this incident in the *Orleans Progress* added: "Truly the way of the transgressor is hard. Tolliver is now meeting the punishment he so richly deserves for his many crimes against law and justice."

Tom's notoriety was made clear in the *Bedford Mail* edition of November 4, 1892, which noted:

> "Tom Toliver, a sporting man whose reputation in his line is almost national, is very ill at the Baker House, with kidney trouble. His recovery is said to be doubtful."

He would live to see his name in print again.

Meanwhile, his partner in crime, Julius "Skip" Chomel, had moved to Indianapolis, where his family owned and published the *Catholic Record*. On April 2, 1894, Skip walked into the Club Bar and asked the bartender for a glass so he could take some "medicine". He then swallowed a large dose of carbolic acid he had just purchased at a nearby drugstore. This was much more effective than his previous suicide attempt. He said, "Goodbye, boys. Skip's gone!" and died before a doctor could arrive. Chomel was only 32 years old.

The *Orleans Progress* reprinted a lengthy and detailed expose from the *Indianapolis State Sentinel* on July 18, 1895, revealing the less than shocking news that open gambling was taking place in West Baden Springs, a resort area in Orange County. The paper was alarmed that this activity was drawing gamblers from Chicago – and even women. Local law enforcement did not seem to be overly concerned by this development and it was alleged that businessmen such as hotel owner Lee W. Sinclair were helping gamblers evade the law. The investigating correspondent applauded a constable named Robert J. Kirkland who "pounced upon" Thomas Tolliver and John Jones and arrested them. Tom's colleague could possibly have been John Wesley Jones, the 28-year-old son of Bent. The prisoners were taken to French Lick, where they appeared before a justice of the peace "in a rude loft over a country store." Their cases were continued and both Tolliver and Jones "readily furnished cash bond." The reporter added: "As to the skin-game grafters of the Jones-Toliver-Scarface Mike-Dan Levy-Deacon Miller stripe, they ought to be drummed out of this country or put to work doing honest toil for the people of the State upon whom they have so long been preying." When Tom appeared in court six months later he was found guilty of "keeping a room to be used for gambling purposes in West Baden". He was fined fifty dollars plus court costs.

Back in 1893 Tom had married Nellie Ferguson, who was twelve years younger. By 1900 they had moved to Washington, Indiana, in Daviess County. According to the federal census taken on June 11 of that year, Tom, Nellie, and their four-year-old daughter Alma were living at 116 Main Street. This would be the final census entry for 43-year-old Thomas Toliver.

Less than four months later, on the night of October 5, 1900, Tom was shot and killed just down the street from his home. The following day's edition of the *Bedford Daily Mail* carried a story written the previous night:

"TOM TOLLIVER KILLED
Shot Down At Washington In a Row Over a Crap Game.

```
Washington, Ind., Oct. 5. - Thomas Tolliver,
a widely known gambler, was shot and killed
in front of a saloon on Main street, to night
at 9 o'clock. He died 15 minutes later. The
```

street fair is going on, and thousands of people were on the streets. Two shots were fired, and people were so excited that they became panic stricken. The second shot struck Joe Slawson, a B & O employe [sic], who was an innocent bystander, and he received a wound that may prove fatal.

No one knows positively who fired the shots. John Massey, a Princeton, Ind., gambler, is in jail as a suspect. He says he knows nothing of the shooting. The row started over a crap game in which loaded dice were used...

Tom Tolliver was born two and a half miles southeast of Mitchell. He came of a good family, but was always a bad and dangerous man, and for many years was one of Bent Jones' lieutenants in the commission of many deeds of outlawry in Lawrence and Orange counties. He was about 50 years of age [actually 44 following a recent birthday] and he was a single man [see above]."

The headline in that day's edition of the *Indianapolis Journal* was **NOTED GAMBLER KILLED,** while the *Richmond (IN) Palladium and Sun-Telegraph* identified Thomas Tolliver as "a well known sporting man".

On October 12 the *Bedford Weekly Mail* reported:

"Tolliver's Slayers Escape.

Jack Massey, the partner of Tom Gleason, who shot and killed Tom Tolliver at Washington Friday night, was given a preliminary hearing before Squire Streeter Saturday afternoon. He was charged with murder, the affidavit having been preferred by Walter B. Meredith, one of Tolliver's gambling partners. He was found not guilty and was released, but was placed under $100 bond to appear as a witness before the Grand Jury. He put up the $100 and left

> town immediately. The chances are that he
> will never return. He got off light."

The article added that there was "no trace of Tom Gleason, who did the shooting." Joe Slawson, the innocent bystander, was reported to be "resting easy", although his doctor was concerned that "the critical period of his trouble will not arrive for about a week or ten days. Dr. Winton thinks the ball that penetrated Slawson's shoulders and lung is a 44 calibre. His chances for recovery are not considered good."

A brief paragraph in the same edition of the *Weekly Mail* reported: "Tom Toliver's body was brought to this place [Mitchell] Sunday from Washington and buried at the Burton graveyard. His sister, Mrs. Lee Jones, and other relatives attended the funeral. Also a number of friends from Seymour and Washington."

His heavily weathered tombstone stands just a few feet away from that of his co-defendant, Lee Jones.

The *Daviess County Democrat*, published in Washington, added some background the following day:

> "The murder grew out of a craps game in Tom
> Riley's saloon. It seems that Tolliver and
> several other sports were conducting the
> game and during the evening three strangers
> entered and began playing. They won money
> with ease and were in a short time about $100
> ahead. Then it was discovered that the men
> had substituted loaded dice and that this
> was the cause of their heavy winnings. The
> men running the game became terribly enraged
> when this discovery was made and compelled
> the three men to return the money they had
> won, after which they were forcibly ejected.
> One of the three men at that time declared he
> would use a gun if he only had one.
>
> Later in the evening while Walter Meredith,
> who was assisting in running the craps game,
> was walking along Main Street he met the three
> men and one of them struck him with brass
> knucks.

> About ten minutes later Tom Tolliver, who had been walking west on Main street, started into Patsy Kelly's saloon. In the doorway stood the strangers. As Tolliver approached one of the strangers, a tall, slender man, jerked a revolver from his pocket and fired at Tolliver. The bullet struck Tom a little below the right nipple, took a downward course, and lodged just beneath the skin in the small of the back. As the stranger pulled his gun Tolliver drew his and both men, it is claimed, fired almost simultaneously. The bullet which Tolliver is alleged to have fired missed the stranger and struck Joseph Slawson, a B & O B W shop employe [sic], in the front part of the right shoulder and passed into his chest. The bullet cannot be located. Slawson is in a critical condition and may die."

The *Washington Gazette* offered the most elaborate headline on October 12, with "**GAME OF CRAPS CAUSES MURDER**" in huge type followed by six additional sub-headlines, including "**DUEL FOUGHT IN A SALOON DOOR And in the Presence of Thousands of People.**" Their story described Tom Tolliver as a gambler "well-known all over Southern Indiana." It concluded:

> "Public opinion is divided as to the justification for the shooting. Some say that Gleason was followed by Tolliver. Others believe it was the other way. So there it is. Some new evidence may be brought out at the Coroner's inquest.
> Tolliver has lived here for many years. He has been a gambler most of his life. He has a wife and a bright little child."

Most accounts suggested that Gleason and Jack Massey were able to avoid immediate apprehension by blending in with the large crowd of people attending the street fair just outside the saloons. However, research by Daviess County historian Don Cosby indicates that the pair ran through the Arcade saloon and out the back door. Meanwhile Tom Toliver – still holding his revolver – staggered toward owner Patsy Kelly and exclaimed, "Patsy, he has killed me!" Toliver and Joe Slawson, the man he had accidentally shot, were both taken across the street to Winton & Smith's drug store at 206 East Main Street for treatment. By this time Tom was unconscious and Dr. Winton discovered that the bullet had penetrated his lung, liver, small intestines, and right kidney. With no hope of recovery, Toliver was moved to his home in the Sum Building, where he died shortly after 10:00 p.m.

At about the same time Washington city policeman William Kermode was walking his beat when he saw two men running east on South Street and heard one of them shout, "We need to get out of this town G-D-quick!" His partner replied, "Where did you get him?" Tom Gleason answered, "I got the S.O.B. in the side." Officer Kermode managed to grab Jack Massey, who then briefly broke loose and dashed west through the crowd on Main Street before he was overtaken by the policeman who then opened an ugly gash on Massey's head with his nightstick.

Two weeks later the *Daviess County Democrat* wrote: "The grand jury failed to find a true bill against Thomas Gleason who shot and killed Thomas Tolliver during the street fair. The jury considered that Gleason acted in self-defense. Gleason, however, was indicted for an assault on Walter Meredith the same night." Massey never returned to testify, as the newspaper reporter had predicted, and Gleason was never apprehended.

Despite the dire prognosis, Joe Slawson recovered and lived until 1932, when he died at the age of 82.

Meanwhile, Nellie Toliver was a 31-year-old widow with a "bright little child" to take care of. Three months after her husband was killed Nellie visited the John Steers family in Orleans. Steers had bought the home where Tom Moody was murdered. By 1910 Nellie and Alma, now fourteen years old, were living in Indianapolis, where Nellie had found work at the telephone company. Alma married a man named Edward Rosenweig, who soon shortened his name to Rose, and in the 1920 census they were living in Chicago. Ten years later the couple had moved to

Los Angeles, where Edward was a furniture salesman and Alma worked for a dentist. At some point Nellie Ferguson Toliver joined her daughter and son-in-law in California. She died in Los Angeles at the age of 96 – sixty-six years after her "sporting man" husband with a nearly national reputation had been killed over a game of craps.

Parks Toliver:
Tricky Tolliver

Milton Parks Toliver may not have looked like a criminal to courtroom observers, as newspaper writers repeatedly suggested, but there was plenty of testimony to support his indictment for murder. According to Eli Lowry, Parks had enough advance knowledge about the plot to have provided ammunition used in the shooting. Lowry also swore under oath that Parks Toliver had been present when Lee Jones fired the shots that killed Tom Moody. After the first jury could not agree on a verdict for him or his younger brother Thomas, Parks had made the surprisingly bold choice to escape from custody while a second jury was still in deliberations. It would later be disclosed that this jury, too, did not reach a unanimous verdict. Instead of being a free man, Parks Toliver became a fugitive from justice.

His escape plan required the advance knowledge and cooperation of at least a few friends or family members and it would not be unreasonable to suspect collusion by locally influential admirers. Regardless, Parks' whereabouts remained unknown for a couple of years. In 1881, when charges against him were dropped, the *Topeka (KS) Daily Capital* wrote that since his escape "he has been a fugitive out in Colorado." An 1885 story in the *Bloomington Saturday Courier* stated that Parks eventually "returned to Mitchell, his old home, and is still there, broken down in health." Another account claimed that he had died in Mitchell. He would reappear and live briefly in Mitchell again later in life, but he was not there in 1885 and died elsewhere.

While Parks Toliver was hiding from the law, his young wife, Ella Belle, and their sons, ages two and four, had moved back in with her parents, Dr. James Pearson and his wife, Martha. Living next to the Pearson's home in Mitchell, according to the 1880 census, were Clarissa Toliver Jones, wife of the imprisoned Bent Jones, and their two sons. Just down the street were two households of Burtons, the family of William Toliver's first wife.

Charges against Parks and his brother were officially dropped in 1881. In the November 25 edition of the *Indianapolis Journal* a story datelined from Mitchell seemed to verify the belief that Parks had fled west:

> "Dr. Parks Toliver, charged as an accessory in the Moody murder of 1875, and gave leg bail about a year ago while the jury had his case under advisement, succeeded, through his counsel in getting his case thrown out of court. His wife, living here, has telegraphed the fact to him in Colorado."

That may have been a red herring. A Toliver family story in the files of Bedford's Edward L. Hutton Research Library claimed that "he is said to have gone to St. Louis in a freight car, then into Arkansas." That appears to be true. On December 14, 1882, the *Mitchell Commercial* reported: "Dr. Parks Toliver, of Arkansas, arrived here this morning, and will take his family to that State with him." That, too, was misleading. In fact, he had already settled in what would become Elnora, Indiana. In 1882 it was an unincorporated village known as Owl Prairie in Daviess County about fifty miles and two counties west of Mitchell. The estimated population was less than thirty inhabitants. Upon his arrival Parks refashioned his identity. From that point forward he was known as Dr. Milton P. Tolliver – with two Ls. That is how he will be identified through the remainder of this book. The town was incorporated and renamed Elnora in 1885, with the arrival of the Evansville and Indianapolis railroad. By 1888 Milton owned a residence near the southwest corner of Adaline and Meridian streets where he practiced medicine as a physician and surgeon. An annual report from the Indiana State Board of Medical Registration and Examination for 1906 lists him as not having a medical degree, although he was apparently a licensed physician.

On February 15, 1889, Ella Belle, his wife of eighteen years and mother of his three sons, died at the age of only 34. This is the woman who had been present – and possibly assisted – when Parks had escaped from custody in Bloomington and who came back to him after he was no longer a wanted man. The cause of her early death and location of her burial are unknown.

Dr. Tolliver was left with three boys to raise, from the ages of four to seventeen. That may partially explain why, less than nine months after Ella Belle's death, he married Letha Alice Stewart. They had two children: Ruth in 1892 and Joseph in 1895. Letha died in 1903 at the age of 44. Parks' oldest son, William, signed her death certificate in three roles: as informant, attending physician, and "Health Officer or Deputy". William had graduated from the Kentucky School of Medicine in Louisville and was practicing medicine with his father in Elnora. The cause of her death is difficult to decipher but appears to be "cerebral hemorrhage". An account in the *Mitchell Commercial* attributed her death to "stomach and brain trouble" and noted that Mrs. Lizzie Jones, widow of Lee Jones, was among the mourners at her funeral. Letha's grave in the Old Elnora Cemetery is unmarked.

The April 14, 1905, edition of the *Bedford Daily Mail* declared that city had been overtaken by friendly visitors:

"KNIGHTS PYTHIAS
Are In Procession [sic] Of
The Stone City Today

"The District Meeting of the Knights of Pythias is in progress in this city today and to-

> night, and many members of that popular order from other towns are in attendance. Beautiful weather has contributed to the success of the occasion, and rendered the profuse decoration of the city with flags and bunting practicable. All incoming trains have brought visitors, and more are expected on the late train this afternoon.
>
> At 2 o'clock this afternoon a splendid parade four blocks in length was given, which strikingly displayed the numerical strength of the order... It was probably the finest public demonstration ever made by a secret order in this city."

The Knights of Pythias is a fraternal organization founded in 1864. In 1905 membership was rapidly growing to reach a high of almost one million members during the Twenties. Among the out-of-town guests noted in the paper was "Dr. M.P. Tolliver, a K of P. of Elnora". His activities that weekend are not known but this visit triggered a surprising series of events. Ten weeks later the *Mitchell Commercial* announced that he was moving back to Lawrence County for the first time since he had escaped from his murder trial in 1879:

> "Dr. M.P. Tolliver of Elnora has decided to go to Mitchell to engage in the practice of his profession. He is a native of Lawrence county, but has lived in Daviess county for eighteen [actually twenty-three] years. Dr. Tolliver is well known in the northern part of the county, and he is generally respected. He is a good man and a kind neighbor, and his Daviess county friends hope that he will find happiness and prosperity in his new field of labor. – Washington Gazette and Herald."

The "generally respected" Dr. Tolliver had another surprise in store for his family, friends, and new neighbors. On July 6, 1905, the *Commercial* announced:

> "On Friday evening [June 30] Dr. M.P. Tolliver, of Mitchell, and Mrs. Mabel Andrew, of Michigan, were united in marriage at Bedford. Mrs. Andrew came here from Michigan Thursday and Dr. Tolliver had rooms engaged at the Putnam in advance. Friday afternoon they drove to Bedford and on their return registered as man and wife.
>
> No one here knew the happy event was even contemplated. However, we wish them unbounded happiness and welcome them as citizens of Mitchell."

Dr. Tolliver was 57 years old. Mabel, his third wife, was only 29. She was born in Altoona, Pennsylvania, in 1875 as Mabel Clara Esther Henderson. When she was seven years old her father was killed in a cave-in at a Michigan mine, leaving her 29-year-old French-Canadian mother with four small children. Mabel married William "Paddy" Andrews when she was sixteen years old. Seven months later she gave birth to a daughter named Antoinette, known as "Nellie". She divorced Paddy Andrews after six years of marriage on grounds of "extreme cruelty".

It is not known how the doctor from Elnora met the single mother from Michigan. Could Mabel have been visiting Bedford during the Knights of Pythias festivities? Possibly, but there is no evidence to support that conjecture.

Dr. Tolliver was soon running display ads in the Mitchell newspaper offering his services as "Physician and Surgeon. Office over Bank of Mitchell. Hours from 8 to 11 a.m. and 1 to 4 p.m." One year later he moved the office to his residence at the corner of Baker (now West Grissom Avenue) and Seventh Street, in what was known as the "M.P. Tolliver addition".

Meanwhile, his son William had also moved to Lawrence County, setting up a practice at 716 East 16th Street in Bedford – "two doors west of hospital" – and was advertising "the Non-Operative treatment of PILES and RUPTURE". Satisfaction was guaranteed.

Part of the new blended household was Milton's daughter

Ruth, from his marriage with Letha Stewart. In August of 1907, when she was fourteen years old, Ruth was aboard a train from Bedford to Mitchell that derailed. Early the following year her father – misidentified in early press reports as "John P. Tolliver" – sued the Baltimore and Ohio Southwestern railroad, making headlines in the *Bedford Weekly Mail*:

BIG DAMAGES
Are Asked Of the B. & O. S.W. For Injuries Sustained By Passengers
YOUNG LADY CRIPPLED
In the Riverdale Wreck Wants $10,000 And Her Father $3,000.

The lawsuit claimed that the track was "in a delapidated condition" and in need of repairs. Milton stated that his young daughter had suffered "personal injuries of such a character that her health has been greatly impaired and that the shock has affected her entire nervous system. The extent of her injuries are such that she can perform little of the duties of life, wherefore she prays judgment in the sum of $10,000". The second suit was based on "the injuries received by his daughter, alleging that he had been deprived of her assistance and has been compelled to care for her and now that she is a cripple her life has been blasted. He also incurred a large doctor's bill for necessary attentions given her and asks that he be given judgment for $3,000." The $13,000 in combined damages would amount to more than $362,000 in 2020 dollars.

The case was to be tried in Lawrence County Circuit Court, but after a jury was sworn in a settlement was reached. Instead of $13,000 in damages, Dr. Tolliver agreed to settle for $200. Ruth would live until 1975, when she died at the age of 82. A Tolliver descendant who remembered her as an elderly great-aunt said she had no apparent disabilities.

While the lawsuit was pending the Tolliver household made headlines for another reason. Sometime before April 1908 Milton and Mabel had relocated from Mitchell to a two-story home in Bedford, where they rented one of the upstairs bedrooms to a local mailman who was in the process of divorcing his wife of 24 years, and another to a single woman. Mabel began selling ladies fashion items from the house, specializing in corsets. Late on the night of April 23 one of their tenants was undressing for bed when he fell out of a window:

"HARB EDWARDS MEETS TRAGIC DEATH
FALLS FROM WINDOW TO STONE WALK
Picked Up Two Hours Later
With Skull Crushed And In
Dying Condition.

Death, in a tragic manner, came to Harbert H. Edwards at an early hour Friday morning, and his sudden demise shocked his scores of friends in the community.

Edwards... roomed at the home of Dr. and Mrs. Tolliver, West Sixteenth street. He occupied an upstairs room and had been down town during the evening. He was seen by several of his friends going home about 10:30 o'clock and 2 hours later was picked up from beneath his window in a dying condition. It appears from a careful investigation of the circumstances that Mr. Edward's death was produced by a fall from the window of the second story room he occupied.

About 12 o'clock Thursday night, Miss Fay Harwick, who rooms at the Tolliver home, was returning from a party and heard groans of distress as she entered the front door. Miss Hardwick proceeded upstairs and the groans were apparently of great volume and appeared to come from Mr. Edwards' room, in which

> a bright light was burning. Miss Hardwick retraced her steps downstairs and awakened Mrs. Tolliver, stating to that lady that she believed Mr. Edwards was ill. Mrs. Tolliver donned a dress and proceeded to the room occupied by Mr. Edwards and entered. She made a minute examination of the room, found a portion of Mr. Edwards' clothing on the floor and the window up and shutters opened. She walked to the window and looked down on a dark object lying on the stone sidewalk beneath."

That "dark object" was poor Harbert, who had been lying there, unconscious, with a broken neck for at least two hours. He apparently sat on the windowsill to remove his trousers, not realizing that the shutters were not hooked. Leaning back, Edwards lost his balance and fell eighteen feet before landing. He was still alive, but efforts by Dr. Morrell Simpson to save him were futile.

The account given above in the *Bedford Weekly Mail* did not address an obvious question: Where was Milton? According to the *Mitchel Commercial*, "Dr. Tolliver was not at home at the time of the accident, being at his office in North Bedford." There was no explanation why he would be at his office at 7th and L Streets after midnight.

But by that time Dr. Tolliver may have been spending many nights "at the office". His marriage to Mabel was quickly falling apart. By February 1, 1909, Mabel had moved out, renting "the handsome new house just completed by J.N. Mallot, on West 17th street" with her upstairs tenant, Fay Hardwick, and Fay's sister, Lucille.

The inevitable divorce was announced in the *Orleans Progress-Examiner* on May 13, 1909:

"Divorce Granted

> Bedford Mail, 12.

> Mrs. Mabel Tolliver was today granted a divorce from Dr. M.P. Tolliver, in the Orange County Circuit Court at Paoli. The court also restored her former name, Mrs. Mabel Andrews.
>
> Dr. Tolliver formerly practiced medicine in this city [Bedford], having his office over Sherwood's Cigar Store. Mrs. Tolliver has resided for some time on West 16th Street."

Mabel moved back to the house at 16th and N streets. Three months after the divorce she began advertising a new "corset parlor" at her home at 1611 West 16th Street in the local newspapers. By the fall of 1910 she was advertising "Customers of Chas. A. Stevens, Chicago, will please call at 1420 K street. Mrs. Mabel Andrews, Rep.". Charles. A. Stevens was a popular department store that had begun as a mail order house specializing in women's clothing.

In the 1910 federal census Milton P. Tolliver had returned to Elnora, was living alone and listed as "widowed" although his most recent wife was very much alive. Later that year he moved to Sullivan, Indiana.

By early 1912 Mabel had moved to Indianapolis and was the apparent corset queen of the state capital in 1922, selling the Spencer Supporting Corset from a shop in the Occidental Building. Mabel would later join her daughter in El Paso, Texas, where Nellie had married a car dealer. She died of cancer at their home in 1937.

But Milton was not finished with matrimony. A story in the January 10, 1912, issue of the *Batesville (IN) Tribune* was picked up in newspapers across the region:

"GRANDMA IS MARRIED, TOO
Mrs. Ellen Hittle and Dr. Milton Tolliver Surprise Grandsons.

> Terre Haute – When B.E. Hutton arranged to have the wedding of his brother, Guy, who is manager of a theater in Ontario, and Miss

> Marie Fancher, of Danville Ill., at his home he did not expect to have a double wedding and thought least of all that his grandmother would be one of the brides. After the Rev. S.E. Hammacker, pastor of the Baptist church, had performed the ceremony for which the guests had assembled, he was asked to repeat it for Mrs. Ellen Hittle of Marshall, who was visiting her grandson, and Dr. Milton Tolliver of Cass. The license had been obtained without notice to the relatives or to the guests. Mrs. Hittle is sixty-eight years old and Dr. Tolliver is sixty-three."

Cass is an unincorporated community in Sullivan County, Indiana, about 25 miles from Elnora. It was her third marriage and Milton's fourth. This one didn't work out, either, as reported in the *Bloomfield News* in 1919: "Milton P. Tolliver v. Ella [sic] Tolliver, divorce. He alleges that she refused to live with him because he moved from Marshall, Parke county, to this county [Greene]. They were married nine [actually eight] years." The 1920 U.S. census placed Milton in Linton, once again "widowed" and living alone. However, Ellen Hittle did not die until February 1, 1923, back in her hometown of Marshall. A coroner's inquest ruled that she had died instantly of "heart trouble". The death certificate gave her marital status as "widow", but her late spouse was listed as John Hittle and there was no mention of her most recent husband.

Perhaps Ellen had discovered that Dr. Tolliver was not as reputable as he must have appeared. When the couple applied for a marriage license in Vigo County on December 26, 1911, Parks stated that he was a "Physician and surgeon" in Sullivan County. But he claimed only one previous marriage, which had ended with the death of his spouse in 1903. It is perhaps understandable that he had not listed Ella Belle, who had been dead for twenty-two years, but there was no mention whatsoever of Mabel Andrews, the wife he had divorced less than three years earlier.

In 1896 M.P. had been elected coroner in Daviess County and served a two-year term. He tried his hand at politics again in

1918 when he ran for the Democratic nomination for the Indiana state senate, to represent Sullivan and Greene counties. When the *Sullivan Daily Times* reported the election results on May 8, with 93% of the precincts reporting, he had finished a poor third in a three-man race with only 10% of the votes.

There was worse to come. Under the headline **ARRESTED AT TERRE HAUTE**, the *Bedford Weekly Mail* reported on September 12, 1919:

> "Milton P. Tolliver, said to be a physician at Linton, was arrested Monday at Terre Haute on the charge of trafficking in morphine sulphate and cocaine. He was temporarily committed to jail at Terre Haute under $1,000 bond."

The *Sullivan Democrat* added: "[He] was formerly located in Sullivan and had an office in the small frame building just opposite the Union office... Dr. Tolliver after leaving Sullivan about four years ago located at Pleasantville [about ten miles from Linton]." It is possible that Parks maintained practices in multiple locations, but it appears that his residence changed often – from Elnora back to Mitchell, to Bedford, back to Elnora, then Sullivan, Cass, Linton, Pleasantville, Westphalia and, eventually, a final return to Elnora.

One month later the *Terre Haute Saturday Spectator* and other newspapers added opium to the list of drugs he was accused of selling. The *Indianapolis Star* reported the outcome of his case on December 2, 1919:

> "Milton P. Tolliver, 72 years old, a Linton (Ind.) doctor, entered a plea of guilty to the illicit employment of morphine, and was fined $300 and costs."

Five years after his guilty plea on illegal drug charges, Dr. Tolliver was one of five physicians called to appear before the state medical board to show cause why their licenses should not be revoked for operating an alleged "diploma mill". Investigators claimed that medical diplomas from a defunct Gary State College were being sold for $250 each. Press reports identified him as a resident of Westphalia, Indiana, less than ten miles west of Elnora. Ironically, that is possibly the closest Doctor Toliver ever got to a medical school diploma.

An entry for his eldest son, William (known to the family as Billy), in a history of Vanderburgh County published in 1922 noted: "Although seventy-five years of age, he [Milton] still follows his beloved calling, and maintains a profitable practice at Elnora...". Billy had left Elnora for brief stays in Bedford and Indianapolis before eventually settling in Evansville. According to the Vanderburgh County history, he "specialized in rectal diseases" and "maintains well-appointed offices at 309 ½ Second Street."

The final year of Milton Parks Tolliver's life was spent in the Elnora home of his son, popular local dentist Harry Cleveland Tolliver. The third son of Parks and Ella Belle was Ralph Thomas Tolliver, a railroad ticket agent in Odon. His son with Letha, Joseph, was a musician aboard the U.S. battleship North Dakota in Mexican waters in 1914. He later immigrated to Canada and became a member of the Royal Northwest Mounted Police.

On February 6, 1926, the *Logansport Pharos Tribune* reported a family tragedy under the headline: **BASKETBALL STAR DIES OF POISONING**. Harry Arthur Tolliver, a 15-year-old son of the dentist and grandson of Milton, had died of blood poisoning resulting from a blister on his foot received at basketball practice.

Just six weeks later the man accused – but never convicted – of participating in the firebombing of the Moody farmhouse and watching Lee Jones fire the shotgun that killed Tom Moody fifty-one years earlier died, on March 23, 1926, at the age of 78. His obituary in the *Odon Journal* remarked: "Besides being a good physician, he was a most active and useful citizen. At one time he was elected to the office of county coroner on the democratic ticket and served one term [1896-98]. Due to ill health the last few years of his life were spent in retirement." There was no mention of his role in the Moody-Tolliver Feud nor of his horseback escape from justice. The man once labeled "Tricky Tolliver" by the press

Bob Moody

had managed to outlive three of his four wives. He is buried in the Old Elnora Cemetery.

BENT JONES: THE TERROR OF INDIANA

ALONZO BENTON JONES WAS THE main instigator of the Moody-Tolliver Feud, to the point where it could more accurately be called the Moody-Tolliver-Jones Feud. He was one of the men who attacked and seriously injured Thomas Moody after the estate sale. He made violent threats against the Moody family prior to the firebombing of their farmhouse in 1871 and continued to boast that he would kill Tom Moody for years before it happened. Eli Lowry told the court that on the day after the murder Bent Jones was in a saloon clicking his heels and chanting, "Tom Moody is dead!" Only after he had been sentenced to life behind bars did local vigilantes feel brave enough to post notices demanding that Bent's wife and his other alleged cohorts in crime leave Mitchell or face the consequences.

By 1898 it had become apparent that many local jurors were so intimidated by the notoriety of some defendants that it was difficult to ensure justice. The *Indianapolis News* addressed this with a story headlined:

"BOLD BANDS OF CRIMINALS
SOME OF THOSE THAT HAVE TERRORIZED COMMUNITIES
Instances in Which Whole Neighborhoods Were Compelled to Suffer

Bob Moody

The Depredations of Lawless Gangs."

The problem, according to the newspaper, was:

"A person accused of crime may take a change of venue to some other county than that in which the crime was committed; but if he refuses to do so, he must be tried at the scene of the crime. The State has no right to a change of venue... when a band of criminals become strong enough to awe the courts and juries, or obtain control of the administration of justice by securing the election of its own members to public office... the criminals will go unwhipt of justice... unless they are so careless as to cross into some other county and commit a crime there.

The first of these was the 'Tolliver gang' that infested Lawrence county, Indiana. The leader of that band was Alonzo B. Jones, a son-in-law of old man Tolliver, who was a wealthy farmer, living near Mitchell. So bold did this band become that its members made little attempt to conceal their identity when they engaged in acts of lawlessness and violence, but they were not even indicted for them. Alonzo Jones was a politician of some local prominence and a member of numerous societies, but so great was the terror that he inspired in the people of Mitchell, that even after he had committed the murder for which he was afterward convicted, an attempt to expel him from the Masonic order failed for lack of an accuser who dared to speak after Jones had finished."

Following a summary of the feud, the *News* pointed out the miscalculation Bent and his gang had made in planning the murder of Thomas Moody:

> "They then returned to Mitchell and undertook to frighten persons there into proving innocence of the crime. But they soon found that the magic of their name did not reach across the county line. They were promptly indicted in the adjoining county, where they were rather hated than feared."

This is a fair assessment of the situation. When the murderers crossed into Orange County they could no longer count on acquittal by a friendly judge or a frightened Lawrence County jury. Indeed, their reception at the Paoli jail was so inhospitable that there was speculation that the "mob" which attacked them there was contrived to boost their eventually successful motion for a change of venue to Monroe County.

Bent Jones had begun lobbying for a pardon by 1881 with a clumsy and ill-conceived appeal to Governor Issac P. Gray, according to the *Bloomington Courier*:

> "It is said that Bent Jones, in his petition to Governor Gray praying for a pardon, made a personal appeal in which he charged Hon. David Huffstetter, of Orange county, one of its oldest and most respected citizens, and a personal friend of the Governor's, with being a counterfeiter. It is already known that Bent was not pardoned."

The *Mitchell Commercial* added on January 12, 1881:

> "Persons who favor peace and order, and who believe in the enforcement of law, will be pleased to learn that Governor Gray did not pardon Bent Jones out of the penitentiary."

A reporter for the *Cincinnati Enquirer* visited the Indiana Prison South in 1883 and learned that Jones was still making futile accusations against the Huffstetter family:

> "In an interview with Bent Jones, he protested his innocence, and claimed that money was used by his enemies to secure his conviction. He said the Huffstetter party had more money than he, and could bribe Lowry to testify as he did. He was not in good health; had been paralyzed in the right foot and arm. His mill burned down shortly after his arrest and lost all of his money with it. He said there had been considerable feeling against him on political grounds, but he and Squire Huffstetter, Jeff's father, were of the same party, and the Squire loaned him $2,000 a short time before the murder. He expressed a hope that he would be pardoned soon."

For years it must have seemed incomprehensible that Bent Jones would ever leave prison alive. Yet he continued to deny his guilt while his friends and family worked behind the scenes to arrange for his pardon or parole. By the time eighteen years of jail time had passed, there was finally reason for Bent to be hopeful.

While the Tolliver family continued to thrive in Orange and Lawrence counties, most of the Moodys had literally died out. Of the nine children born to Alexander and Mezza Moody, only one remained alive by 1889 and he lived in Illinois. Mary Ann "Polly" Moody, whose short and ill-fated marriage to William Toliver had started the feud, died in 1882 – the same year as her brother, William Moody. Joseph had died in 1874, before the murder of Tom, and his fellow life-long bachelor brother John expired in 1888. John had sold the family home on Washington Street to local grocer John H. Steers in 1883. Their only other sister, Betsy, had died at the age of 52 in 1862. Walter Moody had also died at 52 on February 15, 1875 – about two weeks before his brother Tom was murdered. The oldest of the nine children was James, who was 72 years old in 1875 and living southwest of Paoli near Youngs Creek in an area now part of the Hoosier National Forest. James lived until 1883, reaching the age of 80. That left only David, who had moved to Illinois by 1868. A few children and grandchildren remained in the area, but most of them were too young to have experienced the feud first-hand.

Meanwhile, Bent Jones was not a model prisoner, despite apparent efforts to indulge him. An 1885 story in the *Bloomington Saturday Courier* noted "[He] is engaged in the saddlery hardware shops tieing [sic] up packages. He is in poor health and very sullen. The officer say [sic] that he is the hardest man in the prison to please. His work has been changed several times to please him." In 1887 a committee from the Indiana House of Representatives spent two days in Jeffersonville investigating allegations of corruption on the part of Warden A.J. Howard, who had held that post for twelve years. Among the inmates called to testify was Bent Jones. After he was sworn in, Jones said he had been a "trusty" at the prison for "nearly five years". He then presented a lengthy written statement complaining about living conditions ("The new cell-house is a chinchbug harbor... They pretend to give the prisoners pork for dinner four times per week, but the stuff that is given is so fat and strong that not one-fourth of the men eat it...") and accused specific individuals of cruelty, kickbacks, bribery, and theft. Although most inmates who testified were cross-examined by the legislators, the General Assembly's written report noted: "The above sworn statement in writing was delivered to the committee a few moments previous to their adjournment." An audit indicated "a shortage of from $60,000 to $80,000" – as much as $2,159,000 in 2020 dollars. Warden Howard resigned and was held in custody under suicide watch.

In June of 1887 the *Hamilton County Democrat* printed this note:

```
"Bent Jones, a life-time convict from Orange
County, confined in the southern prison, has
been granted a patent on a folding table. The
invention is considered to be very valuable,
and is gotten up on an entire new principle
from others heretofore made. The patent on the
iron castings alone is supposed to be worth
at least $100,000, if the inventor was out of
confinement to properly dispose of them."
```

A.B. Jones had indeed been granted U.S. patent No. 346,660 the previous year for "a new and Improved Folding Table... being more especially designed for use as a lady's work-table, but also applicable to many other uses...". The patent application did not, of course, include the fact that the inventor was serving a life sentence for murder. One month later the *Boonville (IN) Enquirer* noted:

> "John Gladding, of Warrick county, completed a two year sentence for grand larceny at the [Jeffersonville] prison yesterday. He had accepted the position as a traveling salesman for the patent table invented by Bent Jones, a life-time convict. He left yesterday for Evansville, to commence canvassing for orders."

One year later the *Boonville (IN) Standard* mentioned that Alonzo B. Jones had assigned one-half of his folding table patent to "L. Jones of Jeffersonville". This was presumably his brother and fellow inmate Lee, who was still five years away from his eventual release. Nothing more is known about this enterprise although there is no indication that the Jones brother's fortunes were significantly improved.

The August 23, 1887, edition of the *Indianapolis News* published a story that took a circuitous route to address the possibility of a release from prison for two of the convicts. It began:

> "A gentleman familiar with the temper and disposition of the 'White Cap'-infested region of southern Indiana says a peculiarity of the people is that they are influenced by vengeance on the one hand or pity on the other, and the policy of a moderate, even-tempered and inflexible enforcement of the law never commends itself to them. When their blood is up, vengeance is their chief guidance, and their disposition either runs to mob violence or else their worst passions are stirred to make a legal prosecution of the offense,

> vindictive instead of just; and yet this same people, after their blood has cooled, will readily join in an appeal to the authorities to lessen the punishment of the convicted, and so in this way a spirit has been inculcated which has led to defiance of the courts on the one hand, and a feeling of contempt for law on the other, that is now showing itself in these 'White Cap' disturbances. Orange county and the surrounding district is generally racked by some matter of turbulence which frequently takes months to suppress, and even now there is an effort making to secure the pardon by the governor for two of the greatest offenders in the county of Orange, who figured in a vendetta, the bitterness of which has had no parallel, save perhaps in that now raging in Rowan county, Kentucky. And one of the families concerned in the Indiana vendetta was originally from Kentucky and connected by blood with the Tollivers, so conspicuous in the Rowan turbulence."

While actual White Cap vigilantes were not credibly associated with the Moody-Tolliver Feud, the article is correct in its observation about an inclination "to lessen the punishment of the convicted" – in this case, Eli Lowry and Bent Jones. There was apparently no thought yet of releasing the triggerman, Lee Jones. The reference to Kentucky involved what is commonly known as the Rowan County War, although it is sometimes referred to as the Tolliver-Martin Feud. Twenty men were killed and another sixteen wounded in violence that continued between 1884 and 1887 in the vicinity of Morehead, Kentucky. It was a complicated and deadly affair that resulted in the death of several Tolliver men and related family members, including Craig Burton Tolliver, their faction's most prominent leader. But the newspaper was wrong about the origins of William and Delana Toliver's family. They came to Indiana from Alabama. Over the years there were other claims that the Southern Indiana Tolivers were related to the Tollivers in Kentucky. That might be true going back a few generations, but I could find no conclusive evidence that they were direct kinfolk or even acquainted.

The *Indianapolis News* article concluded with some new accusations and confirmation that a plea for Jones's pardon had been filed:

> "The final conviction occurred but a few years ago... and it cost the state a good many thousand dollars before the cold-blooded crime was traced to a final conclusion. It is this which excites the surprise of the gentleman interviewed by The News reporter, for it is a matter of grave wonder to him why the very men then hounding for the conviction of the Joneses and Tollivers should now be working to secure the pardon of Lowery and 'Bent' Jones. He believes, however, that is being done without the knowledge of the law-and-order people of that section. Before 'Bent' Jones became involved in this vendetta, he figured as a member of the 'regulators' of this district, and he certainly participated in the lynching of two thieves at Lost River bridge some years before. It is supposed, also, that he was the leader of the hanging of a negro at Mitchell, who was suspected on no very substantial grounds of horse-stealing. This aided him when he was drawn into difficulty, for many of the best citizens were forced to come to his relief, because they were concerned in these lynchings, and probably had been associated with him in other deeds of violence. The plea for the pardon of Jones, as filed with the governor, is that he is getting old and is in failing health, and for Lowery, that he was a young man at the time of his association with the Tolliver gang, and so completely under their influence that he was afraid to run counter to their wishes. Then again, he was only privy to the plot to kill Moody, not being present when the murder was committed. Jones is said to have secured the signatures

of eleven of the jurors who convicted him, and of the prosecutors and other state officials, and of a large proportion of those who backed and financially aided the prosecution, and to have strong hopes that he will be released. However, The News's informant feels confident that if the governor will call for a record of the trial, and read the evidence submitted, all of which are included in the appeals to the supreme court, he will be slow to exercise clemency in that direction.

In talking with the governor with relation to these cases the chief executive told the representative of The News that he should proceed with great caution. He regarded the crime committed by these men as the worst in the criminal category – cold-blooded, cowardly assassinations, and while it is his duty to consider every petition for pardon that comes before him, he did not talk as if he were prejudiced in favor of these persistent petitioners."

Four days later the *Indianapolis Journal* reported that "Governor Gray has received [another] petition for the pardon of Bent Jones and Eli Lowery, who are serving life sentences in the Jeffersonville Penitentiary for the murder of Thomas Moody, in Orange County, which was the culmination of one of the most desperate family feuds in the history of the State." Less than one month after this article was published Governor Gray – aka "the Sisyphus of the Wabash" – granted Lee Jones a prison furlough to attend his wife's funeral in Mitchell – but he did not issue a pardon or parole for Eli Lowry or either of the Jones brothers.

In 1889 a correspondent of the *Cincinnati Enquirer* visited Bent at the Indiana Prison South in Jeffersonville. The original account began: "Bent Jones. A name associated with the deadliest feud ever waged in Indiana." After a sketchy summary of past events, the writer added:

> "Jones has now been in prison thirteen years, and seems to be resigned to his fate. He declares himself innocent of the crime for which he was convicted, and promises some startling revelation should he ever secure his liberty.
>
> Jones enjoys, or did enjoy, the distinction of having whipped Mood [sic] in a rough and tumble fight. He is employed in the wood-working department, having recently invented a folding table, which is a triumph of mechanism, and which would be worth a fortune to him were he out of prison."

There would be no further mention of the promised "startling revelation."

When the *Bloomington Courier* reprinted the prison visit story it was noted that the *Enquirer* correspondent had neglected to mention the Monroe County connection:

> "The correspondent omits to state that the final act of this tragedy was given in this county in the trial of the parties connected with it."

This was followed with a brief but substantially correct account of the Bloomington trials and Parks Toliver's escape. However, this is also one of the reports that incorrectly claimed that Parks had "returned to his home in Mitchell where he died." It also stated that "The wives of Bent and Lee Jones who stood by them so faithfully during the trial afterwards secured divorces." Bent's wife, the former Clarissa Toliver, had reportedly remarried by 1893, but no record could be found of a divorce between Lee Jones and his wife, Louisa, prior to her death in 1887.

In 1889 the *Cincinnati Enquirer* reported that Bent Jones, while still in prison, had been granted a U.S. military pension of eight dollars per month for his service during the Civil War.

The first indication that the wages of sin might be eventual pardon or parole came on Christmas Day, 1890, when a new

Republican governor, Alvin P. Hovey, pardoned Eli Lowry. When Hovey died the following year his successor, Lieutenant Governor Ira J. Chase, took no further action on petitions for the pardon of Lee and Bent Jones. That changed after Democratic farmer Claude Matthews took office in 1893. On July 20 of that year Governor Matthews pardoned Lee Jones, the man convicted for pulling the triggers in the Thomas Moody murder. That prompted widespread rumors that Bent would soon join his brother as a free man.

Those rumors came true just three months later, on October 23, 1893, when Governor Matthews ordered the release of Bent Jones. There was a noticeable difference between the petition submitted in support of Bent and that of his brother. Lee had gathered the support of the presiding judge, prosecuting attorney, ten jurors, fifty-one named prominent citizens, and 284 others. Bent's petition, submitted on an identical printed form, listed no judge, prosecutor, or juror and a total of only eighteen names alongside conspicuous blank spaces. Milton Moore, founder and president of the Bank of Mitchell, is listed twice, apparently due to a clerical error. First on the list was Moses Clinton, one of Jones's cohorts ordered to leave town by the "vigilants" sixteen years earlier. Other names included his leading advocate, S.J. Glover, his former defense attorney J.W. Gordon, two saloon owners, and other prominent citizens. The reasons given for his pardon were:

1. "Belief he has been sufficiently punished if guilty. Doubt of his guilt."
2. "Think he deserved a pardon and will make a good citizen."

Regardless, Bent's pardon was just as final as that of his brother. In fact, his proclamation didn't even include the "conditionally" notation added to Lee's pardon. Press reports said that one of Bent's two sons brought him the "joyous tidings... with unspeakable joy".

Lee Jones had told the governor "that the crime was committed by a lawless element which Moody opposed, and that it aided in the prosecution of the Joneses to shift the responsibility of the crime. He charged that members of the element were placed on the jury, and that money was furnished for the employment of counsel." There was no explanation why this "element" was not identified during the lengthy trial process other than a futile and discredited attempt to direct blame at Jeff Huffstetter.

Bent Jones had previously announced that he would refuse parole until his much younger brother was released. Of course, nobody had offered to release him before Lee. The story was that "friends had endeavored" to have his case considered first, but that Bent was opposed, saying that Lee – the man convicted of firing the fatal shots – had not participated in the assassination. While that may have been pious, self-serving, and a downright lie, it clearly impressed Governor Matthews, who issued this statement:

> "The closing chapter of the Jones-Moody difficulty shows one of the best phases of manhood that I have ever known. Benton Jones had been in the prison for seventeen years, but he declined to receive his liberty until his younger brother had been provided for. An exhibition of such devotion has not been shown in prison history to my knowledge. I believe that he will become a worthy citizen."

The public relations success of this calculated charade can be measured by a headline that appeared two days after the pardon in the *Middletown (NY) Daily Argus*:

A MAGNANIMOUS MURDERER
Indiana's Governor, in Pardoning Him,
Lauds His Devotion.

Two days after his parole Bent Jones and his youngest son, John, were reported to have returned to Mitchell where "many friends and citizens" welcomed him home. A few days later he was visiting family and friends in Salem, Indiana. On December 9 the *Bloomington Saturday Courier* noted:

> "Bent Jones was here over Sunday to see Mr. Burton the pension examiner on business connected with a patent in which they are both interested. The patent is on a saddle-tree and is the work of Mr. Jones while he was in prison. It is said that the prison contractors at Jeffersonville are now making the saddle-trees at the rate of 50 a day and Messrs. Jones and Burton are to receive $1.00 a dozen royalty. Mr. Jones has just returned from Washington City where he went to get his patent papers. He was considered the most skillful mechanic in the prison, and the officers did not know how they would get along without him when he was pardoned recently. In appearance he has changed but little since he was sent to prison about seventeen years ago. His wife is still living, but married again."

That made Bent Jones appear to be a new man – a talented entrepreneur with prosperity on the horizon. This patent could not be located, but it would not be his last invention.

The spiritualism movement had reached its peak during this time, with millions of Americans convinced that the dead could communicate with the living. In February of 1894 a series of advertisements appeared in the *Bedford Daily Mail* promoting the upcoming appearance of Dr. Charles Slade, "the famous spirit medium" at the Grand Opera House in Bedford. Slade was said to have "appeared before the crowned heads of Europe, and for sixteen months held open light seances at the Egyptian Hall, London, England." He promised "phenomenal manifestations of a startling nature". Among the "fair audience" for the February 21 appearance were Bent Jones and his son, John. Ponder for a moment what messages from the dead a man who four months earlier was serving a life sentence for murder might have anticipated. But he and the audience were to be disappointed. A review in the *Daily Mail* said that "the gentleman whose real or alleged name is Dr. Chas. Slade" was substituting for Kate Fox, one of the nationally renowned Fox sisters, who was said to be absent due to illness. That was an understatement. Kate Fox, who had renounced spiritualism in 1888, had died two years previously. The newspaper claimed that "Instead of calling up the 'spirits' as was expected, Slade gave an exposure of the jugglery and humbug of which state spiritualism largely consists... Some of 'Slade's' sleight of-hand work was good, and some was very common."

Social notices in the Bedford newspapers chronicle several short visits from Bent over the next two years, but in 1896 he was busy in his hometown of Mitchell:

> "Bent Jones and F.B. Wells have bought Chas. W. Burton's Monon restaurant, and will make improvements in the business."

The "improvements" would eventually include a saloon. Then, just three years after being released from prison on a murder conviction, Bent Jones ran for city marshal. He finished third in a four-man race with 16% of the vote. With his law enforcement career thwarted, in 1897 Bent was granted a liquor license. Predictably, he was soon back in trouble. According to the December 10, 1897, edition of the *Mitchell Commercial*:

> "The State of Indiana vs. Alonzo B. Jones is the title of a case in Justice Jones' court to-day. Murtagh O'Donoghue is the complaining witness, and he alleges that Jones assaulted him for failing to liquidate an account for liquids drank."

On June 9, 1898, the *Mitchell Commercial* noted: "Those burglars tried to get into the Gold Mine and Bent Jones' saloon but failed. Must be local amateurs." But on October 26 the *Jeffersonville Evening News* reported that a very serious dispute with a saloon patron had left him near death:

"BENT JONES
Probably Fatally Stabbed in a Saloon Fight.

> Bent Jones, a former inmate of the Indiana State Prison South, is lying at his home in Mitchell in a serious condition from a knife thrust in his throat, inflicted by a man named Dawson. It is believed Jones will die although he may last for several days."

The report added: "Since leaving here [Jeffersonville] Jones is said to have become surly and ready to raise a quarrel at any time. He also drinks hard."

The *Ellettsville Farm* included a similarly terse prognosis:

> "Bent Jones of Mitchell, who was sent to the southern prison on charge of murdering old man Moody, got into a fight Friday night at Mitchell and got his throat cut. It is believed he will die."

On October 27 the *Mitchell Commercial* offered a hometown perspective:

"THROAT CUT.

> The evil that follows in alcohol's train was made horribly apparent last Sunday afternoon when Jack Dawson, the blacksmith at the crusher and Bent Jones, formerly proprietor of the Peoples' saloon, had a bloody and probably a fatal fight. Some days previous they had disputed over an old bar bill and Dawson as he met Jones on the street would not speak in response to his salutation whereupon Jones said, 'D—n you I'll make you speak" at the same time reaching for his gun. He was intoxicated and slower than ordinary and to this fact Dawson probably owes his life for Jones is fearless and a good shot but before he could get action, Dawson whipped out a

common pocket knife, opened the little blade and made a thrust at Jones' throat. The knife blade sank deep, narrowly missing the carotid artery but severing the large muscle on the left side of the neck and cutting across some of the veins.

Dawson was taken into custody and surgeons attended Jones whose condition is precarious owing to the difficulty in staunching the flow of blood while uniting the severed blood vessel.

Dawson is in Bedford jail to await trial and Jones and the surgeons are making a heroic effort to prolong life. Jack Dawson is a blacksmith from New Albany and while fond, too fond, of whiskey, was not considered a bad man."

The *Bedford Mail* reported that Bent was not a compliant patient:

"Jones was badly hurt. He was placed under the charge of surgeons, who succeeded in stopping the flow of blood and sewing up the wound; but during the night Jones got drunk again and torn the stitches out of the wound, which renewed blooding [sic]. He is in a precarious condition today... Bent Jones is well known to the people of Southern Indiana. He is both intelligent and vicious and in his prime terrorized the south part of this county. Though now old, and shorn of his prestige, he is still a dangerous man to quarrel with."

One week later the *Commercial* reported that Bent's condition had improved considerably:

"Bent Jones, while far from well, is recovering and able to be out on the street. Mr. Jones says he was not drunk and the attack on him was entirely unprovoked."

On November 10 Jack Dawson was tried before Bedford Mayor Johnson. He was acquitted and released.

Bent Jones did not die, but only because of a case of mistaken identity. Within three weeks of getting his throat cut, another man had tried to kill him, as reported in the November 17, 1898, edition of the *Mitchell Commercial*:

"MURDERED!
John Flora Killed Jesse O. Burton Monday

Last Monday [November 14], Jesse O. Burton, a respectable young farmer residing near Mt. Horeb, came to town to sell a load of turkeys and transact other business. While waiting for his team to eat he took a walk, starting at Burton's drug-store eastward thence past the Putnam [House hotel] past the Grand [Hotel] to the People's Saloon corner and there he turned north to go back to Main street. He stopped for a brief moment to watch Will Munson who was pasting bills on the big bill boards between the People's and Burton's saloon, then he walked on, little dreaming that he was approaching his doom and as he got opposite the door of Shube Burton's saloon a murderous sheet of flame and shot burst forth striking him on his right side, shattering his arm and lacerating his bowels in a fearful manner.

As Burton heard the fearful roar and felt the pain he turned and saw a man run up the alley. He swayed unsteadily and fell to the ground, writhing in agony. At first those on the street feared to go to the rescue, thinking more shots might be in waiting, but at length willing hands and tender hearts came to his relief.

He was taken to Dr. Byrns' office where an examination was made by Drs. Walls and Byrns who pronounced the wounds fatal and gave him but a short time to live. When asked who did the shooting, he said, "one of the Flora boys." Frank was taken into his presence but he did not think that he was the man. John Flora was shown him and he said "that's the man."

John at first denied his guilt but finally confessed that he had fired the fatal shot but thought he had shot Bent Jones. He had been waiting for a chance to shoot Jones and as each wore a long overcoat and started from the People's Saloon corner about the same time, Flora thought he had killed his man. He expressed sorrow that he had killed an innocent man and one that he did not know. He was also sorry that he had not killed Jones whom he had come up town prepared to slay.

Jesse was taken to the home of his aunt, Mrs. J.K. Hughes on west Main street where everything that could be, was done, to relieve his sufferings. He died Tuesday morning about 9 o'clock, conscious almost to the very last. He was ready to die and cooly gave such instructions to his wife and parents concerning his temporal affairs as were needed.

The funeral was held at Mt. Horeb church yesterday afternoon. Fifteen carriages besides a big buckboard with fifteen of our leading business men attended the funeral in a body. There is not a man, woman or child in Mitchell but what deplores this unfortunate tragedy and all say let there be no temporizing with this man who has shed innocent blood."

The following day's edition of the *Bedford Democrat* began its coverage with:

"Another murder is charged up to the account of Lawrence County. The victim in this instance being an inoffensive young man, whose character is in every way above reproach... About a year ago Flora went to work for Jones, his duty being to open up the saloon of a morning, and later he became Jones' regular barkeeper, a

> position he held until a short time ago, when he was discharged, Jones claiming that he had been robbing him... Flora claims that Jones had made threats that he would kill him, that he considered Jones a dangerous man and feared him, that he had even been afraid to come up town for some time, and finally he concluded that he would stand it no longer, and went up to town to lay in wait for Jones."

The *Bedford Daily Mail* added that when Flora was taken before Burton he exclaimed, "My God! I never meant to shoot you. I thought it was Jones."

Flora was arrested and brought to Bedford where he appeared before Squire Dillman. He pleaded guilty to shooting with intent to kill and was sent to the Lawrence County jail when he was unable to make a $5,000 bond. When word arrived the next morning that Burton had died, the charge was changed to murder. Then Sheriff Dobbins got word that "a mob was being formed in the neighborhood between Georgia and Huron for the purpose of lynching Flora... Many people scouted the idea, believing it to be next to impossible to scare up a mob in Lawrence County to lynch a man." Local law enforcement were so sufficiently convinced of that possibility that the sheriff arranged for a train to Bloomington to make a special stop so he could surreptitiously escort his prisoner on board. The *Democrat* claimed that "Flora, Tuesday night, was perhaps the worst scared man who ever left Bedford. He was so badly frightened on the way to the train that his knees knocked together and he could scarcely walk without assistance." But John Flora's train ride had just begun. Marshal Russell of Bloomington escorted him on the midnight train to Jeffersonville, by way of Indianapolis, where he was placed in the Indiana State Prison "for safe keeping."

Three days later the *Louisville Courier-Journal* offered Flora's perspective:

"KILLED WRONG MAN
John Flora Laments His Bloody Crime.
HE LAY IN AMBUSH
Threatened By a Mob and Brought To the Jeffersonville Reformatory To Escape It.
DESCRIBES HOW HE DID IT.

When a Courier-Journal reporter called upon John Flora, who had been brought to the Indiana Reformatory, in Jeffersonville, for safe-keeping, he looked like a hunted beast. At every noise he trembled, his eyes started, and it was with difficulty that he talked. He does not even feel safe from a mob's vengeance within the strong walls of the Reformatory, but he is perfectly secure from an army of men.

'Poor Jesse Burton; I did not mean to kill him,' was Flora's exclamation [sic] of his action in firing the contents of a shotgun into the man's body. 'I did mean to kill old Bent Jones, though. He is the only enemy I have. He accused me of stealing some money. I told him I was innocent. He insisted that I had taken it. Then I resolved to kill him, for he had threatened my life. Why, I staid at home for two or three days for fear he would kill me. At last I decided to end the matter, and I loaded my shotgun. I went to a saloon in Mitchell and stood behind the door waiting for Jones to come along. I frequently peered out, and when I saw a man approaching that I believed to be him, I got ready to shoot. I knew I would have to be quick. Burton's overcoat caused me to make the mistake. It was like the one Jones wears. Without waiting to catch a glimpse of the man's face I pulled the triggers. As Burton fell I discovered my mistake. I do not think I deserve to be lynched.'

> The people of Mitchell are enraged over the killing of Burton, who was a prominent young man. Sheriff Dobbins had to spirit Flora to Bedford, as a mob was forming. From there he was taken to Bloomington. Word came that a mob would arrive on a train and the prisoner was taken to Indianapolis by Constable Russell. He was so nervous he had to be carried to a cell.
>
> Flora is suffering from nervous prostration and is partially paralyzed. By occupation he is a bar-tender. Flora's brother, George Flora, is serving a term in the Reformatory for stealing.
>
> Bent Jones at present conducts a saloon and restaurant in Mitchell..."

The *Courier-Journal* then gave a brief account of the Moody-Tolliver Feud, Jones's murder conviction, and his pardon, adding:

> "At first Bent Jones was a desperate man in prison, but after a time he became reconciled. He was a genius in prison and made all of the machines that were used by the saddle-tree company.
>
> A few days ago at Mitchell, he had a fuss with one Dawson, who cut his throat."

The unfortunate Jesse Burton was a recently married 23-year-old. It would have been difficult to intentionally select a worse victim. The "celebrated Burton family", related by marriage to the Tolivers, were pillars of the community. Three of them were named on the petition for Lee Jones's pardon and two Burtons were listed among those in favor of releasing Bent. Jesse Burton was laid to rest in the same family cemetery as Lee Jones and Tom Toliver.

Bent wasted no time in releasing a letter that appeared in the *Bedford Daily Mail* and other local papers:

"Mr. Editor: —I wish to correct some mistakes published in your paper concerning the shooting of Jesse Burton, mistakes which I think are liable to cause people to think my wrongs were the cause of his death.

In the first place I did not quarrel with Flora. I simply told him in a rough manner that he had stolen my money and he was a low down thief, and I wanted him to get out and stay out of my saloon and after that he came in when he knew I did not want him there almost daily, until Monday morning, he come in and took a seat, smoking a cigar, and I considered that too much audacity for a man who I knew had my money in his pocket and I said to him (but very civilly this time) that I wanted him to get out and do his loafing elsewhere for I did not want any thieves laying around there, and he went out on the walk and swore he would kill me before night. I then put a man to watch him and the man soon reported to me that he had borrowed a gun and taken it in the back way to Shube Burton's saloon, so I walked on the opposite side of the street after that well prepared for him. Now he tries to lighten his crime by saying I had threatened his life and he was afraid of me. There is not a man of any morality who will say he ever heard me threaten any man's life unconditionally nor ever knew me to strike a man with any kind of a weapon, and there is no man afraid of me doing so; and there is no man afraid of me anyway unless he has willfully and maliciously wronged me, and then he is not afraid of me killing him nor using weapons on him. What was Flora lying around my saloon for almost daily if he was afraid of me?

BENT JONES."

One week after the murder Bent Jones was arrested on a charge of illegal sales of liquor. He put up a $200 cash bond with

Sheriff Dobbins and was released pending trial. Four days later the *Louisville Courier-Journal* declared that the man Governor Matthews had thought would prove to be a "worthy citizen" was no longer welcome anywhere in the state:

"EXIT JONES
Terror of Indiana To Leave the State.
CHIEF OF AN OUTLAW BAND.
Sentenced To Life Imprisonment, But Pardoned.
ONCE AN UPRIGHT MAN.

Financially and physically broken down and bent with age, 'Old' Bent Jones, at one time a terror in the counties of Lawrence, Orange and Washington, over in Indiana, has promised to leave the State to escape punishment.

Jones was said to be at the head of the outlaws who killed Dr. Moody, in Lawrence county, in 1876, and with his brother, Lee, and Eli Lowry, a paid servant, was sent to the Jeffersonville prison for life. In the last few years they were released either by pardon or parole. Lee was killed by accident at Mitchell, and Lowry died at Terre Haute.

Bent Jones went back to Mitchell and started a saloon. Brawls were frequent and a few weeks ago he was stabbed and narrowly missed being murdered. Following this came a quarrel with John Flora, who finally went into ambush to kill Jones. While he was on watch he mistook Jesse Burton for his enemy and shot him dead. A mob went after Flora, and he is now in the Jeffersonville Reformatory for safekeeping.

Jones was indicted on two counts for selling liquor on Sunday, and when taken before Judge Martin, at Bedford, Tuesday he wept like a child. He did not want to go to jail to satisfy a fine he could not pay and begged the court for mercy. Judge Martin finally agreed

> to suspend sentence if Jones would promise to leave the State. This he was glad to do, and he is now arranging his few belongings to take his departure.
>
> Twenty-five years ago he was the most influential man in Lawrence county. He had money and friends to back him in all his schemes. He coveted the office of Trustee of the township where he lived, and although he was a Democrat and the county largely Republican he ran for the office and was elected without trouble. With this additional money at his command he became overbearing, and organized a band of outlaws who followed his bidding."

The number of errors in this account re-emphasize the effect of time on the recollections of events nearly a quarter century past. Tom Moody was murdered in 1875, not 1876, in Orange County rather than Lawrence. He was not a doctor, nor was he called that in his lifetime. Bent Jones may have been the most *notorious* man in Lawrence County at one time, but there were certainly more influential residents. After an account of the trials and the 1877 vigilante revolt against Jones and his cohorts, the *Courier-Journal* concluded:

> "This stopped outlawry in the section for many years, but there is again a feeling that the committee's work is needed, and it is probably for this reason that 'Old' Bent Jones desires to get away before John Flora is taken back to Bedford for trial."

An account in the *English (IN) Crawford County Democrat* added that Jones had agreed "to leave Indiana for good" and that "Several weeks ago he came near having his throat cut from ear to ear in a quarrel with an infuriated customer..."

A year later John Flora was convicted of murder in Orange County circuit court and was sentenced to life in prison for the unintended murder of Jesse Burton. On July 27, 1899, the *Mitchell*

Commercial offered additional details about that incident and included an update on the whereabouts of Bent Jones:

> "John Flora intended to shoot Bent Jones and was lying in wait for him with a double-barreled shot gun in Shube Burton's saloon. Jones' saloon was the first door south of Burton's and Flora expected him to pass by but Jesse, who came by and was mistaken for Jones, was shot down.
>
> Jones' life has been a stormy one and he has had more turmoil than usually falls to man. Once an honored citizen filling an enviable position in political and social life, he became entangled in the Moody-Tolliver feud and was sent up for life. He was paroled after seventeen years imprisonment, returned to Mitchell, lived quietly for awhile and then embarked in the saloon business.
>
> John Flora, formerly a section hand on the B. & O., S-W Ry. but who had been partially paralyzed and unable to work on the section was installed as bar tender. Disagreements arose and Jesse Burton… was shot…
>
> Shortly after this, Jones left town and is now living at Natchidoches, La.
>
> The crime sent a thrill of horror over Mitchell and the citizens determined to visit the author of it with punishment. It has come to him, notwithstanding delays, continuances and the visitation of a maniac confined in the Paoli jail, who came near saving the expense of a trial. After a trial he is found guilty and given a life sentence but is to have a re-hearing and so the end is not yet."

John Flora's sentence was upheld and he was sent to the Indiana State Prison North in Michigan City. His brother, Henry Flora, made news in 1900 for being "the only man that has been discharged from the Reformatory by expiration of sentence for some time." A story in the *Jeffersonville Evening News* added new details to John Flora's ordeal after he killed Jesse Burton by mistake. He had been confined with "an insane person" named Sherman Walls who was awaiting transportation to "the insane hospital." Flora was beaten so badly with a wooden poker used in the jail stove that he was able to convince many people that he was in no condition to stand trial. The headline read:

"FLORA'S MIND IS ABOUT TO GO LAPSE.
Slayer of Jesse Burton on the Verge of Becoming a Maniac.
Talks Incoherently and Stares Like a Madman at His Visitors.
Bent Jones Only Enemy He Had"

John Flora eventually admitted that he had been "shamming" and would serve about eight years of his life sentence before dying in prison. A newspaper story reporting that his remains had been returned to Mitchell for burial added the helpful note that Flora had been "near sighted". He was buried at the Mitchell City Cemetery.

Bent Jones may have been gone from Mitchell, but he was not forgotten. In fact, the quarrelsome saloon owner left behind an ironic legacy, as reported by the *Indianapolis News* on June 20, 1900:

"A VERY DRY TOWN
Mitchell Has Wiped Out All the Saloons.
(Special to The Indianapolis News)

MITCHELL, Ind., June 20 - For the first time in its history this town is without a saloon. There is great rejoicing among the temperance people, for during the past Mitchell has had a reputation for murderous feuds that was scarcely equaled by old Kentucky, and the saloon was always a prominent factor in the record of bloodshed and crime. The last tragedy was the killing of Jesse Burton by John Flora, who was lying in wait for Bent Jones, against whom he had a grudge. Flora is now serving a life sentence at Michigan City, while his enemy, Bent Jones, is in Louisiana. As a result of the indignation caused by the wanton killing of an innocent man, 615 voters out of a total of 832 signed a remonstrance against the issuance of licenses to any one. Not content with that, the Anti-Saloon League put up a straight temperance ticket, and elected every man. The county commissioners held that the "agency" arrangement was valid, the various remonstrances were sustained, and Mitchell is, for the first time in its history, a "dry town."

On December 8, 1898, the *Mitchell Commercial* stated simply: "Bent Jones has gone to Shreveport, La.". By early the following year he had moved 75 miles southeast to Natchitoches, Louisiana. At the time there were just over 33,000 residents in the entire parish, but numbered among them was Bent's son John, now known as J. Wesley Jones, and his growing family. The 1900 federal census showed "J. Wesley Jones", his wife Stella, four children ranging in age from nine months to twelve years, and "father" Alonzo B. Jones living in a rented house on Second Street. Bent's marital status was "widowed", suggesting the possibility that the reportedly re-married Clarissa Toliver Jones was deceased. His age was listed as 67 years – although he was only 62 – and his occupation was "carpenter".

John Wesley Jones's occupation was listed as "Book Agt". On February 28, 1899, Bent, his son "J. Wesly [sic] Jones", and a man named Walter S. Trichel had appeared before a notary public to sign the legal paperwork forming a Natchitoches-based corporation called The Growers Guide Co., Ltd. According to public notices printed for several weeks in the *Natchitoches Enterprise*, its purpose was to "acquire, by purchase or otherwise, the sole and exclusive control of a book or publication known as and sold under the name of The Growers Guide." They would "employ agents, solicitors, and salesmen" to sell and distribute this publication. They would issue up to 250 shares of stock at $100 per share. J.W. Jones would serve as president, Alonzo B. Jones would be vice-president, and Mr. Trichel was named secretary and treasurer. The only other board member was Bent's ill-fated brother-in-law Thomas J. Toliver, who was living in Washington, Indiana. No further details have been found about this business venture.

There was another potential source of income: in 1900 the United States Patent Office issued patent No. 649,129 to Alonzo B. Jones and John Wesley Jones of Natchitoches, Louisiana, for a new and improved Stalk-Cutter. This was a heavy-duty rotary cutting device designed to remove vines and other underbrush. As with the earlier patents for a coffee grinder and folding table, it is not known if this invention ever went into production and on to market.

The next printed reference to Bent Jones appeared in a social note from the *Salem (IN) Leader* that was reprinted on September 21, 1905, in the *Orleans Progress-Examiner*:

> "Benton Jones, who formerly resided at Mitchell, and at one time was a prominent citizen and business man of that place, is visiting Salem relatives and friends. On the 22nd of June, 1876, Thomas Woody [sic] was murdered at Orleans, being shot from ambush with a double barreled shot gun loaded with buck shot. Jones, Lowery and others were implicated and sentenced to prison, Jones serving sixteen years 4 months and 10 days. His sentence was for life but Gov. Matthews pardoned him. Mr. Jones spends most of his time traveling, having recently returned from a trip through the west. He was 39 years of age when sentenced to prison and is now 67. He claims that he had nothing whatever to do with the killing of Woody [sic]."

Once again, the errors in this report point to the passage of time and resulting lack of accurate information. Not only was Tom Moody's last name wrong, but the actual date of his murder was March 2, 1875.

Little information had previously been known regarding the whereabouts of Alonzo Benton Jones following his agreement to avoid jail by leaving Indiana in late 1898. New research for this book discovered his move to Louisiana and the 1905 visit to Salem, Indiana, most likely to visit his sister, Mary M. Giles. This story would not be complete, however, without knowing where and how Bent Jones spent the remainder of his life. It took years of work and more than a little luck to find the answer, which requires some background information.

After the Civil War, veterans who had volunteered for service were not eligible for medical care at facilities dedicated to active career military personnel. One of the last acts signed by President Abraham Lincoln before his assassination was legislation to create what was initially known as the National Asylum for Disabled Volunteer Soldiers and Sailors of the Civil War. A few years later that name was shortened to the National Home for Disabled Volunteer Soldiers. By 1929 there were ten branches distributed geographically across the United States, including one in Marion, Indiana. These facilities would eventually be merged into the U.S. Veterans Administration system.

Admission to what were more commonly known as "Old Soldiers Homes", was voluntary and veterans could request permission to live in the location of their choice. Residents could check themselves out at any time and could apply for readmission later. The men were issued blue uniforms and were assigned to a "company" under the supervision of a sergeant. Bugle calls awakened them each morning, called them to meals in the dining hall, and sounded "lights out" at night.

On December 16, 1906, Alonzo B. Jones was admitted to one of the National Homes for Disabled Volunteer Soldiers. He chose not to defy the court by returning to Indiana. Instead, Bent Jones became a resident of the Pacific Branch in sunny Sawtelle, California. That location is now part of the Los Angeles metropolitan area – about halfway between Beverly Hills and Santa Monica. The facility was home to more than one thousand veterans by 1900 and covered 500 acres, plus a twenty-acre cemetery and a new hospital. Renowned architect Stanford White is said to have designed the original barracks, while palm trees, pines, and eucalyptus groves were planted as part of the landscaping. By the time Bent arrived it was a regular stop for tourists on streetcar tours. Real estate developers were already building residential subdivisions nearby.

There is no doubt that he was a veteran of the Union army. The official register at Sawtelle states that Alonzo B. Jones enlisted in Company I of the 50th Indiana Infantry at Mitchell, Indiana, on November 15, 1861. He was discharged on January 5, 1865, in Indianapolis. Bent's rank was listed as "Musc." This was confirmed by official military rosters and a one-paragraph note on the front page of the *New Albany Daily Ledger-Standard* on June 9, 1877 – about one week after his conviction for first-degree murder – written by the paper's Salem, Indiana, correspondent:

> "Bent Jones, of murder notoriety, was for a long time a resident of this county. His father was considered pretty hard, but Bent was looked upon as a good boy. Bent was chief bugler of the 50th Indiana regiment, and belonged to Capt. A.H. Miller's company."

By the time he arrived at the facility, more than forty years after the Civil War had ended, the definition of "disability" had been expanded to take into consideration the age and infirmity of many applicants. In Jones's case the "kind and degree of disability" was given as "chronic rheumatism" contracted in January 1862 at Camp Wickliffe in Larue County, Kentucky. During his residence in California, Bent Jones was also treated for "hypertropy of prostate" – an enlarged prostate gland – and "senility".

The official register at the home includes vital statistics and descriptions of each resident. Bent was listed as a 68-year-old widower, born in Ohio. His occupation was "carpenter", his religion was "Protestant", and he was able to read and write. Bent's height was 5 feet, 5 ½ inches – three and a half inches shorter than listed on his Indiana State Prison admission log. Weight was not a category on this standard form. His complexion was "fair", he had gray eyes and his hair had turned gray. Next of kin were his son, John W. Jones, whose address was given as Durango, Colorado, and his sister, Mary M. Giles, of Salem, Indiana. Bent Jones's pension rate while residing at the home was $30.00 per month, but he instructed that $8.00 be sent monthly to his sister in Salem.

The 1910 U.S. census located the Pacific Branch of the National Home for Disabled Volunteer Soldiers as part of Malibu township in Los Angeles County. Bent Jones, now 72, was still listed as an "inmate". According to his record he never checked himself out after he was admitted.

It isn't known why John Wesley Jones was in Colorado in 1906 nor how long he stayed, but he and his family had joined Bent in California no later than 1909 – although it isn't clear how much (if any) contact he had with his father. John Wesley Jones's obituary appeared in the *Los Angeles Times* the day after he died at the California Hospital on October 2, 1909. No cause of death was given. The rest of the family was recorded in the 1910 federal census as living in a rental house at 1438 15th Street in Santa Monica. Curiously, the head of household was "J. Wesley Jones", but this person was clearly designated as "Female" and "Widowed". Since he was dead, and his wife Stella was living but not listed among the family members, there must have been either some confusion or deliberate deception. Also living in the house were nineteen-year-old son Roland, fifteen-year-old Dorothy, and ten-year-old daughter Weslie. The enigmatic "J. Wesley" was unemployed, but Roland was listed as an "apprentice cable splicer".

In 1919 Bent's granddaughter, Dorothy Jones, married a New Albany, Indiana, native named Roscoe Conkling Sarles. He was a pioneer race car driver; less than a month before the marriage he had competed in the Indianapolis 500. In the 1920 federal census Stella Jones reappears as part of the new couple's household on West 43rd Place in Los Angeles. Roscoe's occupation was given as "Auto Racor". Weslie, now twenty years old, was working as a stenographer at a music store. Mother-in-law "Estella" was recorded as a fifty-year-old widow.

By this time, however, Alonzo B. Jones had finally drawn his last breath. On June 12, 1918 – more than forty-three years after the murder of Thomas Moody; twenty-five years past his pardon from a life sentence in prison; and almost twenty years since he had been declared "physically broken down and bent with age" when ordered by a judge to leave the state of Indiana – "Old" Bent Jones died at the Old Soldiers Home in Los Angeles at the probable age of 79. No cause of death was listed in the record; there is merely an asterisk. According to the official register, he had $5.35 in cash when he died, along with $180.00 in accumulated pension money. His total personal effects were valued at only thirty-five cents.

The old soldiers who died at the home were buried in the nearby Los Angeles National Cemetery. It is the final resting place of 85,715 United States military veterans and spouses (as of 2020), including fourteen Medal of Honor recipients. There, in section 36, row G, plot 20, lie the remains of "the terror of Indiana". His military headstone reads:

ALONZO B JONES
MUSICIAN
CO I
50TH IND
INF
JUN 12 1918

At his murder trial in 1877, prosecutor George W. Friedley suggested an epitaph for Bent Jones when he paraphrased part of a poem by Lord Byron:

"And when thou fain would weary heaven with prayer
Look on Moody's grave and despair.
Down to the dust, and as thou rot'st away
Even worms shall perish on thy poisonous clay…"

Afterword

In 1912 the *Orleans Progress-Examiner* remembered the Moody-Tolliver Feud with a story that included a description of the Moody family farmhouse that was attacked in 1871: "For years afterward the effect of the attempted assassination could be seen in the residence which was a log structure. The log ceiling and joists were filled with slugs of iron, nails, and buckshot." That home was rebuilt and remodeled several times before it had to be demolished in 2018 when the structure became dangerously unstable.

The home in Orleans where Thomas Moody was murdered is also no longer standing, although some foundation stones were still visible on the otherwise vacant lots 247 and 248 on West Washington Street in 2020. The same 1912 Orleans newspaper story noted that "[S]ome of the bullit marks, if not covered and painted over now, were for years visible in the door facing." A local source told me that floorboards just inside the door were still faintly stained with blood as late as 1981.

Tom Moody's final resting place is unknown. No details regarding his funeral or burial could be found. This might have been intentional given that Joshua Younger had testified that Bent Jones told him he wanted Thomas Moody's skull, bones, and "hide" to make household utensils and clothing accessories. Eli Lowry added that on the night after the murder Bent was offering $300 for Moody's scalp.

There is evidence that some members of the Moody and

Wright families were buried together on the Wright family farm in the early to mid-nineteenth century, but at some point the Wright burials were moved to Liberty Cemetery in Orleans while the Moody graves remained on private property. Regardless, the location of graves for Thomas, Polly, James, William, John, and Joseph Moody remain elusive.

George W. Friedley, the Bedford attorney whose seven-hour speeches were effective in securing a conviction of Bent Jones and his brother, Lee, was offered the governorship of Wyoming in 1882 by President Chester A. Arthur. He declined the honor and took a position as legal counsel for the Louisville, New Albany & Chicago Railroad. He dropped dead at the National Hotel in Bloomington (while reading the *Louisville Courier-Journal*) in 1889 at the age of 49. His friend Daniel O. Spencer accompanied Friedley's body on the train taking him home to his grand funeral and burial in Bedford's Green Hill Cemetery.

Judge A.C. Voris left the legal profession and, as founder of the Dark Hollow Stone Company, became a pioneer of the stone industry in Indiana. He was a founder and long-time president of the Citizens National Bank of Bedford. "Arch" Voris died in 1911 and is also buried at Green Hill Cemetery.

Prosecutor Robert W. Miers was later a state representative and served as a member of the board of trustees of Indiana University. He was judge of the tenth judicial district in Indiana from 1883 until 1896, when he was elected to the U.S. Congress, where he served until 1905. He was buried at Rose Hill Cemetery in Bloomington.

Professor Cyrus F. McNutt moved to Terre Haute, where he was elected as Superior Court judge for Vigo County before he moved to California in 1896. McNutt died in 1912 and is buried at the Evergreen Cemetery in Los Angeles. His grandnephew, Paul Vories McNutt, was elected Governor of Indiana in 1932.

The main buildings of the Indiana State Prison South are still standing, although the site is now officially designated to be in Clarksville rather than Jeffersonville. In 1897 – four years after Bent Jones was pardoned – the facility was renamed as the Indiana

Reformatory and was used exclusively for men between the ages of 16 and 29. Older inmates were transferred to the Prison North in Michigan City. After a fire at the Reformatory in 1918 the state legislature passed a bill making the Michigan City facility the sole Indiana State Prison.

The Colgate-Palmolive company bought the prison site in 1923 and used it as a factory until 2007. During those years Colgate installed what is said to be the world's second-largest functioning clock on top of the former cellblock building. The Colgate Clock is still visible in Clarksville and across the Ohio River in Louisville, although it works only sporadically. The main building has been used for warehouse space, although efforts had been underway to convert it for use as offices or condominiums when a hotel chain announced plans to renovate the site in 2020. That project was delayed indefinitely due to the pandemic.

In 1921 Roscoe Sarles, the young race car driver married to Bent Jones's granddaughter, Dorothy, finished second in the Indianapolis 500 driving a Duesenberg. Nevertheless, Roscoe told his wife and others that 1922 would be his final year of racing. He had begun doing some work for the motion picture studios in Los Angeles and his plan was to return to California to work full-time as a stunt driver. In September 1922 he agreed to a final race at a new high-banked track in Kansas City. A mechanical malfunction caused a multi-car accident and Sarles's car jumped the top rail, dropped 25 feet and trapped him beneath the wreckage. According to the *Sacramento Union*:

> "Persons who reached the car a few seconds after the accident found Sarles still alive. He begged for assistance, they said, but before they could help him, flames enveloped the wreckage."

Sarles died in the fire. He was 30 years old. His wife lived until 1976. Dorothy and Roscoe Sarles are both buried in the Hollywood Forever Cemetery in Los Angeles.

One final note: On December 12, 1912, the *Orleans Progress-*

Bob Moody

Examiner published a letter to the editor from E.S. Lynd, a former Indiana resident living in Garland, Wyoming. Garland, located in Park County just east of Yellowstone National Park, had been a boom town a decade earlier but lost population when it was bypassed by a new railroad. Most of the letter gave details of the Wyoming landscape, explained irrigation issues, and described his "farm or ranch they are called here". Then there is this:

> "I enjoy the McCoy history fine, so does A. Jones, a merchant here who left Mitchell, Ind., 40 years ago and went to Nebraska. He has been here six years. He delights to tell me of the old times and of the Bent Jones and Moody scrape of which he was a witness.
>
> He used to run the ax-handle factory at Mitchell 40 years ago and more. He seemed surprised at the change and great improvements around Orleans and Mitchell I tell him of. Said I was the first person he had seen from that country for many years and that it made him homesick to see the old places once more, especially the old caves at Hammer's and Donaldson's or the old Jimmy Lynd cave (a great uncle of my father) it was called then.
>
> Send the Progress-Examiner along regular. I can't do without the home news if it costs $5.00 a year.
>
> Yours truly,
> E.S. Lynd"

"A. Jones" was former saloon owner Abram "Abe" Jones, who was whispering to Bent Jones in a corner of his saloon the night of Tom Moody's murder. He was last seen making a hasty departure from Mitchell to Evansville thirty-six years earlier following robust encouragement by local vigilantes who numbered him among the evil associates of "the terror of Indiana".

Acknowledgments
For the Second Edition

THIS BOOK WOULD NOT EXIST if two people I'd never met had not taken the time to make a phone call forty years ago to tell me about the Moodys in their cornfield. I cannot think of a better place for my ancestors to rest than on Jim and Sheila Salkeld's land.

During a visit to Orleans in 1981 I had the good fortune to meet the late Elma Allegre Payton, who was a direct descendant of Walter Moody. She showed me the house where Tom Moody was killed. I only wish that I had taken photos and asked more questions.

When my car arrived unannounced on Bob Radcliff's driveway, he must have wondered what I was selling. After I explained that the Moody farmhouse, scene of the 1871 firebombing attack, was located on his property, Bob graciously gave me a tour of the site and provided important background information. He also put me in touch with talented local photographer Tamera Noble. With no inkling of the historical significance of the house, she had been attracted by its character and took a series of remarkable photos shortly before its demolition. With her kind permission, some of those photos can be viewed on the "Terror of Indiana" Facebook page.

Roger Moon retired after more than thirty years as a beloved newspaper columnist in Orange and Lawrence counties. His columns about the Moody-Tolliver Feud in the *Bedford Times-Mail* generated feedback that provided valuable information. Roger and his wife, Valerie, continue their work to preserve and protect local history.

Among the most valuable local archives are those at the Lawrence County Museum of History & Edward L. Hutton Research Library in Bedford. Rowena Cross-Najafi, President of the Board of Directors of the Lawrence County Museum of History, and her husband, Reza, are dedicated preservationists and gracious hosts with special knowledge regarding the old county jail where several folks in this book found occasional free accommodation. Library Director Joyce Shepherd became an immediate ally and provided more documentation and encouragement than anyone. Joyce is also a fellow fan of traditional country music. You don't find many librarians with whom you can also discuss Larry Cordle and Junior Brown.

Robert F. Henderson, longtime Orleans Town Clerk, Executive Director of the Orleans Chamber of Commerce, and President of the Orange County Historical Society is the type of historian and preservationist most localities can only wish for. His archives and extensive contacts have been invaluable, and I look forward to working with him to further commemorate the Moody-Tolliver Feud in its proper context.

Danny Woodson and I grew up together in the Fairgrounds neighborhood of Pine Bluff, Arkansas. We both attended Dollarway Elementary, Junior High, and Senior High School (all on the same campus). No person outside of my family has known me longer or knows me better. He read early drafts of this book and kept a backup copy in case of an emergency. Danny's friendship is one of my life's greatest blessings.

Nobody would have enjoyed this book more than my father, Henry John Moody. He and my mother drove more than one thousand miles roundtrip from Arkansas to Orleans to visit the family graves soon after I became aware of them. He had a keen interest in the information I was able to find up until his death in

2008 and I regret that the technology had not yet advanced enough for him to read the rest.

My passion for this story went beyond the normal diligence required to write a book. I felt – and still feel – that portraying the events accurately and bringing fresh attention to an almost forgotten chapter in history was a debt I owed to my ancestors. There were several almost mystical instances of vital information appearing from unexpected sources at just the perfect time. Along the way I came to recognize that the feud was an ordeal for the Tollivers, too, and I have tried to be as fair as possible. The most unforeseen blessings were the friendships and support I have received from several of their descendants.

My wife of more than thirty-three years, Karen, listened to me "thinking out loud" about events that took place nearly 150 years ago and ignored the loud mumbling coming from my desk upstairs. She accompanied me on research trips across Indiana, including memorable visits to Paoli, Orleans, Mitchell, Bedford, Elnora, Washington, and Bloomington, and tolerated the time and expense required to fulfill my family obligation. I am grateful for her patience and hope she is proud of the result.

Bob Moody
Jeffersontown, Kentucky
January 2021

About the Author

Bob Moody is a native of Arkansas and a direct descendant of James Moody (1803-1883), the eldest of Alexander and Mezza Moody's nine children. His nearly fifty-year career as a radio personality and programmer included stops at top-rated stations in San Antonio, Denver, Detroit, Louisville, Shreveport, and Baltimore. He served on the board of directors of both the Academy of Country Music and the Country Music Association and is a member of the Country Music Radio Hall of Fame. In 1990 he was honored as Honorary President of Scotland's Auchinleck Boswell Society. Bob and his wife, Karen, live in Jeffersontown, Kentucky.

For interviews or information on presentations for historical societies, schools, libraries, and civic groups, contact him at bobmoody@bobmoody.com

For photos, illustrations, links, and updates on this book, go to the "Terror of Indiana: Bent Jones & The Moody-Tolliver Feud" Facebook page: https://www.facebook.com/bobmoodybook

Moody-Toliver Feud Timeline

24 Feb 1869	William Toliver marries Mary Ann "Polly" Moody.
17 Aug 1870	William Toliver killed in wagon accident.
30 Sep 1870	Estate sale in Mitchell. Thomas Moody assaulted by Tolivers and Bent Jones.
Mar 1871	Thomas Moody files lawsuits for slander, trespass, and assault.
29 Mar 1871	Settlement of slander suit reported.
25 Jun 1871	Firebombing of the Moody farmhouse.
7 Sep 1872	Indiana Supreme Court upholds judgment in slander case.
9 Apr 1874	Firebombing trial begins in Bedford.
11 Apr 1874	Judge Bicknell orders jury to deliver "not guilty" verdict.
2 Mar 1875	Thomas Moody murdered in Orleans.
31 May 1876	Bent Jones arrested and charged as accessory to murder.
10 Jun 1876	Preliminary examination of Bent Jones concludes.
16 Jun 1876	Bent Jones and Cole Smart released on bail. Lowry and Patterson remain in jail.

23 Jun 1876	Bent Jones, Lee Jones, Eli Lowry, Parks Toliver, and Thomas Toliver indicted for first-degree murder.
29 Jun 1876	Eli Lowry turns "state's evidence" and pleads guilty.
9 Jul 1876	Mob makes early morning attack on Paoli jail. Prisoners return fire.
10 Jul 1876	Joneses and Tolivers transported to New Albany jail.
23 Jul 1876	Vigilantes attack Abe Jones's saloon in Mitchell.
2 Nov 1876	Prisoners returned to Paoli jail.
16 Dec 1876	Habeas corpus hearing begins in Bloomington.
19 Dec 1876	Judge Pearson denies bail for prisoners.
24 Jan 1877	James Murray arrested.
15 May 1877	Trial of Bent Jones begins in Bloomington.
1 Jun 1877	Bent Jones found guilty of first-degree murder.
21 Jun 1877	More than 200 vigilantes post warnings in Mitchell.
6 Oct 1877	Trial of Lee Jones begins in Bloomington.
15 Oct 1877	Lee Jones found guilty of first-degree murder.
13 Mar 1878	All charges against James Murray dismissed.
5 Jun 1878	Trial of Parks Toliver and Tom Toliver begins in Bloomington.
12 Jun 1878	Mistrial declared for Parks Toliver and Tom Toliver.
Apr 1879	Indiana Supreme Court upholds conviction of Bent Jones.
24 Nov 1879	Conclusion of testimony in Toliver retrial.
25 Nov 1879	Parks Toliver escapes from custody in Bloomington.
1 Dec 1881	All charges dismissed against Parks and Tom Toliver.
30 Oct 1885	Eli Lowry's sentence affirmed by Indiana Supreme Court.

10 Sep 1887	Louisa Toliver Jones dies in Mitchell.
25 Dec 1890	Eli Lowry pardoned by Governor Hovey.
20 Jul 1893	Lee Jones pardoned by Governor Matthews.
21 Oct 1893	Bent Jones pardoned by Governor Matthews.
14 Jan 1894	Eli Lowry arrested for robbery in Terre Haute.
13 Dec 1895	Eli Lowry dies in Terre Haute.
22 Jun 1897	Lee Jones killed in industrial accident in Mitchell.
14 Nov 1898	John Flora kills Jesse Burton by mistake.
22 Nov 1898	Bent Jones agrees to leave Indiana in exchange for his freedom.
Jun 1900	Bent Jones listed in federal census at Natchitoches, Louisiana.
5 Oct 1900	Thomas Toliver murdered in Washington, Indiana.
21 Sep 1905	Bent Jones visits his sister in Salem, Indiana.
10 May 1906	Bent Jones admitted to the National Home for Disabled Volunteer Soldiers in Sawtelle, California.
12 Jun 1918	Bent Jones dies in Los Angeles, California.
23 Mar 1926	Dr. Milton Parks Tolliver dies in Elnora, Indiana.

BIBLIOGRAPHY
NEWSPAPERS AND PUBLICATIONS

<u>United States</u>

Albany (NY) Evening Journal

Argos (IN) Reflector

Daily Kennebec Journal (Augusta, ME)

Baltimore (MD) Sun

Deutsche Correspondent (Baltimore, MD)

Batesville (IN) Tribune

Bedford (IN) Daily Mail

Bedford (IN) Banner

Bedford-Mitchell (IN) Banner

Bedford (IN) Democrat

Bedford (IN) Lawrence Mail

Bedford (IN) Mail

Bedford (IN) Progress Examiner

Bedford (IN) Star

Bedford (IN) Weekly Mail

Bloomfield (IN) News

Bloomington (IN) Courier

Bloomington (IN) Gazette

Bloomington (IN) Progress

Bloomington (IN) Republican Progress

Bloomington (IN) Saturday Courier

Bloomington (IN) Telephone

Bloomington (IN) World

Boonville (IN) Enquirer

Boonville (IN) Standard

Boston (MA) Herald

Boston (MA) Post

Bowling Green (IN) Review

National Opinion (Bradford, VT)

Brazil (IN) Democrat

Jackson County Banner (Brownstown, IN)

Buffalo (MO) Reflex

Buffalo (NY) Commercial

Cambridge City (IN) Tribune

Delaware County Daily Times (Chester, PA)

Chicago (IL) Tribune

The Inter-Ocean (Chicago, IL)

Cincinnati (OH) Commercial Tribune

Cincinnati (OH) Daily Gazette

Cincinnati (OH) Enquirer

Cincinnati (OH) Daily Star

Cleveland (OH) Plain Dealer

Clinton (IL) Public

Columbus (IN) Democrat

Columbus (IN) Republic

Der Westbote (Columbus, OH)

Daily Corrine (UT) Reporter

Elkhart (IN) Daily Review

Elkhart (IN) Sentinel

Elkhart (IN) Weekly Review

Ellettsville (IN) Farm

English (IN) Crawford County Democrat

Eureka (NV) Daily Sentinel

Evansville (IN) Journal

Fall River (MA) Daily Evening News

Fort Wayne (IN) Daily News

Fort Wayne (IN) Sentinel

Fort Wayne (IN) Morning Gazette

Daily Fort Worth (TX) Standard

Fredericksburg (IN) Blue River Gazette

Goshen (IN) Weekly News

Greencastle (IN) Banner

Greencastle (IN) Star Press

Greensburg (IN) Standard

Greenville (OH) Democrat

Harrisburg (PA) Telegraph

Hickman (KY) Courier

The Daily Democrat (Huntington, IN)

Indianapolis (IN) Evening News

Indianapolis (IN) Journal

Indianapolis (IN) People

Indianapolis (IN) News

Indianapolis (IN) Sentinel

Indianapolis (IN) Star

Indiana State Sentinel (Indianapolis, IN)

Indianapolis (IN) Times

Jasper (IN) Weekly Courier

Jeffersonville (IN) Daily Evening News

Jeffersonville (IN) National Democrat

Daily Journal of Commerce (Kansas City, MO)

Lafayette (IN) Journal & Courier

Lancaster (MO) Excelsior

Lawrence (KS) Daily Journal

Western Home Journal (Lawrence, KS)

Lincoln (KS) Sentinel

Nebraska State Journal (Lincoln, NE)

Arkansas Democrat (Little Rock, AR)

Logansport (IN) Pharos-Tribune

Loogootee Martin County (IN) Tribune

Los Angeles (CA) Times

Louisville (KY) Daily Commercial

Louisville (KY) Courier-Journal

Martinsville (IN) Weekly Gazette

Memphis (TN) Daily Appeal

Daily Memphis (TN) Advance

Public Ledger (Memphis, TN)

Middletown (NY) Daily Argus

Star Tribune (Minneapolis, MN)

Mitchell (IN) Commercial

Mitchell (IN) Enterprise

Mitchell (IN) Times

Republican Banner (Nashville, TN)

The Tennessean (Nashville, TN)

Natchitoches (LA) Enterprise

New Albany (IN) Daily Ledger

New Albany (IN) Daily Ledger Standard

New Albany (IN) Independent

New Albany (IN) Ledger

Courrier des Etats-Unis (New York, NY)

The Sun (New York, NY)

New York (NY) Times

New York (NY) Tribune

Newport (IN) Hoosier State

Hamilton County Democrat (Noblesville, IN)

Odon (IN) Journal

Orleans (IN) Progress

Orleans (IN) Progress Examiner

Paoli (IN) American Eagle

Paoli (IN) Republican

Paoli (IN) Weekly News

Philadelphia (PA) Inquirer

Marshall County Independent (Plymouth, IN)

Princeton (IN) Clarion-Leader

Richmond (IN) Palladium and Sun-Telegram

The Daily Republican (Rushville, IN)

Sacramento (CA) Union

Daily Bee (Sacramento, CA)

Saginaw (MI) Herald

Deseret Evening News (Salt Lake City, UT)

Salt Lake Tribune (Salt Lake City, UT)

St. Louis (MO) Globe-Democrat

Saint Louis (MO) Post-Dispatch

Missouri Republican (St. Louis, MO)

Westliche Post (St. Louis, MO)

Salem (IN) Democrat

Salem (IN) Leader

Sandusky (OH) Daily Register

San Francisco (CA) Chronicle

Sioux City (IA) Journal

Springfield (MA) Republican

Steuben Republican (Angola, IN)

Sullivan (IN) Daily Times

Sullivan (IN) Democrat

Sullivan (IN) Union

Terre Haute (IN) Saturday Evening Mail

Terre Haute (IN) Saturday Spectator

Topeka (KS) Daily Capital

Topeka (KS) State Journal

Daviess County Democrat (Washington, IN)

Washington (IN) Gazette

Washington (IN) Gazette and Herald

West Baden Springs (IN) Journal

Democratic Advocate (Westminster, MD)

Wheeling (WV) Daily Register

Wilmington (DE) News Journal

Canada

Halifax (Nova Scotia) Citizen

Bowmanville (Ontario) Canadian Statesman

Great Britain

Birmingham Daily Post

Western Mail (Cardiff, Wales)

Exeter Flying Post

Lancaster Gazette

Leeds Mercury

Liverpool Mercury

The Guardian (London, England)

London Magnet

London Standard

Manchester Weekly Times and Examiner

Royal Cornwall Gazette, Falmouth Packet, and General Advertiser (Truro)

Bowen, B.F. *History of Lawrence and Monroe Counties, Indiana: Their People, Industries and Institutions.* Indianapolis, Indiana: B.F. Bowen & Co., 1914.

Boyd, Gregory A. *Family Maps of Orange County, Indiana, Deluxe Edition.* Norman, Oklahoma: Arphax Publishing, 2010.

Cosby, Don. *Revisiting the Past.* Shoals, Indiana: Whispering Pines Publishing, 2012.

Edwards, James W. *History of Mitchell and Marion Township, Indiana.* Mitchell, Indiana: Mitchell Tribune, 1916.

Goodspeed *History of Lawrence, Orange, and Washington counties, Indiana: from the earliest time to the present; together with interesting biographical sketches, reminiscences, notes, etc.* Chicago: Goodspeed Bros. & Co., 1884, Internet Archive Edition.

Fulkerson, Alva Otis (editor). *History of Daviess County, Indiana: Its people, industries and institutions… with biographical sketches of representative citizens and genealogical records of many of the old families.* Indianapolis, Indiana: B.F. Bowen, 1915.

Iglehart, John E. (editor). *An Account Of Vanderburgh County From Its Organization.* Included in Volume 3 of *History of Indiana From Its Exploration To 1922,* edited by Logan Esarey, Ph.d. Dayton, Ohio: Dayton Historical Publishing Co., 1922.

Illustrated Historical Atlas of the State of Indiana. Chicago: Baskin, Forster & Co., 1876.

Indiana General Assembly, House of Representatives. *Report of the House committee on investigation of the Affairs of the State Prison South.* Indianapolis, Indiana: Wm. B. Burford, 1887.

Indiana State Board of Medical Registration and Examination, *The Eighth Annual Report.* Indianapolis, Indiana: Wm. B. Burford For State Printing and Binding, 1906.

Martin, Augustus N. (Official Reporter). *Reports of Cases Argued and Determined in the Supreme Court of Judicature of the State of Indiana, with Tables of the Cases Reported and Cases Cited and an Index, Vol. LXIV, Containing Cases Decided at the November Term, 1878, Not Reported in Vols. LXIL and LXIII.* Indianapolis, Indiana: Sentinel Company, Printers, 1879

Orange County Historical Society *Reflections of Orange County, 1816-2016.* Greensburg, Indiana: Winters Publishing, 2015.

Rader, Owen R. *History of Elnora, Indiana 1885-1985 (2016 Facsimile Edition).* CreateSpace Independent Publishing Platform: 2016.

Shepherd, Joyce. "The Friedley Family of Lawrence County." *The Seedling Patch*, Vol. III, No. 65. Bedford, Indiana: The Lawrence County Historical & Genealogical Society, Inc.: Winter 2019-20.

Souvenir Indiana State Prison South. New Albany, Indiana: C. Heimberger & Son, 1890.

Stroud, Dorothy Alice. *My Legacy for Mitchell, Indiana.* Paoli, Indiana: The Print Shop, 1985.

Indiana Archives and Records Administration, Indianapolis, IN.

Lawrence County (IN) Historical Museum family history files, Bedford IN.

Lawrence County (IN) Historical Museum probate files, Bedford IN.

Lawrence County (IN) courthouse records, Bedford, IN.

Monroe County (IN) courthouse records, Bloomington, IN.

Orange County (IN) courthouse records, Paoli, IN.

Union List of Sanborn Fire Insurance Maps.

U.S. Indexed County Land Ownership Maps, Indiana: Daviess, 1888.

WPA Death Index, 1882-1920, City Health Office, Terre Haute, IN.

Online Resources

www.ancestry.com

www.archive.org

www.findagrave.com

www.digitalarchives.in.gov

www.ingenweb.org/inorange/cemeteries/wright.htm

www.newspaperarchives.com

www.newspapers.com

https://newspapers.library.in.gov

www.officialdata.org

http://www.tolliverfamily.com

www.wagonhound.com

www.webster-dictionary.org

www.wikipedia.com

Lane, Robert E. *The Tolivers of Lawrence & Orange Counties, Indiana: A Family History*: http://www.ingenweb.org/inorange/familyfiles/toliver_family.htm

Public Speaking in an Outspoken Age: Oratory in 19th Century America: http://www1.assumption.edu/ahc/rhetoric/oratory.html

www.ingramcontent.com/pod-product-compliance
Lightning Source LLC
Chambersburg PA
CBHW071336080526
44587CB00017B/2857